TAX INCREMENT
FINANCING
AND ECONOMIC
DEVELOPMENT

SUNY series in Public Administration
Peter W. Colby, editor

TAX INCREMENT FINANCING AND ECONOMIC DEVELOPMENT

Uses, Structures, and Impacts

edited by

CRAIG L. JOHNSON
and
JOYCE Y. MAN

State University
of New York
Press

Published by
State University of New York Press, Albany

Production by Susan Geraghty
Marketing by Patrick Durocher

Printed in the United States of America

For information, address State University of New York Press,
90 State Street, Suite 700, Albany, NY 12207

Library of Congress Cataloging-in-Publication Data

Tax increment financing and economic development : uses, structures, and impacts /
Craig L. Johnson and Joyce Y. Man, editors.
  p. cm.
Includes index.
ISBN 0-7914-4975-0 (alk. paper) — ISBN 0-7914-4976-9 (pbk. : alk. paper)
  1. Tax increment financing—United States. 2. Urban renewal—United States—Finance.
I. Johnson, Craig L. (Craig Lawrence) II. Man, Joyce Y.

HT175 .T38 2001
336.22′0973—dc21

                                                                00-057392

10 9 8 7 6 5 4 3 2 1

CONTENTS

PART II

INDEX OF
FIGURES AND TABLES

CHAPTER 9

CHAPTER 10

CHAPTER 11

CHAPTER 12

CHAPTER 13

ACKNOWLEDGMENTS

This book would not have been possible without the generous support of the Ameritech Fellowship Program of the Institute for Development Strategies, Indiana University, and the Center for Urban Policy and the Environment, Indiana University.

The Institute for Development Strategies was initially established by the Indiana University Trustees in 1984 as the Regional Economic Development Institute. The institute was created to further research, graduate-level education, and scholarly exchange in the area of economic development and development policy.

The Center for Urban Policy and the Environment is part of the nation's largest school of public policy and affairs, the School of Public and Environmental Affairs of Indiana University. The center's mission is to work with state and local governments and their associations, neighborhood and community organizations, community leaders, and business and civic organizations in Indiana to identify issues, analyze options, and develop the capacity to respond to challenges.

CHAPTER 1

Introduction

Joyce Y. Man

In the past several decades, economic development has become one of the top priorities on the public policy agenda of many state and local governments in the United States. A variety of policies, programs and strategies have been designed to provide assistance, directly or indirectly, to businesses for the purpose of promoting economic development in a community. While they differ in specifics, the direct economic development policies all invariably attempted to reduce costs to businesses by assisting them with tax and financial subsidies, new or improved infrastructure facilities, or services in order to encourage investment and thus promote development. Various economic development incentive programs at the state and local levels consume billions of dollars every year in expenditures and forgone tax revenues.

One of the most widely used state and local economic development policies is tax increment financing (TIF). TIF has been implemented primarily as a means to finance public investments and infrastructure improvements needed for economic development in specific geographic areas, usually blighted areas. The TIF program largely freezes the assessed valuation of all property parcels in a designated area (the TIF district) for a specific period of years. Property taxes levied on this frozen tax base continue to accrue to local taxing bodies, but taxes derived from the increases in assessed values (the tax increment) resulting from new development are used to pay for infrastructure needs and development expenditures in the TIF district. Thus, TIF serves as a geographically targeted tax, expenditure, and regulatory inducement to a specific location. Since it was first used as a funding technique in California in 1952, forty-eight states have passed legislation authorizing the use of TIF by local governments (Johnson and Kriz, this volume).

1

CURRENT DEBATE ON THE USE OF TIF

The increasing popularity of TIF programs has also raised many issues concerning the appropriate use of this technique as an economic development tool. The use of TIF has created debates on issues associated with the effectiveness, efficiency, and equity aspects of TIF programs. Effectiveness is the criterion often used to judge whether and to what extent a TIF program has achieved its objectives of enhancing property value growth and economic development. The efficiency criterion addresses issues such as whether benefits achieved through the TIF program in terms of revenue growth outweigh the costs associated with the implementation of TIF. The criterion of equity is commonly used to evaluate whether one group of taxpayers benefits from the TIF program at the expense of other groups or whether a government policy creates an inequitable tax treatment for some of the communities' residents or businesses. Researchers and practitioners have evaluated TIF programs against these three criteria and have drawn different conclusions. As a result, a wide spectrum of views has emerged regarding the use of TIF as an economic development tool.

Perceived Benefits of TIF

An Example of Public-Private Partnership   Proponents of TIF programs claim that such programs have made significant contributions to the beneficial restructuring of intergovernmental and public-private relationships. It has been argued that TIF programs have worked as a strong unifying force in the economy, which induces normal antagonists—developers, neighborhood groups, and local government officials—to form a public-private partnership to deal with urban problems and to restructure the otherwise deteriorating areas.

A Tool of Correcting Market Failure   Advocates of the use of various economic development programs argue that, as an economic development policy, TIF has become a valuable tool used by government to correct private market failures (Bartik 1990). Market failure is the failure of private markets to achieve economic efficiency on their own. It occurs when individuals who are out of work are willing to work at the prevailing wage for jobs for which they are qualified or when workers who are currently employed want high-paid jobs for which they are qualified. In the presence of the market failure, relying solely on the private sector to increase capital investment would result in an undersupply of capital in certain jurisdictions or areas. Therefore, it becomes necessary for government to intervene by offering tax and other incentives to induce private investment that otherwise would not have occurred. The local incentives provided through TIF may generate significant capital investment to certain types of development projects that are economically feasible but would not have been funded without TIF. In particular, TIF programs may provide residents in depressed urban areas with nonmarket benefits by reducing involuntary unemployment and underemployment.

A Self-Financing Mechanism Proponents of TIF argue that TIF is a self-financing mechanism to undertake significant projects that have economic development impact without direct public investment or an increase in tax burdens. Under TIF, development projects are financed from the increased tax revenues that projects generate rather than being subsidized by taxes from other overlapping governments (Greuling 1987). The TIF-enacting government spends money for projects only when enough revenues have accumulated in the TIF fund. If TIF bonds are issued, the increased tax revenues generated by the new investment are used to pay off the debt. Once the bonds are retired and all projects are completed, the entire property tax base is returned to the original tax rolls, generating additional tax revenues for all affected local governments. If no new investment is attracted to the community, no increases in property tax revenues would accrue to the TIF-adopting government. Thus, property owners pay no more than the normal taxes, and there is no increase in their tax burdens. As a result, no real loss to the community occurs from using the incremental tax dollars for infrastructure financing.

An Effective Economic Development Tool Proponents believe that incentives provided through TIF are effective in attracting firms to locate or expand their business in the targeted area, resulting in increased economic activities, more jobs, lower unemployment, higher wages, greater property values, more tax revenues, and the revitalization of the blight areas. TIF development projects may create economic growth both inside and outside the TIF district, especially if the development is industrial or commercial (DeBoer, McNamara, and Gebremedhin 1992). Workers employed by the new businesses will probably live outside the TIF district, so the market value of the property tax base of the enacting and overlapping governments will increase. In addition, economic and population growth associated with the TIF program may generate increases in other local government revenue sources, such as local income taxes, sales taxes, and motor vehicle excises taxes. This argument derives from recent research that provides evidence that differences in state and local taxes and expenditures have significant effects on the level of economic activity (Bartik 1991). The new research findings reinforce the belief that reducing business costs by offering tax incentives, financial subsidies, or new or improved infrastructure facilities will attract more businesses to locate and expand in the targeted area and stimulate economic growth in the entire hosting community.

A Flexible and Politically Attractive Tool   Flexibility has been attributed as one of TIF's principal strengths. According to Paetsch and Dahlstrom (1990), TIF can be applied to any area meeting broad statutory standards and to any project proposal for that area demonstrating financial feasibility. The TIF process can be initiated at any time when a city perceives a development opportunity. Also, project funds can be used for almost any incentive purposes. Furthermore, TIF can be used with other economic development programs simultaneously. For example, TIF funds can be part of a tax and financial incentive package used to attract or retain businesses. TIF funds can also be used for rehabilitation of an old neighborhood that may produce no new jobs but can make the community a more attractive place to live.

TIF is also politically popular largely because of the widespread presumption that a TIF project will pay for itself. In addition, it is claimed that the development or redevelopment of a targeted area may produce larger tax revenues than would have been produced had no development occurred. Thus, for taxpayers, it seems reasonable to earmark a portion of the increased tax revenue for the purpose of paying some of the costs of that development (Klemanski 1990). TIF is also viewed as preferable to many other tax incentive programs, the tax abatement program in particular, because TIF may stimulate economic activities without giving away tax breaks to businesses or reducing the community's total tax revenues for future years.

Criticism of TIF

An Ineffective Economic Development Tool   Despite its increasing popularity among public officials, TIF programs are not without critics. One fundamental criticism is based on the widely held belief that most economic development programs, including TIF, are ineffective and inefficient. It is perceived that incentives provided by state and local governments usually account only for a small portion of a firm's production cost so that they are unlikely to affect business location choices or expansion decisions (Cummings 1988). This argument has its root in the longstanding debate on whether state and local tax and financial policies have any effect on the location of capital investment. Critics of these policies usually rely on two sources of evidence to illustrate their points: (1) surveys of business firms; and (2) econometric studies of the determinants of state and local job growth in the 1970s. Surveys of business firms often show a low ranking of state and local taxes as a location determinant. Many executives in private companies claim that state and local taxes played little, if any, role in their firms' location decisions. Consistent with their opinions, most pre-1980s studies (Oakland 1978) found no significant statistical relationship between state and local taxes and economic growth. In addition, critics of TIF argue that the use of TIF by one city is likely to lead other cities to adopt it as a defensive policy. As a result, TIF is likely to become increasingly ineffective over time.

A Zero-Sum Game State and local economic development programs are also criticized as a zero-sum game for the country as a whole. According to this argument, when one state wins by convincing a firm to locate within its boundaries, the other forty-nine states lose. Thus, states and cities compete with each other without increasing the number of jobs available nationwide. Zero-sum games are particularly likely to occur when communities within a particular region or metropolitan area compete for businesses, even though the firms have probably already decided to locate somewhere in the region. Even if the offer of a local incentive package has a marginal effect on firms' location decisions, other cities may offset this effect by making similar counteroffers. The marginal effect may decline and disappear. At the closing of a bidding war, little change is realized in the distribution of economic activity.

A Budget-Manipulating Instrument Used by Municipalities TIF is a way of sharing the costs of local development projects among the governments that benefit from an expansion of the local tax base. TIF-enacting cities (or other eligible jurisdictions) receive the property tax revenues assessed on the growth in property value from school districts, the county, and other local government jurisdictions whose tax boundaries overlap the TIF district. The TIF mechanism involves implicit subsidies across local government units to the TIF-enacting government. Among the most vocal critics of TIF are those school districts and other overlapping jurisdictions within the TIF districts. Their resentment to TIF derives from their perception that they have "lost" their own revenue and have to spend more to cover increased local service costs generated by development or redevelopment in the TIF district. They view TIF development as a subsidy of tax revenues from the overlapping jurisdictions to the enacting jurisdiction. Some critics even allege that TIF is nothing but a budget-manipulating instrument adopted by growing cities to capture property tax revenues that otherwise would have gone to the township, the school corporation, or other overlapping jurisdictions (see Anderson 1990). According to the conceptual framework underlying the use of TIF, all the taxing bodies within the TIF district ultimately benefit from the development project in the district. But those benefits are often fifteen years or more into the future. This accusation may turn out to be true if TIF programs fail to increase the property tax base or never return increased tax revenues to other overlapping jurisdictions because the length of time to capture the tax increment has been extended indefinitely.

Complexity and Costliness   Many critics argue that TIF programs are too complicated and costly. A typical TIF implementation process requires an eligibility report based on a market study for the project area, an inspection of the project area, real estate valuation data, and a financial feasibility analysis supported by services of real estate appraisers, civil engineers, financial analysts, and consulting planners (Paetsch and Dahlstrom 1990; Klacik and Nunn, this volume; Johnson and Kriz, this volume). For this reason, TIF opponents claim that TIF represents a more complex process than does grant administration. Tax increment bonds or revenue bonds issued to finance infrastructure investment in the designated TIF district are more expensive, more complex, and more uncertain than general obligation bonds, because these bonds normally contain no general obligation contingency provision pledging a city's full faith and credit.

Lack of Voters' Participation   A number of legal arguments against TIF have also been articulated in judicial processes. In some states, decisions to adopt TIF are made without a vote by the citizens or without participation by other jurisdictions whose tax boundaries overlap the TIF district. It has been argued in courts that TIF constitutes an improper delegation of legislative power. The creation of TIF authorities also raises the questions of accountability because decisions concerning millions of dollars are made by individuals who are often not elected by voters (Klemanski 1990).

Abused Use of TIF   Some opponents of TIF charge that some cities abuse the use of TIF by designating large areas as TIF districts for the purpose of capturing tax increments not directly related to the public investment or improvement financed through TIF. Many TIF projects are designed to maximize the potential property tax increment or sales tax receipts rather than eliminate blight. Although local governments claim to adopt the TIF program as an incentive to induce development in an area that would have otherwise not occurred, in some cases it could be argued that such development would have occurred without the incentive provided through TIF. There are also charges that local incentives under TIF mislead some firms to an inappropriate location and that government subsidies are provided to firms or affluent areas that do not need them, thus wasting taxpayers' money. It is even argued in certain legal cases that some local authorities misused TIFs to solidify patterns of residential segregation in an attempt to escape public attention and legal scrutiny (Reingold, this volume).

ISSUES ADDRESSED IN THIS BOOK

These conflicting views on the value of TIF programs at a time when local government officials are eager for new economic development strategies create a need for a thorough evaluation of TIF programs. However, the number of studies of TIF is very limited, and our knowledge of TIF is far from adequate. This book provides a comprehensive yet detailed discussion of the uses, structures, and impacts of TIF programs. Illustrated with specific examples, cases, surveys, and empirical evidence, it addresses such issues as how TIF works, why TIF is adopted, and what impact TIF has on local economic development. Our goal is to offer a comprehensive description and analysis of this increasingly significant mechanism of state and local economic development finance.

This book reflects a collective effort of a team made up of practitioners, consultants, and academics with training and expertise in the fields of urban and regional planning, political science, economics, law, finance, and sociology. It is divided into fifteen chapters and organized in two parts. Part I describes the TIF process and the debt-financing mechanism, analyzes TIF legislation in different states, evaluates factors influencing the municipal TIF adoption decision, and reviews the evidence on the effectiveness of TIF as an economic development tool. Part II presents a detailed analysis of TIF programs in a specific state or city or for a specific project through a survey analysis or a case study. Starting with a brief overview of the current debate on the use of TIF in the introduction, this book addresses the following questions:

What Is TIF and How Does TIF work?   Answers to this question are provided by J. Drew Klacik and Samuel Nunn in chapter 2. This chapter presents a thorough description of the generic TIF planning and implementation process. The authors discuss seven broad steps involved in this process and subtasks within each discrete task, along with major questions that local administrators should address as they enter and close each step. They offer definitions to a number of terms essential to the understanding of the TIF process and ways of calculating the incremental revenue stream. Using a scenario of a hypothetical five-year TIF plan covering five jurisdictions, they discuss some of the issues, such as the risks of projecting TIF incremental revenues and inter-jurisdictional consequences associated with the use of TIF. Also, they predict the prospect of the future use of TIF as an economic development tool.

Do the Laws Governing TIF Vary among States?   In chapter 3, Craig L. Johnson and Kenneth A. Kriz provide a review of the diverse legal frameworks that states have chosen to authorize, stimulate, regulate, and constrain TIF districts across the nation. By comparing state laws governing

TIF, they have identified differences in the processes, requirements, and restrictions in the use of TIF. They point out some major problems in each stage of TIF initiation, formulation, adoption, implementation, and termination. They also discuss the interjurisdictional impacts of TIF and propose possible solutions to those problems through legal provisions. In this chapter, they argue that TIF is a process for allocating public resources, not just a technique for redevelopment finance. Based upon this conviction, they suggest that the state laws governing the TIF process be structured to channel the process in ways that should provide a balance among efficiency, equity, and accountability concerns.

Can TIF Be Financed by Revenues Other Than Property Taxes?   TIF is usually perceived as synonymous with property tax increment financing. But according to information presented by John L. Mikesell in chapter 4, at least seven states have used incremental sales and/or business tax revenues to finance economic development. Mikesell's chapter provides the first national analysis of nonproperty tax increment programs and expands our understanding of alternative TIF programs. By comparing the strengths and weaknesses associated with the use of the sales tax TIF with those of the traditional property tax TIF, he concludes that nonproperty taxes are less suited for use in TIF programs than are property taxes.

What Are the Issues Associated with TIF Debt Finance?   TIF projects are financed using either the "pay-as-you-go" method or the debt mechanism or a combination of both. The pay-as-you-go method allows cities to spend money on TIF projects only when enough tax revenues have been accumulated in the TIF fund. The debt-financing mechanism involves issuing bonds to generate a large amount of cash upfront to be repaid by future tax increment revenues. Since it usually takes many years for cities to accumulate enough tax increments to finance large-scale public investment projects, debt finance is usually preferred. In chapter 5, Craig L. Johnson analyzes the structure of the TIF debt market and the risks associated with TIF debt for both bond issuers and investors.

Why Do Cities Adopt TIF?   Although hundreds of cities in forty-eight states have adopted TIF, many more do not use TIF programs. One may ask the following questions: why do cities adopt or not adopt TIF? What are the common characteristics of the cities that adopt TIF? Does a city adopt TIF because it wants to mimic its neighbors' behavior? Are growing cities or financially strained and economically distressed cities more likely to adopt TIF? Does fiscal pressure play a significant role in the municipal TIF adoption decision? Joyce Y. Man provides answers to these fundamental questions in chapter 6 by identifying the possible factors that may influence the municipal TIF adoption decision. After reviewing survey results and empirical evidence from recent research, she suggests that the municipal TIF adoption decision is influenced by a set of factors that describe the city's economic and fiscal environment, the availability of alternative economic development programs, inter-jurisdictional competition for businesses, and the expected growth that may result from the implementation of TIF.

Is TIF Effective in Stimulating Economic Development? Another issue of great interest and importance to state and local government officials and the general public is the effectiveness of TIF as an economic development tool. In chapter 7, Joyce Y. Man discusses the possible effects of TIF upon local economic development. But the evidence uncovered by national surveys and recent empirical studies has yielded conflicting conclusions about the effectiveness of TIF programs. There is evidence suggesting that the TIF-adopting cities in Michigan experienced faster property value growth than non-TIF cities and that TIF programs in Indiana raised property value and employment in a city beyond the level that would have been expected had the TIF district not been created. But such positive effects of TIF on property value were not found in the study using data drawn from municipalities in the Chicago metropolitan area. Since the evidence on the effectiveness of TIF is conflicting and inconclusive, she points out the directions for future research on the effects of TIF on economic development.

Are Fiscal Stresses and the Use of TIF Closely Related? This question was answered in chapter 8 by Jeff Chapman, who provides a historical overview of California's experience in the use of TIF. He suggests that the fiscal stresses experienced by local governments after the passage of property tax limitation legislation (e.g., Proposition 13 in 1978) play a significant role in the genesis and development of TIF in California.

Are School Districts Likely to be Harmed by the Use of TIF? Proponents of TIF often provide justification of the use of TIF on the grounds that public investment projects financed through TIF pay for themselves with costs covered by the increased tax revenues generated by the projects. Thus, they believe that other jurisdictions whose tax boundaries overlap the TIF district are not harmed in the redistribution of tax revenues through TIF. This may not be the case, according to the study conducted by Robert G. Lehnen and Carlyn E. Johnson in chapter 9. Their study reveals that the redistribution of funds among local jurisdictions in Indiana through TIF programs may have a detrimental financial impact on school districts. In addition, they present the steps and procedures that certain states have taken to reduce the potential adverse impact of TIF on school districts.

What Can We Learn from the TIF Experience in Texas? Enid Arvidson, Rod Hissong, and Richard L. Cole present their findings of a survey of municipal governments in Texas in chapter 10. Their investigation and review of the Texas TIF experience confirm that TIF has some advantages and disadvantages as an economic development tool in Texas. They find that on the whole, a wide variety of Texas cities have had successful experiences with TIF. Most of the cities claim to have attained the expressed goals of increasing the tax base and attracting new businesses.

Does the Use of TIF Vary within a State? By adopting a survey approach similar to the one employed by Arvidson, Hissong, and Cole, J. Drew Klacik offers insights into the legislative and administrative decisions that have led to the current variety of TIF district structures found in Indiana. In chapter 11, he reveals that TIF programs within a state can vary widely in terms of types of activities financed, financing methods chosen, size and type of areas selected as TIF districts, and length of time required to complete the projects. His findings remind us that because of wide variations in the uses and structures of TIF, we should not base our judgment of TIF on our assessment of merely one good example or one bad one.

Is TIF Suitable to Finance Affordable Housing? Although TIF may be well suited to develop central business districts that contain a predominantly commercial and industrial base, this mechanism can also be applied to finance affordable housing as Andrea Elson, Garrit Knaap and Clifford Singer have pointed out in chapter 12. They present a financial analysis of the use of TIF in providing affordable housing in Urbana, Illinois. Illustrated with a flexible and detailed financial model, this chapter demonstrates how the purchase, redevelopment, and sale of affordable housing affect the flow of funds in a TIF district. It also reveals how their model can be used to evaluate alternative TIF projects and the achievement of multiple public policy objectives using TIF.

Can TIF Be Misused? In chapter 13, David A. Reingold provides an answer to this question. By investigating the case of Addison and Chicago, Illinois, he demonstrates that TIF programs can be misused to regulate patterns of residential segregation. His findings suggest that the use of TIF needs to be closely monitored by state and local governments.

Can TIF Be Used to Finance an Environmental Cleanup? In chapter 14, Jeff Zachman and Susan D. Steinwell present a case study of how Minnesota uses TIFs to redevelop Brownfields, properties with significant environmental problems. They demonstrate that local government can create a special type of TIF district to use the tax increment to finance the costs of cleaning up contaminated sites.

At the end of this volume, Craig L. Johnson provides a summary of the findings contained in this book. Putting it all together, these chapters combine prior research with the latest findings on the fundamental issues of TIF programs to provide a comprehensive analysis of TIF throughout the nation. We believe that the information contained in this book will be of interest to state and local officials, economic development practitioners, academic researchers, college students, and members of the general public who are concerned with state and local economic development policies. University instructors may also find this book useful as a supplemental textbook for economic development courses.

REFERENCES

Anderson, John E. 1990. Tax increment financing: Municipal adoption and growth. *National Tax Journal* 43(2): 155–163.

Bartik, Timothy J. 1990. The market failure approach to regional economic development policy. *Economic Development Quarterly* 4(4):361–370.

Bartik, T. J. 1991. *Who Benefits from State and Local Economic Development Policies?* Kalamazoo, Michigan: W. E. Upjohn Institute for Employment Research.

Cummings, S., editor, 1988. *Business Elites and Urban Development*. Albany: State University of New York Press.

DeBoer, L. K., K. T. McNamara, and T. G. Gebremedhin. 1992. Tax increment financing: An infrastructure funding option in Indiana. Department of Agricultural Economics, Purdue University.

Greuling, John E. 1987. Tax increment financing: A downtown development tool. *Economic Development Review* (Winter): 23–27.

Klemanski, John S. 1990. Using tax increment financing for urban redevelopment projects. *Economic Development Quarterly* 4(1): 23–28.

Oakland, William. 1978. Local taxes and intra-urban industrial location: A survey. In *Metropolitan Finance and Growth Management Policies*, ed. G. Break. Madison: University of Wisconsin Press.

Paetsch, James R., and Roger K. Dahlstrom, 1990. Tax increment financing: What it is and how it works. In *Financing economic development: An institutional response*, ed. R. Bingham, E. Hill, and S. White. London: Sage Publications.

PART I

CHAPTER 2

A Primer on Tax Increment Financing

J. Drew Klacik
and
Samuel Nunn

INTRODUCTION

Two themes combine to establish tax increment financing (TIF) as an attractive way of funding urban development projects: the neverending and increasingly difficult search for creative local financing mechanisms and the desire to establish local revenue and expenditure systems that reflect the longstanding benefit principle of public finance. The use of TIF establishes a geographic area for which debt instruments are issued (in some cases a TIF district may opt to spend revenue as it is collected) to finance specific public improvements that will presumably enable economic development or redevelopment, usually by installing physical infrastructure that makes a particular project or series of projects possible. It is assumed that these improvements will engender new private investment so that the expected increase in property tax revenues (i.e., the "increment") can be captured to amortize the public facility debt. Since municipal managers are able to connect expenditures with tax revenues more explicitly by using TIF, it is assumed that, for the residents within the TIF district, "each taxpayer contributes in line with the benefits which he [sic] receives from public services" (Musgrave and Musgrave 1989)—the textbook definition of the benefit principle. The presumed beauty of TIF approaches for municipal managers is that they are able to leave a property tax base in place that is designed to pay for the package of basic public services the TIF district already receives. The new private investment creates a new "revenue increment" that will pay for the infrastructure but may not pay for the new services required by and delivered to the development project.

Apart from this theoretical elegance, using TIF has become a popular economic development tool for other reasons as well. TIF is one of the few locally controlled funding options available to local economic development practitioners that can be used for investment in infrastructure improvements they deem necessary for economic growth. Furthermore, local control means there are none of the bureaucratic delays and reporting components associated with intergovernmental revenue (Davis 1989). TIF also allows local economic development officials to consider a broader scope of projects than other redevelopment tools (Davidson 1979). Using debt financing allows officials to raise large amounts of preproject revenue for development initiatives. For example, TIF made possible more than $150 million of public spending for the city of Indianapolis's Circle Centre project (an expansive, enclosed downtown shopping mall), which represented the redevelopment of several blocks of deteriorating central business district real estate. Local officials also like TIF because, unless the debt mechanism is a general obligation bond, TIF debt does not count against general obligation debt limits (Klemanski 1990). Some have also argued that TIF is a means for local officials to avoid referendum-style voter approval campaigns for the issuance of bonded debt (Davis 1989).

For many local officials, the use of TIF is also justified because it is one of the few mechanisms available to a locality to generate money for infrastructure incentives that leverages private investment and aids community growth. In its purest form, revenue from the development project pays to make the project possible. Stinson (1992, 241) notes that "if the development would not have occurred without a subsidy, TIF may be cost-free to local taxpayers other than those whose property benefits from the subsidy." When the project is paid for, all incremental AV reverts to the general taxing district, thus generating either new revenues or reducing tax rates for taxpayers. It is also argued that during the course of the project, indirect economic and fiscal benefits accrue to residents and taxing districts. Many users of TIF would also argue that in most instances, TIF only involves real property; thus, all personal property within the districts accrues to the general taxing districts.

But TIF can create fiscal dangers as well. By layering numerous TIF districts over a local jurisdiction in order to promote economic development and enable specific public-private deals, municipal authorities are segmenting the local fiscal structure and restricting how the revenue associated with new assessed value can be used to pay for general public services and facilities. Using TIF adds to the problems associated with overlapping taxation and fragmented fiscal authority created by TIF bonds that, in effect, place liens against specific portions of the local property tax base in order to pay debt retirement for certain designated public facilities. This can make local fiscal management and planning more challenging for public administrators, as well as create serious problems in vertical and horizontal equity problems among a jurisdiction's citizens.

This chapter offers a brief overview of tax increment financing. It starts first with a historical overview and description of the generic TIF process. Second, it offers a summary of TIF calculations that public administrators should understand, including a discussion of some of the issues associated with using TIF to build public infrastructure and promote economic development within communities. Then, a brief explanation of the expected economic and fiscal impacts of TIF is presented, followed by conclusions about the administrative implications and future use of TIF as an economic development tool.

HISTORICAL OVERVIEW AND TIF BASICS

The simple explanation of tax increment financing (TIF) is that property tax revenue generated by new construction in a designated area is deposited in a special fund and used to pay for public improvements within the same designated area. A more formal explanation of TIF is that new tax revenue generated by increased assessed value within the designated district resulting from direct and indirect real estate investment is captured by the TIF authority and used to pay for public development costs rather than to pay for general government services (Michael 1987). Those who advocate the use of TIF believe in the right and ability of localities to play a significant role in attracting and directing business investment and economic activity to their local community. Advocates of TIF also realize the important role infrastructure plays in economic growth. Combined with this is a view of TIF as a way to finance public facilities by directly connecting the population that requires the infrastructure to the allocation of expected property enhancement effects and related property tax burdens.

TIF originated in California in 1952 as a means to provide local matching funds for federal grants (Huddleston 1979). In California, TIF increased in popularity in reaction to the adoption of Proposition 13, which limited local property tax increases. Huddleston (1979) argues that from the fiscal perspective of the benefit principle, TIF has been viewed as a mechanism to distribute the cost of local development incentives among the various taxing units benefiting from a longterm increase in the local tax base. Without the use of TIFs, the general tax base of the city alone would bear the cost of providing the local incentives necessary to obtain certain economic development projects, rather than relying on the more site specific TIF approach to link tax payments to service or facility benefits. By 1984, twenty-eight states permitted the use of TIF (Greuling 1987). According to surveys in 1986 and 1987, at least thirty-three states had adopted TIF-enabling legislation (Klemanski 1990). By 1992, Forgey (1993) reported that forty-four states had authorized TIF. Johnson and Kriz (this volume) report that TIF-enabling legislation is on the books in forty-eight states. Nationally, the use of TIF has expanded in reaction to the decreased availability of federal funds for economic development projects and infrastructure improvements. Fifty-six percent of cities with populations over one hundred thousand in 1975 have used TIF. The majority of these cities first used TIF after 1980 (Clarke and Galle 1992).

After adoption of the plan and establishment of the TIF district, states allow a wide variety of financing mechanisms, but there are typically two ways to use TIF revenues. TIF sponsors may use incremental revenues as they are received to pay for infrastructure construction. Alternatively, the TIF sponsor may choose to incur debt based on anticipated future revenue streams. In most states, incremental revenue is generated by all taxing jurisdictions within the TIF district, including schools, counties, and special districts (Harbit 1975). In Florida, California, Illinois, and Wisconsin, school districts are excluded from the TIF process (Klemanski 1990).

A generic TIF planning and implementation process, based on the procedures used in Elgin (IL), is described by Paestch and Dahlstrom (1990). It involves at least seven broad steps that, in turn, require a variety of subtasks within each discrete task. Figure 2.1 summarizes the broad steps, along with the key questions that local administrators should address as they enter and close each step. The first concern of municipal officials is straightforward: Are the project and its financing feasible? Another major consideration in the earliest stage of the project is to determine whether there are private-sector actors who are interested and willing to participate in the proposed project. Assuming feasibility is present, the next requirement is a determination of blight elimination or significant economic benefit as a reason for overlaying a TIF district. Associated with this step is the need to determine the geographical boundaries of the district. This step is obviously important because TIF is an inherently geospatial technique in economic development; it applies to a specific, bounded space within the community, which ultimately has crucial legal and jurisdictional meaning with respect to the allocation and distribution of incremental tax revenues. The third step is the establishment of an agreement between the TIF authority and the developer involved in the project, which according to

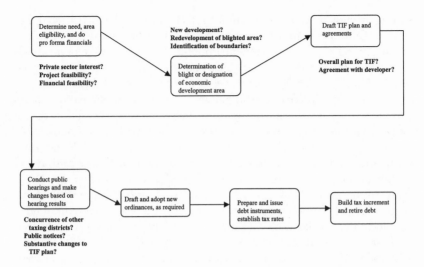

FIGURE 2.1

A Generic TIF Process

Source: Adapted from information contained
within Paetsch and Dahlstrom (1990)

Paestch and Dahlstrom should include an overall development (or rede-velopment) plan for the district. After drafting a (re)development plan and an agreement, public hearings are required to allow for input from citizens and especially from other taxing districts that are within the TIF boundaries; it is assumed that if justified by the findings of the public hearing(s), changes can then be made to the plan and agreement. The last steps in the process involve the creation of new ordinances, the issuance of debt, the establishment of TIF tax rates for the district, and the implementation of the project.

The generic process is designed in a way that suggests TIF is attrac-tive because it insures, to at least some degree, the private market will test development ideas and projects. It is assumed that private investor scrutiny will guarantee that only projects with acceptable risks go for-ward (Greuling 1987). For instance, during the latter stages of the TIF process, the public sale of TIF bonds invites intense inspection by poten-tial investors. Presumably, if the project appears in danger, the bonds would not be purchased. Proponents of this view argue that informed private investors are most capable of making investment decisions—if they are unwilling to invest in a project, then neither should local gov-ernment (Stallard 1991). Furthermore, the generic TIF process presup-poses that local government officials are working closely with private-sector business firms to ascertain a project's practical and financial feasibility. Conversely, in those instances of TIF utilization that are unilateral decisions of local governments, public officials can take precautions to expose the TIF plan to private financial and business interests or bond-rating agencies in order to verify a project's feasibility.

The generic TIF process also allows for planners, administrators, and citizens to focus on a critical question concerning proposed TIF projects: would the project have been implemented anyway without TIF assistance? Answering this question is important because opponents of TIF and other supply-side economic assistance programs argue that locationally based incentives rarely affect business location decisions (Schmenner 1982; Swanstrom 1988; Wolman 1988; Barnekov and Rich 1989). Even acknowledging the potential of incentives to affect intrametropolitan business locations, critics note that many other factors can affect such decisions by wandering business firms (Ritter and Oldfield 1990; Dabney 1991). Furthermore, evidence indicates that many economic development incentive programs may help redistribute growth from distressed urban areas to rapidly growing suburban areas (Dewar 1990). This may be especially true in states that do not require blight findings as a prerequisite for TIF declaration and may also affect states that are rather lenient in blight scrutiny. If TIF is available for suburban development, many private interests are likely to be unwilling to take on redevelopment of the most blighted areas of a city, instead concentrating on areas currently experiencing gentrification or other areas for which there are indicators that private investment, supported by public capital, can prosper. Blighted areas experiencing the most serious economic and social deterioration may not be likely targets of TIF-backed redevelopment. Thus TIF planners should spend time determining how critical TIF assistance is to propose projects. The generic TIF process described here suggests that these considerations should be given close attention in the earliest stages that are designed to take place before the development of a TIF agreement.

TIF TERMINOLOGY, CALCULATIONS, AND PROJECT RISKS

A number of terms are essential to the understanding of TIF and TIF calculations. They are as follows:

- *Base Year*—the year that the TIF district is established;
- *Base Assessed Value*—the assessed value of property within the TIF district in the base year;
- *Incremental Assessed Value*—the assessed value in the TIF district in any postbase year, minus the base assessed value;

- *Incremental Revenue*—incremental assessed value, multiplied by the overall tax rate of the TIF district;

- *Sponsoring Jurisdiction*—the organization that creates and activates the TIF district, usually a redevelopment commission;

- *Contributing Jurisdiction*—the taxing units whose assessed value is at least partially contained within a TIF district.

Figure 2.2 presents a visual representation of the interaction of the terms essential to understanding the TIF process. Before the TIF is established, all contributor jurisdictions share in the tax proceeds of the assessed value. As shown in the graphic, assessed values within the proposed TIF district could have been stable, climbing, or declining until the base year is established. For example, assessed values would probably be stable or declining in an inner-city residential area outside the commercial business district (CBD); values could be stable or climbing on the fringe of a commercial area within the CBD. The overall assessed value situation is likely to be related to the geospatial placement of the final TIF district boundaries. After the base year is established, only the property tax revenue generated by the base AV goes to the contributing jurisdictions, while the increment (if it appears) flows to the sponsor jurisdiction. Again, it should be noted that *after* the base year (as before it), assessed value could be climbing, declining, or stable. Clearly, if the assessed value declines after the base year, there will be two critical impacts: (a) the revenue going to the contributing jurisdictions decreases, and (b) the

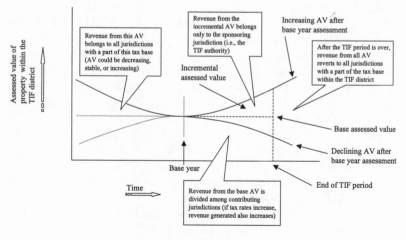

FIGURE 2.2
Schematic of TIF Assessed Value and Revenue Structure

TIF sponsor authority will not have the incremental revenue needed to pay for infrastructure expenditures. Likewise, if the base assessed value remains the same, contributing jurisdictions will be no worse off than before the base year, but the sponsoring jurisdiction will face a shortage of incremental revenue. Under the expected ideal situation, assessed values begin to climb after the infrastructure or other physical improvements made possible by TIF financing are installed, and in that case the revenue from the incremental assessed value accrues only to the sponsor jurisdiction (i.e., the TIF authority). Accordingly, the dynamics of assessed value are of great interest to TIF administrators.

TIF calculations are typically performed on assessed value. Table 2.1 shows a simple example of the base year and incremental allocation for a hypothetical five-year TIF plan covering five jurisdictions. Base assessed value is calculated by summing the base year assessed value of all tax parcels within the TIF district. The simplified example assumes that the TIF district geospatially encapsulates all five jurisdictions depicted. Revenue from the base year assessed valuation is divided among the sponsor and contributor jurisdictions based on their respective tax rates. If any of the jurisdictions elect to increase their tax rates, the base year revenue would of course increase commensurately. The TIF district applies the combined tax rates from the five jurisdictions against the incremental assessed values. In the example, the assessed value of the selected property totals to five hundred thousand dollars which represents the base year value. The sponsor jurisdiction and the four contributor jurisdictions share in the base year value according to their respective tax rates, as shown in the table. Until or unless any jurisdiction changes its tax rate, its share of tax revenues will stay the same (unless base year assessed value actually goes down). The TIF district can work only with the incremental assessed value that develops after physical improvements, which in this case are assumed to bump up assessed values beginning in base year plus two years. The incremental assessed value is the sum of the current assessed value of all tax parcels within the TIF district minus the base assessed value. The incremental revenue is calculated the same way, by multiplying incremental AV by the TIF district tax rate. The tax *rate* for a TIF district is the total of the tax rates for all taxing units contained within a TIF district. However, the tax *revenues* for the TIF district would accrue as shown in table 2.1. According to this hypothetical scenario, by the end of the five-year TIF period the TIF district will have captured nearly 30 percent of total tax revenues, while the other jurisdictions' shares will have declined, although their base collections would have remained constant.

Regarding tax impacts, table 2.1 also shows that taxpayers within this hypothetical TIF district will in fact see increased tax payments dur-

TABLE 2.1
Base Year and Incremental Revenue Allocation

	Tax rate per $100 AV	Tax increment financing period — Assessed value						Post-TIF period begins; assessed value
		$500,000	$500,000	$550,000	$600,000	$700,000	$700,000	$700,000
		Base year	Base year +1	Base year +2	Base year +3	Base year +4	Base year +5	
Jurisdiction								
Sponsor jurisdiction	$1.25	$6,250	$6,250	$6,250	$6,250	$6,250	$6,250	$8,750
Contributor jurisdiction 1	$0.75	$3,750	$3,750	$3,750	$3,750	$3,750	$3,750	$5,250
Contributor jurisdiction 2	$0.85	$4,250	$4,250	$4,250	$4,250	$4,250	$4,250	$5,950
Contributor jurisdiction 3	$1.00	$5,000	$5,000	$5,000	$5,000	$5,000	$5,000	$7,000
Contributor jurisdiction 4	$0.90	$4,500	$4,500	$4,500	$4,500	$4,500	$4,500	$6,300
Total TIF district tax rate	$4.75							
Tax revenues								
Base year (to contributor jurisdictions)		$23,750	$23,750	$23,750	$23,750	$23,750	$23,750	$33,250
Incremental revenue (to TIF district)		$0	$0	$2,375	$4,750	$9,500	$9,500	$0
Total		$23,750	$23,750	$26,125	$28,500	$33,250	$33,250	$33,250
Revenue allocation								
Share to TIF district		0.0%	0.0%	9.1%	16.7%	28.6%	28.6%	0.0%
Share to sponsor & contributor jurisdictions		100.0%	100.0%	90.9%	83.3%	71.4%	71.4%	100.0%

Notes:

1. This assumes the TIF district exactly contains sponsor and contributor jurisdictions.
2. The example shows a five-year TIF period. Typically, the TIF period would correspond to the length of the bond issues (e.g., twenty years).
3. The example would apply to real property only; changes in personal property would accrue to jurisdictions according to their respective tax rates.
4. Variations in state laws governing TIF implementation would affect the allocation of revenues depicted in this table.

ing the TIF period. Total tax collections would rise 40 percent during the five years, from $23,750 to $33,250 based on the change in assessed values generated by the physical improvements made possible by the TIF plan. In this context, planners for TIF districts should also consider the likely incidence of the TIF district tax rates on different income groups. For example, some critics argue that *in general* many incentive packages are regressive in nature and that there is little indirect economic return or fiscal impact accruing to sponsor jurisdictions (Cummings 1988; Rosentraub and Swindell 1991). This is especially true for incentives such as physical infrastructure that offer few restrictions on who can use them, to the extent that many users are not required to pay for the facilities (i.e., suburban commuters into inner-city TIF districts). In this vein, an additional criticism is that those who pay for a TIF may not be the ones who benefit. Lawrence and Stephenson (1995) cite evidence from Huddleston's TIF studies in the 1980s "that tax increment financing may demand cost subsidization by taxpayers geographically and politically separate from the decision-making sponsor." Some critics claim that if all tax revenues from the project are used for infrastructure, then other taxpayers must contribute to the costs of providing police, fire, roads, trash, and other services to the project. Others believe that TIF unfairly helps TIF property owners at the cost of other property owners (Davis 1989).

For TIFs that are funding projects through the pay-as-you-go method, incremental revenue is generated on an annual basis, and TIF revenue is collected and deposited in a TIF fund and spent without incurring debt. TIFs that fund projects through debt generally have immediate access to larger amounts of revenue than pay-as-you-go TIFs. TIFs that assume debt incur increased risk because incremental revenue must be projected annually for the duration of the debt. The calculation of the incremental revenue stream requires projections of direct project-specific AV growth and may require projections of indirect or spin-off AV growth. Incremental revenue projections must also take into account changes to the tax rate and the effects of reassessment. Typical growth projections for incremental AV may include (a) the specific project for which the TIF was created; (b) other construction under way but not completed and assessed; (c) projects committed to but not initiated; (d) known city land purchases; (e) anticipated demolitions; and (f) increased AV resulting from the expiration of tax abatements.

The calculation of TIF revenue projections presents a variety of challenges to municipal administrators and their consultants, especially when public debt is incurred and public spending occurs before private spending. Possible detrimental events affecting the realization of TIF AV projections include (a) project failure; (b) a reduction in project size and investment; (c) a delay in construction schedule, possibly related to weather or labor conditions; or (d) the failure of the project to achieve the projected amount of AV. Failure to achieve projected AV can result because AV often is projected from preconstruction design drawings and financial pro formas. These risks can at least partially be offset through binding agreements with the private developer that designate a specific amount of revenue the private development must generate. If this revenue is not generated through property taxes resulting from the project, the developer must make up the difference through direct payments to the sponsor jurisdiction.

Because contributor jurisdictions are often involved in a TIF plan, interjurisdictional relationships can be affected by the spatial and fiscal apportionment of tax bases required for TIF to work. There have been many interjurisdictional disputes over the use of TIF. Principal opposition comes from school districts, and at least four states (California, Florida, Illinois, and Wisconsin) have omitted school district revenues from the TIF increment (Klemanski 1990). The school authorities in some jurisdictions may be concerned about TIF's impact and whether TIF would result in increased obligations without an increase in revenue (Jung 1991). This fear strikes school districts deeply, especially for residential TIFs (Davis 1989).

Other projection risks can be associated with either the specific projects or other property within the TIF district. Unanticipated successful tax appeals can reduce the assessed value for specific parcels. Financial difficulties can lead to failure of affected private firms to pay property taxes, resulting in a delay in revenue availability. Catastrophic events such as fire, tornado, or hurricane can dramatically reduce the supply of AV in a district. An economic downturn can lead to vacant buildings and reduced tax revenues. A changing political climate or changes in state and federal mandates or funding can slow tax rate growth or perhaps even cause reduced local property tax rates. In states where AV is not directly market related, mandated reassessment could affect AV. Ostensibly, the intent of reassessment is to distribute the property tax burden fairly; and while reassessments are intended to be revenue neutral, and while this may occur on a countywide basis, within a TIF district revenue neutrality is not assured. In states where AV is market-driven, an economic downturn, coupled with the sale of an existing property at a reduced price, would have a negative effect on TIF revenues. Finally, the use of tax abatements by city governments when they are engaged in interjurisdictional competitions for economic development activity can result in a reduction of the tax base that would complicate or undermine the use of TIF approaches.

In some states, the tax rate is the final variable in the property tax equation. The net assessed value and the tax levy or amount of revenue required by the taxing unit is known before the tax rate is established. For TIF districts, the tax rate and assessed value are known before the levy or tax revenue is calculated. This method of calculating TIF revenue adds an element of risk to the TIF financing process. Of course, many of these risks can be ameliorated to some degree through conservative assumptions, the use of debt reserve funds, and a high ratio of debt coverage.

CONCLUSIONS AND ADMINISTRATIVE IMPLICATIONS

As a technique useful in local economic development, tax increment financing has a history more than four decades long. The basic concept of TIF is the same everywhere, based on the principal that within the district, increased assessed value and revenue are captured by the TIF sponsor and used to pay for development costs rather than general government services. For its proponents, the use of TIF ensures that the sponsor government does not bear the sole burden of financing the economic development project.

From a public management and an administrative perspective, a proliferation of TIF districts has the potential to make local fiscal administration more difficult, if for no other reason than the increased number of tax rates that must be calculated and administered by local government authorities. The institution of TIF districts requires a spatial delineation of the TIF project area in relation to the other taxing units, as well as the monitoring of the TIF's impact on the taxing unit's fiscal position. If a variety of projects within a local jurisdiction use a TIF approach to initiate economic development projects, a great deal of fiscal fragmentation within the same unit of local government is bound to occur, further complicating what is often an already complex local fiscal economy. The following scenario illustrates some of the potential challenges associated with widespread use of TIF districts.

Imagine a local fiscal economy that is composed of literally dozens of different taxing districts, all administered by the same local government authority, with each district composed of a different and partitioned tax base that is designated specifically to pay for only certain types of public facilities and public services. Each taxing district has a base assessed value that can be used to finance (up to a limit established by the tax rate) the provision of a basic package of services, as well as another incremental portion of assessed value ("above" the base) that can be used only for a separate and different set of public services and facilities. These revenues cannot, or at least should not, be mixed. An arbitrary decision must be made concerning the exact boundaries of service benefits for specific public facilities so that only the persons residing within these boundaries pay taxes that finance those facilities, even if other persons residing elsewhere can travel within the boundaries and enjoy the benefits provided by the earmarked facilities. As a result, there are as many different effective tax rates as there are taxing districts, even though the same local government authority is administering all districts. Similarly, residents within the different taxing districts are provided with different levels and packages of public facilities and public services, with the composition of each package dependent upon the facilities and services financed within each district. Certainly, a fiscal economy such as this will create an extraordinary public administrative burden and, just as certainly, a potentially wide range of interdistrict inequities among citizens. Yet, taken to its logical spatial conclusion, this is exactly the type of fiscal system toward which the widespread use of TIF districts by a single jurisdiction will evolve.

Clearly, then, issues of fiscal equity are always involved in decisions about TIF boundaries, project costs and payments, and the use of debt instruments. The jurisdictional influence of a TIF sponsor (i.e., the formal political boundary) often goes beyond just the project area and encompasses land parcels that are not even adjacent to the project but that, presumably, will receive some benefits from the public facilities financed by TIF bonds. If these nonadjacent areas fail to capture any of the fiscal or economic benefits anticipated from the TIF project, residents within those areas are faced with paying part of the debt service for facilities from which they receive few if any benefits. This is, of course, the case with many traditionally financed public capital facilities; but because one of the presumed advantages of TIF is its explicit implementation of the benefit principle, it is ironic that when such mismatches occur, vertical and horizontal equity in the local fiscal system may be damaged rather than improved by the TIF approach.

Yet the need to create economic development opportunities for metropolitan regions is as great as ever, and there are no compelling reasons to expect a diminution of local government interest in tax increment financing approaches to economic development. Apart from the administrative complexity of TIF, the problems underscored by critics of TIF (e.g., subsidies to or by TIF districts and fiscal fragmentation and management) are not terribly severe, particularly when considered in the context of the overall fiscal environment of modern local administration. City governments continue to be pressured to keep taxes low, to tie service delivery benefits to quid pro quo payment schemes, to provide constant levels of local services in the face of declining federal and state revenue transfers, and to offer public capital investment in support of private-sector development projects. Faced with such pressures, it is unlikely that local government managers will abandon the use of TIF even if subsidization issues remain. Far less attention has been given to what could be considered the growing administrative burden of managing TIF districts and the variety of tax rates, revenue distribution rules, and interjurisdictional transfers that are created by tax increment financing. The administrative complexity of managing TIF districts could become more serious for local government managers, especially if the reinventing government movement continues to reduce the staffing levels of city governments. As more case studies and cross-sectional analyses of TIF districts are published, more will be learned about how best to administer tax increment financing in the interests of project participants and citizens at large.

REFERENCES

Anderson, J. E. 1990. Tax increment financing: Municipal adoption and growth. *National Tax Journal* 43(2): 155–163.
Barnekov, T., and D. Rich. 1989. Privatism and the limits of local economic development policy. *Urban Affairs Quarterly* 25 (December): 4.
Clarke, S. E., and G. Galle. 1992. The next wave: Postfederal local economic development strategies. *Economic Development Quarterly* 6(2) (May): 187–198.
Cummings, S. 1988. *Business elites and urban development.* Albany: State University of New York Press.
Dabney, D. Y. 1991. The industrial location decision. *Economic Development Quarterly* 4(2) (May): 154–156.
Davidson, J. M. 1979. Tax increment financing as a tool for community redevelopment. *Journal of Urban Law* (56): 404–444.
Davis, D. 1989. Tax increment financing. *Public Budgeting and Finance* 1(9): 63–73.
Dewar, M. E. 1990. Tax incentives and public loans and subsidies: What difference do they make on nonmetropolitan economic development? In *Financing economic development,* ed. R. D. Bingham, E. W. Hill, and S. B. White. Newbury Park, CA: Sage Publications.
Forgey, F. A. 1993. Tax increment financing: Equity, effectiveness, and efficiency. *The Municipal Yearbook,* Washington, D.C. International City Management Association, 25–33.
Greuling, J. E. 1987. Tax increment financing: A downtown development tool. *Economic Development Review* (Winter): 23–27.
Harbit, Douglas A. 1975. *Tax increment financing.* National Council for Urban Economic Development Information Service no. 1 (September). Washington, DC: National Council for Urban Economic Development.
Huddleston, J. R. 1981. Variations in development subsidies under tax increment financing. *Land Economics* 57(3): 373–384.

———. 1982. A comparison of state tax increment financing laws. *State Government* 55(1): 29–33.

———. 1984. Tax increment financing as a state development policy. *Growth and Change* 15(2): 11–17.

———. 1986. Intrametropolitan financial flows under tax increment financing. *Policy Sciences* 19(2): 143–161.

———. 1986. Distribution of development costs under tax increment financing. *Journal of the American Planning Association* 52 (Spring): 194–198.

Jung, Lynne. 1991. No tax relief seen for schools in '92. *Lafayette Journal and Courier* (November 10).

Klemanski, J. S. 1990. Using tax increment financing for urban redevelopment projects. *Economic Development Quarterly* 4(1): 23–28.

Lawrence, D. B., and S. C. Stephenson. 1995. The economics and politics of tax increment financing. *Growth and Change* 26(1) (Winter): 105–137.

Michael, Joel. 1987. Tax increment financing. Local development finance after tax reform. *Government Finance Review* 3(5): 17–21.

Musgrave, R. A., and P. B. Musgrave. 1989. *Public finance in theory and practice*. New York: McGraw-Hill Book Company.

Paetsch, J. R., and R. K. Dahlstrom. 1990. Tax increment financing: what it is and how it works. In *Financing economic development: An institutional response*, ed. R. D. Bingham, E. W. Hill, and S. B. White. Newbury Park, CA: Sage Publications.

Rosentraub, Mark S., and D. Swindell. 1991. Just say no? The economic and political realities of a small city's investment in minor league baseball. *Economic Development Quarterly* 5 (May 2): 152–167.

Ritter, K., and K. Oldfield. 1990. Testing the effects of tax increment financing in Springfield, Illinois: The assessor's role in determining policy outcomes. *Property Tax Journal* 9(2): 141–47.

Schmenner, Roger W. 1982. *Making business location decisions*. Englewood Cliffs, NJ: Prentice-Hall.

Stallard, M. A. 1991. Tax increment financing: Flying a public/private banner. *Corporate Cashflow*: 40–41.

Stinson, T. F. 1992. Subsidizing local economic development through tax increment financing: Costs in nonmetro communities in southern Minnesota. *Policy Studies Journal* 20(2): 241–248.

Swanstrom, Todd. 1988. Semisovereign cities: The politics of urban development. *Polity* 21(1) (Fall): 83.

Wolman, Harold. 1988. Local economic development policy: What explains the divergence between policy analysis and political behavior? *Journal of Urban Affairs* (10): 19–28.

CHAPTER 3

A Review of State Tax Increment Financing Laws

Craig L. Johnson
and
Kenneth A. Kriz

INTRODUCTION

Following the rapid post-World War II development, the first law authorizing the use of tax increment financing (TIF) was passed in California in 1952 (after approval of an amendment to the state constitution in 1951) (Huddleston 1982). TIF use grew quickly in California after passage of the law, but it was relatively slow to spread to other states. By 1970 only six additional states (Minnesota, Nevada, Ohio, Oregon, Washington, and Wyoming) had joined California in authorizing this form of financing (Wyatt 1990). However, from the mid-1970s to the late-1980s several states passed enabling legislation, and the use of TIF expanded throughout the nation. This expansion was due to a number of factors, most important, a decline in federal aid, a steady economic and concomitant social decline in some urban areas, and substantial public pressure against general tax increases (Paetsch and Dahlstrom 1990; Klemanski 1989; Klemanski 1990).

By 1997, forty-eight states had passed legislation authorizing TIF. Only North Carolina and Delaware do not authorize TIF. The North Carolina legislature enacted a TIF law in 1982 but made it effective only on passage of an amendment to the state constitution. Such an amendment was proposed in 1982 but was defeated, and the law never took effect. Besides these two states, the fate of West Virginia's law is uncertain. In 1996 the state Supreme Court of Appeals ruled in *County Com-*

missioners of Boone County v. Ed Cooke that the Tax Increment Financing Act passed in 1995 was unconstitutional (Resnick 1996).

While almost all states authorize TIF, there is substantial variation in its actual use. In 1987, 467 cities in California had operating TIF districts (TIDs). In contrast, Hawaii, Mississippi, and New Jersey all had laws authorizing TIF since at least 1985, but none had an operating TID (Klemanski 1987). There is also great diversity in the provisions of TIF legislation across states. The laws range from extremely basic (Alaska's law is only one printed page) to very detailed (California's provisions take over three hundred printed pages). This chapter reviews the current state of TIF legislation throughout the nation and provides a framework for understanding the broad and diverse nature of TIF in the United States.

FRAMEWORK: TIF AS A PROCESS

TIF is an innovative financing tool, but it should also be understood as a comprehensive process for allocating scarce public resources. Successful TIF programs require an extensive, long-term, and costly administrative effort. The TIF redevelopment process progresses through five stages: (1) initiation, (2) formulation, (3) adoption, (4) implementation, (5) evaluation and termination. Tables 3.1 and 3.2 provide a schematic of the enabling legislation that exists for each stage of the process in each state. The first stage is initiation of the redevelopment process. During this stage, the problem of an underdeveloped (or "blighted") area is recognized by private- or public-sector decision makers, and the actors in the process begin to take steps to address the problem. The second stage is marked by formulation of a redevelopment plan. Various choices are made during this process that involve trade-offs between the costs and expected benefits from increased development. Once the plan is formulated, there is a specific set of procedures that must be followed prior to adoption. There is an opportunity at this third stage for government to make the process as open or closed to the public as they wish. Once adopted, the plan must be implemented. This involves property value assessment and the allocation of tax increment revenues, including the disposition of surplus funds. Decisions on these and other administrative issues have far-reaching consequences for the effectiveness and efficiency of TIF projects. Finally, when the plan is implemented, it should be subject to evaluation and set to terminate within a specified time. These provisions effectively place constraints on the project, both in terms of requiring measurable results and requiring development to be completed within a predetermined time limit.

TABLE 3.1
TIF Enabling Statute Provisions for the Project Initiation, Plan Formulation, and Plan Adoption Stages

STATE	AK	AL	AR	AZ	CA	CO	CT	FL	GA	HI	IA	ID	IL	IN	KS	KY	LA	MA	MD	ME	MI	MN	MO	MS
PROJECT INITIATION																								
Authorized Agency:																								
Municipality	X	X	X	X	X	X	X[a]	X	X		X	X	X	X	X		X	X[b]	X[c]	X	X	X	X	X
Redevelopment or other authority		X								X						X							X	X
County		X		X	X	X		X	X		X			X			X		X					X
PLAN FORMULATION																								
Blight finding:																								
Quantified	X	X		X	X	X		X	X		X	X		X	X			X		X				X
Not quantified			X		X				X				X	X								X	X	
"But for" required										X			X											
Plan requirements:																								
Conformance with existing plans		X		X	X	X	X	X	X	X	X	X		X	X		X				X	X	X	X
Special features				X	X			X	X	X			X	X	X[d]		X			X	X			X
Project costs				X	X			X	X	X			X	X			X	X		X	X			X
PLAN ADOPTION																								
Hearings required:																								
At plan adoption		X	X[e]	X	X	X	X	X	X	X	X	X	X	X	X		X			X[f]	X	X[g]	X[h]	X
At district creation		X	X									X	X	X			X			X	X	X	X	
Add'l participatory mechanisms						X	X				X						X			X	X	X	X	

(continued on next page)

TABLE 3.1 *(continued)*

STATE	MT	ND	NE	NH	NJ	NM	NV	NY	OH	OK	OR	PA	RI	SC	SD	TN	TX	UT	VA	VT	WA	WI	WV	WY
PROJECT INITIATION																								
Authorized Agency:																								
Municipality	X	X	X	X	X[i]	X	X	X	X	X	X	X	X	X	X	X	X	X	X	X	X	X		X
Redevelopment or other authority								X[j]															X	
County	X		X				X			X	X	X	X	X	X	X		X	X		X			
PLAN FORMULATION																								
Blight finding:																								
Quantified																								
Not quantified	X	X	X			X		X	X	X	X	X		X	X		X	X			X	X	X	X
"But for" required					X							X		X			X	X[k]				X		X
Plan requirements:																								
Conformance with existing plans	X	X	X	X	X	X		X		X	X	X	X	X	X	X	X	X			X	X		X
Special features	X		X	X	X	X	X	X		X	X	X	X	X	X		X	X			X	X		
Project costs																				X				
PLAN ADOPTION																								
Hearings required:																								
At plan adoption	X	X	X	X	X	X	X	X		X	X	X[l]		X	X	X	X	X[m]		X	X	X[n]	X	X
At district creation	X		X	X		X	X[o]			X	X	X		X		X[p]	X	X	X			X		
Add'l participatory mechanisms			X			X			X			X						X						

(continued on next page)

TABLE 3.1 (*continued*)

[a] Also requires approval by state agency or commission.
[b] Also requires approval by state agency or commission.
[c] Maryland's statute excludes Baltimore City.
[d] Project costs required in separate feasibility plan.
[e] Hearings at plan adoption and district creation can be held concurrently.
[f] Hearings at plan adoption and district creation can be held concurrently.
[g] Hearings at plan adoption and district creation can be held concurrently.
[h] Hearings at plan adoption and district creation can be held concurrently.
[i] Also requires approval by state agency or commission.
[j] In New York City, the "Board of Estimate" may establish project areas.
[k] Required in a separate report is an analysis of whether the proposed development might reasonably be expected to occur in the foreseeable future solely through private investment.
[l] Hearings at plan adoption and district creation can be held concurrently.
[m] Hearings at plan adoption and district creation can be held concurrently.
[n] Hearings at plan adoption and district creation can be held concurrently.
[o] District is created at same time as redevelopment plan is approved. One hearing is required prior to the simultaneous plan adoption and district creation.
[p] Allowed but not required.

PROJECT INITIATION

In the first stage of the process the enabling legislation can be structured to quickly initiate a tax increment project by delegating the authority to establish districts to redevelopment authorities. It can also force a more formal and lengthy process by requiring local governing bodies (such as city or county councils, school districts) to adopt ordinances establishing districts. A more formal process that involves all affected local governing bodies may result in the costly delay of some worthwhile projects,[1] but it is more likely to increase public confidence in the process and assure accountability over the long run.

There is evidence that formal, more inclusive, district establishment procedures are necessary. Among the states that authorize TIF, only Kentucky allows redevelopment agencies statewide to establish tax increment or redevelopment districts. Within the forty-seven states that do not delegate the power to establish districts to authorities, twenty-three allow counties to establish projects. This is important for TIF project initiation in those states. The traditional relationship between counties and the state has been that counties, as creations of the state, are subject to their authority and serve their purposes. Allowing counties to create TIDs can create a situation where local control over the planning process is diminished since counties have only marginally independent decision-making authority. In Hawaii and West Virginia, the sole authority to establish districts resides with counties. Connecticut, Illinois, Massachusetts, and New Jersey go a step further toward centralized control. In these states, development plans drafted by municipalities must be approved by a state agency in order for a project to be established. In Illinois, for example, once the municipality has adopted an ordinance approving an economic development plan and authorizing the use of TIF, it must submit certified copies of the ordinance, along with supporting documentation to the state Department of Commerce and Community Affairs for approval and certification as an economic development project area (Illinois General Assembly 1996).

PLAN FORMULATION

Once the redevelopment process is initiated, the next stage typically involves the formulation of a redevelopment plan. The increasing use of TIF has created at least two concerns regarding plan formulation and adoption. First, in some states, TIF has been used for general governmental purposes (Johnson 1997). Second, there have been concerns raised that the definition of the term *blight* has been pushed to a meaningless extreme, with parts of affluent areas such as Palm Springs, California, being TIFed (Hitchcock 1995).

The first requirement relates to the basic nature of TIF as a tool for redevelopment. Tax increment financing was not envisaged to be a financing source for general government expenditures. A finding of blight in the area creates the link between the activities of private developers and the public purpose necessary for government to exercise the powers of eminent domain and fund a project using tax revenues (Davidson 1979). This point has been upheld in one recent court case, wherein a South Carolina court held that the state's Tax Increment Financing Law and its application to the issuance of revenue bonds by a city did not violate Article I, section 3 of the South Carolina Constitution. The court reasoned that the legislation directly benefited the public since it was designed to eliminate decaying and unhealthy areas within a city, which would significantly increase the tax base within the area, and the redevelopment was expected to stimulate growth and development in the areas immediately adjacent to the redevelopment area (South Carolina State Supreme Court 1985).

At one time, a municipality wishing to engage in redevelopment activities had only one option—to participate in federally funded low-income housing projects. The federal Fair Housing Act of 1949 (United States Congress) expanded the authority of subnational governments to engage in broader redevelopment projects. However, to qualify for federal aid on new projects, the local authority administering the project had to furnish a "workable program" including a redevelopment plan for dealing with slums and blight, which had to conform to overall federal planning objectives. In drafting local legislation to enable redevelopment projects, attempts were made to create a broad definition of the conditions necessary to create a public purpose. The notion of a blighted area redevelopment came out of these efforts.

This type of redevelopment seeks to ameliorate the causes of slums in an area that is deteriorating, but before the area becomes unusable (Purver 1996). The notion of the public interest was thus expanded to include private development of areas before they reached a point of disrepair that required widespread condemnation. This broad definition of conditions warranting a redevelopment effort has been upheld by several courts. One court held that blighted area legislation was intended to allow municipalities the latitude to make "proper development" of property in the community and arrest deterioration (New Jersey State Supreme Court 1971). However, a recent court case in Addison, Illinois, a suburb of Chicago, illustrates the potential abuse of the blight finding. The case turned on the Village of Addison's alleged misuse of the blight designation in order to justify pushing existing Hispanic residents out of the community. Without admitting guilt, the Village of Addison settled the case out of court for an estimated cost between $20 and $25 million (see Reingold, this volume).

The second problem—that of expanding definitions of blight—is more complex. California and thirty-two other states require some form of blight finding. However, this finding can take many forms. An important dimension of a blight finding is whether it is required to be in quantifiable or nonquantifiable terms. Quantified blight findings limit projects undertaken to those that meet prespecified and measurable adoption criteria. Some courts have rejected the notion that a blight finding has to be quantified or even explained. An Illinois court, for example, held that laws cannot state specific degrees of deterioration or dilapidation or mathematical measurements of the extent of overcrowding of residences, schools, and other community facilities, "for the combinations which will produce the condition at which the legislation is aimed are highly variable" (Illinois State Supreme Court 1963). Nevertheless, requiring a quantified blight finding may strengthen the link between the need to alleviate blight and the expenditure of public funds for private development efforts. Currently, however, only seven states (Alabama, Arkansas, California, Maine, Minnesota, Nebraska, and South Dakota) require some form of a quantified blight finding. An example of the language in a quantified blight finding is found in the Alabama statute:

> The local governing body shall adopt a resolution . . . which: . . . Contains findings (which shall not be subject to review except after a showing of fraud, corruption, or undue influence) that: . . . Not less than 50 percent, by area, of the real property within the tax increment district is a blighted area and is in need of rehabilitation or conservation work. (Alabama State Legislature 1996)

Twenty-six other states require a nonquantified finding of blight in order to begin the redevelopment process. In some states TIF is explicitly permitted for general economic development. In such cases some form of nonquantified notion of blight is usually incorporated into the enabling legislation, but it is not the sole or primary factor for establishing a TID. Indiana's statute is illustrative:

> The commission may determine that a geographic area is an economic development area if it finds that: . . . (1) The plan for the economic development area: (A) Promotes significant opportunities for the gainful employment of its citizens; (B) Attracts a major new business enterprise to the unit; (C) Retains or expands a significant business enterprise existing in the boundaries of the unit; . . . (Burns Publishing 1996)

An issue related to blight considerations is whether the development for which tax dollars are being expended would have occurred without the public investment, the "but for" test. Again, the primary consideration here is that the government or the authority that is designated to carry out redevelopment is expending public funds that serve a public purpose. If the development would have happened without the expenditure of public funds, then a larger public purpose was not served. However, determining whether development would have occurred is an extremely difficult matter. Many states require projects to cross some form of but for hurdle prior to project approval, but the tests are usually very low hurdles and not uniformly or rigorously applied. Kansas is among the few states that require the preparation of a comprehensive feasibility study before adoption of redevelopment plans (Kansas State Legislature 1996). However, no guidelines are offered in the legislation on how to accomplish such a study.

Most states have resorted to a simple finding by the authorizing governmental body that development would most likely not occur without the assistance and public funds supplied by the government. Currently TIF laws in fourteen states contain language requiring a but for finding. Minnesota's required finding provides an example:

> Before or at the time of approval of the tax increment financing plan, the municipality shall make the following findings, and shall set forth in writing the reasons and supporting facts for each determination: . . . (2) that the proposed development or redevelopment, in the opinion of the municipality, would not reasonably be expected to occur solely through private investment within the reasonably foreseeable future (Minnesota State Legislature, 469–175, 1996)

Along with these fourteen states, some states have required findings that come close to a but for test but lack some of the specificity of Minnesota's. Michigan, for example, requires that a redevelopment plan must include "a statement of the reasons that the plan will result in the development of captured assessed value that could not otherwise be expected" (Michigan State Legislature, 213, 1996). Probably because of the broad, nonspecific language contained in typical but for findings, there have been few challenges to this aspect of TIF laws. The court in an early case in California held that a blight finding that is based on substantial evidence is sufficient to outweigh a speculative argument that the redevelopment would take place without public intervention (California State Legislature 1964).

The redevelopment plan serves many purposes, but primarily it is a planning tool that sets forth the objectives, project timetable, and forms the written basis for communicating these matters to the taxpayers in the community. The plan is a statement of the objectives of the redevelopment project and should reflect the interests and existing plans of the community as a whole, which are commonly described in a community master plan.

The master plan of a community typically lays out several aspects relating to zoning, densities of residential and commercial properties, the provision of affordable housing, and other matters integral to community development. A redevelopment plan that differs greatly from the goals and desires embodied in the master plan changes the overall course of development in a community. Most states require the redevelopment plan to conform to the existing community plan and sometimes require a written statement from the planning body opining on the contents of the redevelopment plan. This requirement is usually a straightforward part of the enabling statute (it usually is a separate requirement, plainly observable). What is less clear is what the term *conformance* means. None of the statutes reviewed had definitions of conformance, and it appears that individual communities are at least the initial judge of when the conformity hurdle is crossed.

States that do not have a conformance requirement (along with those that do) may require the redevelopment plan to list specific planned uses for the redevelopment area. An example is provided by Illinois, which requires the following items in an economic development plan:

> a general description of any proposed developer, user, or tenant of any property to be located or improved within the economic development project area; a description of the type, structure and general character of the facilities to be developed or improved in the economic development project area; a description of the general land uses to apply in the economic development project area. (Illinois General Assembly 1996)

The second type of plan requirement relates to both the planning and the communication functions of redevelopment plans. The plan may be required to include an estimate of project costs. This requirement provides affected taxpayers with an estimate of how much they will be paying for redevelopment and begins the public debate on the appropriateness of the public expenditure. An informed public may take the opportunity to voice concerns or support at a public hearing or through other citizen participatory mechanisms. Currently, thirty-one states require an estimate of project costs to be captured in the redevelopment plan. In addition to these states, Kansas's feasibility study must show that "benefits derived from [a] project will exceed the costs" (Kansas State Legislature 1996).

The final component of the redevelopment plan concerns special features that must be incorporated into the plan. Some states require that their economic development plans explicitly mandate that development projects preserve and protect the local environment. Arizona has incorporated such a provision into their statute, which states: "The land uses and building requirements proposed in a redevelopment plan shall be designed with the general purpose of accomplishing . . . , adequate provision for light and air, the promotion of healthful and convenient distribution of population, . . . the promotion of sound design and arrangement" (Arizona State Legislature 1996). California and New York require neighborhood impact statements, which among other provisions require statements describing the effect of redevelopment on environment quality. In addition, Maine and New Hampshire require statements addressing the environmental controls to be applied to economic development projects.

Another type of special feature that some states have written into their laws is a statement of maximum density or the amount of open space in a jurisdiction. This feature relating to the human geography of redevelopment is found in the laws of nine states (Colorado, Indiana, Michigan, Montana, Nebraska, New Hampshire, New Mexico, Washington, and Wyoming). These states are all relatively low population density states (though densities are higher in Michigan and Indiana). It appears that these states are taking a more active role in preserving natural resources while still encouraging development. A similar type of special feature, this type relating to physical geography, is found in the laws of Louisiana and Mississippi, which require statements of waterfront or shoreline development. These states are evidently concerned about the impact of large-scale redevelopment on their coastal areas. A last type of special feature can be characterized as a set of equity concerns. Florida and California require statements relating to the impact of redevelopment on affordable housing in the area of the project. Illinois requires "a commitment by the municipality to fair employment practices and an affirmative action plan with respect to any economic development program to be undertaken by the municipality" (Illinois General Assembly 1996).

PLAN ADOPTION

The enabling provisions that affect this stage of the TIF process are requirements for public hearings prior to approval of a redevelopment plan or the creation of a redevelopment district, and requirements for certain additional participatory mechanisms. These requirements constrain the process by placing additional public accountability restrictions on the planning effort.

Public hearings are a "good government" tool, generally proposed with

the intent that projects that use public funds should involve public participation. Of the forty-eight states with enabling statutes, only six (Alaska,
Kentucky, Massachusetts, Maryland, Ohio, and Rhode Island) do not
require public hearings prior to plan approval or district creation; thirty-five
states require a hearing on adoption of a redevelopment or tax increment
finance plan; twenty-three states require a hearing on the creation of a TID
or redevelopment district. Some states thus have a requirement for a hearing on both occasions. However, in several states only one public hearing is
required if plan adoption is concurrent with district creation.[2] Additionally,
at least two states (Nevada State Legislature 1995; Pennsylvania State Legislature 1996) establish districts and approve plans in one ordinance and
require one meeting prior to passage of the ordinance.

In addition to the requirement for hearings, some statutes encourage
greater public participation by requiring that additional participatory hurdles be crossed. There is a tremendous range of input and control provided by these mechanisms. At one end of the spectrum, some states allow
for input from taxing districts affected by the TIF project. Oregon's
statute reflects this orientation: "An urban renewal plan and accompany-
ing report shall be forwarded to the governing body of each taxing district
affected by the urban renewal plan and the agency shall consult and con-
fer with the taxing districts prior to presenting the plan to the governing
body of the municipality for approval" (Oregon State Legislature 1995).

Another approach reflected in the laws of some states is the establishment of a formal commission. Such an approach is exemplified in
Michigan's law:

> [T]he governing body shall then approve or reject the plan, or approve
> it with modification, by resolution based on the following considera-
> tions: (a) The findings and recommendations of a development area
> citizens council, if a development area citizens council was formed. . . .
> A development area citizens council shall be established if the proposed
> development area has 100 or more persons residing within it and a
> change in zoning or a taking of property by eminent domain is neces-
> sary to accomplish the proposed development program. (Michigan
> State Legislature, 3.540[218 and 220], 1996)

At the most restrictive end of the continuum, states may require
approval from affected taxing districts to establish a TIF project. New
Mexico has required this of their municipalities:

> [T]he tax increment method shall be used only upon prior approval by
> a majority of the units of government participating in property tax rev-
> enue derived from property within an urban renewal project. The local
> government of the municipality shall annually request such approval.
> The governor, or his authorized representative, shall approve or disap-

prove the use of the method for the state government: the governing body of each other participating unit shall approve or disapprove by ordinance or resolution the use of the method for their respective units. (New Mexico State Legislature 1996)

Obviously, given the wide range of potential control over the plan adoption process, there are tradeoffs to decisions regarding the amount of input to grant overlapping jurisdictions. Those states that have adopted the strongest provisions (e.g., New Mexico) are evidently following an egalitarian method of policy adoption. They are attempting to minimize the tax loss for overlapping districts. Since the districts as a unit ultimately have veto authority on projects, one would be surprised to see projects undertaken that did not distribute net benefits to all overlapping jurisdictions. This choice of provisions may maximize equity at the possible sake of efficiency.

At the opposite end of the spectrum, those states without provisions for formal input mechanisms are obviously discounting horizontal equity concerns in favor of approving more projects, some of which may not produce net benefits for all affected taxing entities. States with participatory mechanisms that give affected taxing districts some influence over the process, without giving them complete veto power, are granting them a measure of input without unduly constraining the authorizing body. This balanced approach will probably yield the best results in terms of the mix of efficiency, effectiveness, and equity concerns. The law should require TID officials to design projects that proportionately spread benefits and costs across all affected jurisdictions.

PLAN IMPLEMENTATION

Once a redevelopment or TIF plan is adopted, work commences on developing the project area. The actual development work is guided by the needs of the area and the possible types of development. The administration of the project area is guided by the restrictions laid out in the enabling statutes, which define how the TIF project proceeds.

Project Finances

The first broad set of restrictions relates to project finances. TIF projects are usually large financial undertakings that impact local government finances for several years. By setting financing restrictions at the outset of a TIF project, local governments can develop financial plans under less uncertainty. A vivid example is provided in the set of laws that authorizes and constrains the ability of a redevelopment agency to leverage their finances through the issuance of long-term debt securities. Of the forty-eight states that have authorized TIF, forty-six allow the

44   CRAIG L. JOHNSON AND KENNETH A. KRIZ

authority to issue bonds and other indebtedness (only Massachusetts and Tennessee do not allow the use of leverage).

Local governments in states that allow bond issuance must be prepared to have their ability to tap into their property tax base somewhat impaired while debt is outstanding. In some states, the impact of TIF on the long-term ability of municipalities and school districts to raise tax revenues can be severe. A recent study indicates that in California and Wisconsin, the statewide captured value of TIFs (the size of the property tax increment) is greater than the statewide frozen base assessed valuation (Johnson 1997).

The impact on local government finance can be substantial if the bonds issued to finance redevelopment are considered obligations of the overlapping tax districts. This is due to the fact that in many states, stringent limits are in effect on the amount of debt taxing authorities can issue or have outstanding. There are at least three different ways that states have chosen to deal with the relationship between TIF debt and debt limits in their statutes. The first way is the most often used and the least restrictive on the finances of overlapping tax districts. Thirty-six states allow the issuance of debt to be repaid from tax increments and expressly set forth in the enabling statute that this debt shall not be counted in calculating a taxing district's debt outstanding for purposes of a debt limit.

The next least restrictive way of defining the relationship is to make TIF debt not subject to constitutional debt limits, but to place separate restrictions on the amount of debt that can be issued or outstanding. This is done through setting limits within the redevelopment plan. Three states (Arizona, California, and Oregon) take this course. The California statute is illustrative: "If the [redevelopment] plan authorizes the issuance of bonds to be repaid in whole or in part from the allocation of taxes . . . , the plan shall establish a limit on the amount of bonded indebtedness which can be outstanding at one time without an amendment of the plan" (California State Legislature, 33334.1, 1996). Either of these first two methods could have the unintended consequence of transferring power and future resources from overlapping jurisdictions to the authority responsible for administering the TIF project. The final method is one of omission. Six states do not explicitly address debt limits in the enabling statute. This choice may indicate that a state is willing to let municipalities set their own debt parameters within the context of existing state law. This, however, leaves municipalities open to potential court challenges, especially regarding whether TIF debt will count against local debt limits. Whatever the intent of the state, it has become increasingly clear that courts are finding against municipalities that issue debt authorized under TIF laws that exceed debt limits.[3] The tactic of remaining silent on this issue in the context of the enabling statute may ultimately be the most restrictive on TID finances.

TABLE 3.2
TIF Enabling Statute Provisions for the Plan Implementation, Evaluation, and Termination Stages

STATE	AK	AL	AR	AZ	CA	CO	CT	FL	GA	HI	IA	ID	IL	IN	KS	KY	LA	MA	MD	ME	MI	MN	MO	MS
PLAN IMPLEMENTATION																								
Tax increment bonds:																								
Allowed,not subject to limit		X	X	X[ii]	X[iii]	X	X	X	X	X	X	X	X	X	X	X	X			X		X[i]	X	X
Allowed,subject to limit	X																							
Tax increment management:																								
Excess return allowed but not mandated		X	X	X	X	X		X		X	X		X	X			X		X	X		X	X	X
Return mandated			X[iv]												X									
Losses reimbursed					X				X					X					X		X			
School district exclusion									X[v]			X				X					X			
Development types allowed:																								
Residential			X	X	X	X		X	X	X	X		X	X		X	X		X	X	X	X		X
Industrial			X	X	X	X	X	X	X	X	X		X	X		X	X	X	X	X	X	X		X
Commercial			X	X	X	X	X	X	X	X	X		X	X		X	X	X	X	X	X	X		X
Size limits:																								
Area		X	X	X	X	X			X	X	X	X		X	X		X			X				
Property value		X	X															X		X				
EVALUATION																							X[vi]	
TERMINATION																								
Time limits		X	X	X	X	X		X			X			X	X		X	X		X	X	X	X	

(continued on next page)

TABLE 3.2 *(continued)*

STATE	MT	ND	NE	NH	NJ	NM	NV	NY	OH	OK	OR	PA	RI	SC	SD	TN	TX	UT	VA	VT	WA	WI	WV	WY
PLAN IMPLEMENTATION																								
Tax increment bonds:																								
Allowed, not subject to limit	X	X	X	X	X	X	X	X	X	X	X^{vii}	X	X	X	X^{viii}		X	X			X	X	X	X
Allowed, subject to limit																			X	X				
Tax increment management:																								
Excess increment return allowed but not mandated	X			X	X			X	X	X^{x}	X	X	X				X^{ix}	X						
Return mandated		X																		X				
Losses reimbursed				X										X							X	X	X	
School district exclusion									X			X												
Development types allowed:																								
Residential	X					X			X	X	X	X	X	X	X		X^{xi}	X			X	X		
Industrial	X	X	X		X	X		X	X	X	X	X	X	X	X		X	X			X		X	X
Commercial	X	X	X		X	X		X	X	X	X	X	X	X			X	X			X		X	X
Size limits:																								
Area			X	X						X	X	X	X		X^{xiii}		X	X				X		
Property value				X			X			X	X	X						X				X		
EVALUATION					X			X^{xii}	X					X										
TERMINATION					X																			
Time limits	X		X			X	X		X	X		X			X			X			X	X		

(continued on next page)

TABLE 3.2 *(continued)*

i   Only debt of an independent authority is not subject to debt limits. If the authority is the same as the municipality (the municipality chooses not to establish an independent authority), debt issued is considered a municipal obligation for purposes of debt limits.

ii   Limit is set forth separately in redevelopment plan.

iii   Limit is set forth separately in redevelopment plan.

iv   The amount of school district exclusion is limited to the amount of property taxes obligated to retire school district bonds.

v   School district ad valorem taxes are excluded in cases where the school district has the power to set its own tax rate and does not specifically consent to be included in the redevelopment plan.

vi   Requires public hearing on progress of redevelopment plan.

vii   Limit is set forth separately in redevelopment plan.

viii   The statute is silent regarding the relationship between TIF debt and the state debt limit. However, in *Meierhenry v. City of Huron* (354 NW 2d 171), the court ruled that increment debt is subject to the limit.

ix   The city of El Paso is excluded from the provisions allowing a return of excess increment and optional school district exclusion.

x   Overlapping taxing districts may agree to alternative uses of excess increment in lieu of the mandated return.

xi   Residential projects are limited to 10 percent of property by area in the redevelopment project area.

xii   New York requires that each legislative body approving TIF projects conduct, at least biennially, a public hearing for the purpose of reviewing the redevelopment plan for each redevelopment project within its jurisdiction and evaluating its progress.

xiii   Required in previous versions of the statute, South Dakota's evaluation provision was repealed in 1982.

Receipt and Distribution of Tax Increments

The other major set of financial management restrictions deals with how a redevelopment authority handles the tax increment it receives. These restrictions go to the very heart of a TIF project, the accumulation and use of tax increments. Since a TIF project diverts funds to a redevelopment project that otherwise would have gone to municipalities and other taxing districts (especially schools), the concern regarding increment accumulation and use is fundamental to the efficient use of TIF resources.

In an ideal situation, the increase in assessed value produced from redevelopment will generate just enough tax revenue to pay development costs, administer the project, and service any debt incurred. Balances in excess of those necessary to provide an adequate debt service reserve may accumulate in the fund (for municipal authorities) or account of the redevelopment authority. These balances consist of excess increments, which are idle funds and not needed to fulfill redevelopment needs.

To deal with this problem, twenty-nine states have included provisions in their statutes that address the issue of returning excess increments to overlapping jurisdictions. Thirteen of these states have chosen to simply "allow" the return of excess incremental revenues. This is usually accomplished by allowing a redevelopment authority to choose among alternative uses of the excess, where one of the alternatives is the return of funds to the local department in charge of revenue collection. Minnesota's law provides an example:

> In any year in which the tax increment exceeds the amount necessary to pay the costs authorized by the tax increment financing plan, . . . the authority shall use the excess amount to do any of the following: (1) prepay any outstanding bonds, (2) discharge the pledge of tax increment therefor, (3) pay into an escrow account dedicated to the payment of such bond, or (4) return the excess amount to the county auditor who shall distribute the excess amount to the municipality, county, and school district in which the tax increment financing district is located in direct proportion to their respective local tax rates. (Minnesota State Legislature, subd. 2, 1996)

The second restriction relating to project finances involves the initial stages of the physical improvements. In the initial phase, land is purchased, cleared (if there are any structures that will be demolished and replaced), and prepared for future development. Often the assessed land value in the project area will fall initially, and the tax revenues for the overlapping districts will fall relative to where they may have been. Also, municipalities may have to expend regular property tax revenues to pay for initial phase improvements prior to the point where increment financing produces positive cash flow (the end of the following assessment cycle) (Huddleston 1982). If these "losses" and "advances" go unreimbursed by the authority in charge of redevelopment, then the proposed TIF project is not strictly financed through increments. Again, this gets at the very nature of TIF. Financing redevelopment in a self-supporting way has always been the primary selling point for municipalities seeking a technique to redevelop previously blighted areas.

Despite the basic importance of this requirement, only seven states currently have provisions regarding reimbursement of municipalities for tax loss or redevelopment expenditures in their enabling statutes. North Dakota's law provides the prototype, where the county auditor must certify all tax losses. Then,

> [u]pon receipt of any tax increments in the fund the county treasurer, at the times when the county treasurer distributes collected taxes to the state and to each political subdivision for which a tax loss has previously been recorded, shall also remit to each of them from the tax increment fund an amount proportionate to the amount of that tax loss, until all those tax losses have been reimbursed. (North Dakota State Legislature 1995)

The final major restriction that may be placed on TIF project finances defines the relationship between school districts and the project. School districts have traditionally been one of the larger benefactors of property tax revenues. As discussed earlier, there is a concern that the diversion of property tax revenues to a TIF project can place undue burdens on overlapping jurisdictions, especially school districts, in terms of lost property tax revenues. This concern is exacerbated in areas where the primary and secondary school age population is growing.

As a response to concerns of TIF projects "siphoning" off needed funds from school districts, fourteen states have included some form of an exclusion of the property taxes generated in the TIF project area that were to go to overlapping school districts. Within these states, however, there is a wide amount of variation in the nature of the exclusion. Three methods of exclusion have been developed. The first two are mandated in the enabling statutes. The most restrictive of any exclusion is the mandated full exemption of school districts in four states (Kentucky, Louisiana, Maryland, and Washington). Washington does give school districts the choice to participate in the increment: "Any other taxing unit in a municipality *is authorized* to allocate a like amount of such [increment] to the municipality or municipalities in which it is situated" (emphasis added) (Washington State Legislature 1996).

A somewhat less restrictive but still mandatory exclusion is provided in four states (Arkansas, California, Idaho, and Michigan). Arkansas weakens the exclusion by allowing it only on "that amount of the general property taxes . . . obligated to retire any bonded indebtedness of the school district in a redevelopment property district" (Arkansas State Legislature 1995). Michigan's restriction is of the following form: "The percentage of taxes levied for school operating purposes that is captured and used by the plan shall not be greater than the plan's percentage capture and use of taxes levied by a municipality or county for operating purposes" (Michigan State Legislature 1996).

The last method is the least restrictive. Four states (New Hampshire, Ohio, Pennsylvania, and Texas) allow school districts to vote on an optional exclusion. Ohio's optional exclusion is unique in that Ohioans can choose to either lose tax increment revenues on the full assessed value of a property for ten years or lose 75 percent of the revenue for thirty years (Ohio State Legislature 1997). In Pennsylvania (Pennsylvania State Legislature 1996) school districts can opt to retain the full tax increment and not participate in the redevelopment project. In Texas school districts may decide to contribute anywhere from 0 to 100 percent of its incremental revenue to a project (Arvidson, Hissong and Cole, this volume).

Georgia and South Carolina offer special cases of school district exclusion. Under Georgia law, school district ad valorem taxes are excluded in cases where the school district has the power to set its tax rate and does not specifically consent to inclusion in the revenue allocation plan (Georgia State Legislature 1996). South Carolina has a rather complex exclusion stating that overlapping taxing districts (including school districts) can object to the formation of the TID. In this case, the increment value for that district cannot be included in the amount of the increment that goes to a redevelopment fund. However, this exclusion applies only after the first fifteen years of debt service on TIF-backed bonds. If the initial term of the bonds or the time remaining to retirement (for refunding bonds) of the issue is less than fifteen years, no consent is needed to include the increment of the overlapping districts (South Carolina State Legislature 1996).

Another set of features that may appear in enabling statutes is a set of limitations on the types of redevelopment projects allowed in the TID. There is no one way to describe all potential types of redevelopment in a project area. Thus, some state laws and two earlier studies of TIF laws[4] referred to the types in broad categories of residential, industrial, and commercial. We continue this practice as merely a means of simplification.

These redevelopment-type limitations describe a vision of what a completed redevelopment project will look like in terms of land uses.

This vision in turn may offer clues as to the type of redevelopment that states value most. Consider the examples of California and Massachusetts. California requires the following:

> Not less than 20 percent of all taxes which are allocated to the agency pursuant to [tax increment financing] shall be used by the agency for the purposes of increasing, improving, and preserving the community's supply of low- and moderate-income housing available at affordable housing cost ... to persons and families of low or moderate income ... and very low income households . . . [income levels are elsewhere defined]. (California State Legislature, 33333.2, 1996)

This requirement is a specific incentive offered to increase the supply of low- and moderate-income housing in the state. Therefore, mixed-use development should be a predominant type of project found in California TIDs.

By contrast, Massachusetts allows the proceeds of their TIF program to be used solely for attracting and retaining industrial and commercial projects (Massachusetts State Legislature 1996). Thus, residential development in project areas is only accomplished through private initiative. Furthermore, the redevelopment authority might not be able to "capture" the assessed value of said residential development. One would expect to see very little residential development in Massachusetts TIDs.

Most states have chosen not to restrict certain types of redevelopment projects. Twenty-eight states allow residential, commercial, and industrial projects. Texas does allow residential development projects, but limits the area they occupy to 10 percent of the overall project area (Texas State Legislature 1997). Seven states restrict residential development entirely through permitting only industrial and commercial development. Ohio is the only state to allow only residential projects. Wisconsin allows only industrial redevelopment (Wisconsin State Legislature 1996). New Hampshire allows only commercial projects (New Hampshire State Legislature 1996).

The laws of nine states do not explicitly or implicitly refer to the types of allowed projects. There are at least two ways to view this silence. One could reasonably infer that these states have decided that the allowed project should be determined by local zoning ordinances. Another possibility is that the states wanted redevelopment authorities to concentrate on developing the land to the point where any type of development was feasible and then let the private market determine the development type most suited to the TID.

Limiting the type of redevelopment projects allowed in the project area is just one example of limitations on administration of a project.

Another example is a limitation on the extent of redevelopment allowed in a municipality. Redevelopment authorities may have incentives to expand their area of authority to capture as much area and property as possible. Since redevelopment authorities lack the ability to change the tax levy, the only avenue for growth is to capture more property value either through creating new projects or expanding the borders of the current project area.

Twenty-one states restrict either the physical area that can be encompassed by TIDs or the percentage of assessed value that can be captured. Eight states use the method of restricting the physical area of TIDs. Within this group, Kansas places no specific restriction on the area of TIDs but places it on the percentage of land that can be in conservation areas and enterprise zones (Kansas State Legislature 1996). These two types of development areas are the only areas that can be placed into redevelopment districts and funded through TIF. Eighteen states restrict the percentage of total assessed value of the municipality that can be placed in a redevelopment area. The statutes in five states (Maine, New Hampshire, Oklahoma, Oregon, and Utah) contain both limitations.

EVALUATING AND TERMINATING A TID

The last stage of a TIF project is the evaluation and termination of the redevelopment effort. One can view this stage as the culmination of redevelopment activities. Properly handled, TIF projects can produce gains in employment, income, and civic pride in a local area. Successful projects such as the Los Angeles Skid Row renovations have been put forth as shining examples of the potential of TIF to spur the redevelopment of a blighted area (Hitchcock 1995). However, there also have been notable failures in TIF redevelopment. The Riverfront Authority established in the city of Littleton, Colorado, provides a vivid example. The authority was created to make commercial improvements to a redevelopment area consisting primarily of small retail development. Occupancy rates in the completed project were well below expectations and failed to generate sufficient incremental sales and property tax revenues. The authority eventually defaulted on its TIF bonds (Johnson 1997). As late as August 1996, the principal building financed by the authority stood nearly empty in an otherwise vibrant commercial area, and no long-term net increase in employment occurred that can be specifically tied to the Littleton Riverfront development project.

A set of legal provisions that require the evaluation of a project's progress toward meeting the objectives laid out in the enabling ordinance is an important mechanism to isolate and contain problems inherent in redevelopment projects. If problems such as those in Littleton, Colorado, can be identified early in the redevelopment venture, then the authority can act to alleviate the problems. Currently, only nine states have provisions in their TIF laws requiring evaluations. Massachusetts has one of the more robust provisions. It requires the state Economic Assistance Coordinating Council to "conduct a continual evaluation of economic opportunity areas and the projects certified for participation in the economic development incentive program" (Massachusetts State Legislature, 23A:3C, 1996). In addition, New York State requires a public hearing every two years on the redevelopment plan to review progress made (New York State Legislature 1996).

Another limitation that can be placed on the administration of TIF relates to the termination of projects. A redevelopment authority with the ability to TIF can capture resources that would normally go to overlapping jurisdictions for a period of time far in excess of the effects of a specific project. A "perpetual" TIF district was likely not envisioned by those seeking to promote current redevelopment in an area. If TIDs are not limited in the period of time they may collect diverted taxes, authority members may inappropriately use such revenues for purposes not explicitly approved in the capital planning process.

Twenty-four states have chosen to address this issue through setting maximum time limits for either projects or the use of TIF by an authority. There is a great amount of variation in the number of years one can use TIF financing for a specific project. For example, California places an effective thirty-year time limit on TIF projects (Chapman, this volume). Contrasted with this very liberal policy, New Mexico places strict five-year (ten years for projects initiated under the metropolitan redevelopment provisions of the statutes) time limits on the tax increment financing method. Under this restriction, the redevelopment area can live on perpetually, but the tax increment is restricted. This may act to focus effort early in the development undertaking, but may preclude the efficient use of debt financing.

CONCLUSION

This chapter has described the salient features of state laws governing tax increment financing. These laws reflect the evolutionary process of tailoring a legal framework to meet the diverse economic development needs of many different states and municipalities.

We have portrayed TIF as a process for allocating public resources, not just a redevelopment finance technique. The laws of a state that govern the TIF process must be structured to channel the process in ways that further the public interest. This channeling should provide a balance among efficiency, equity, and accountability concerns. States must not sacrifice equity and public accountability, for the sake of expediency and efficiency—an appropriate balance must be struck. Also, states should increase their use of program evaluation to measure the effectiveness, efficiency, and equity of TIF programs. In the absence of other strong limiting factors, the presence of strong evaluation requirements could protect the interests of the public while allowing the redirection of funds to extremely worthy projects.

Whatever course is chosen by states in refining their laws, the basic realization that TIF is a process must be present. Decisions made about the restrictions, requirements, and processes at one stage have important implications for all other stages. Decisions about what type of redevelopment to allow, for example, need to be coupled with decisions on how much public input to require. There are markedly different equity concerns among commercial, industrial, and residential project types, and these concerns need to be reflected consistently in all areas of enabling statutes. In summary, what we have found is an amalgam of TIF law that has emerged out of the dialectic nature of redevelopment. What is called for is a more thoughtful and consistent redesign of the law in accordance with the wishes of the citizens of states utilizing tax increment financing and the concerns of planners and policymakers in those states.

NOTES

1. See Holupka and Shlay (1993) for a case study of a successful attempt to stop a proposed development project.
2. See for example Minnesota State Legislature, *Revised Statutes*, 469–175 subd. 3 (1996) and Missouri State Legislature (1996).
3. See for example Iowa State Supreme Court (1975), South Dakota State Supreme Court (1984), Wisconsin State Supreme Court (1992), and Oklahoma State Supreme Court (1995).
4. See Huddleston (1982) and Wyatt (1990).

REFERENCES

Alabama State Legislature. 1996. *Alabama State code*, 11–99–4.
Arizona State Legislature. 1996. *Revised statutes*, 36–1479.
Arkansas State Legislature.1995. *Code of 1987 annotated*, 14–168–203.
Burns Publishing Company. 1996. *Indiana Code annotated*, 36-7-14–41.
California State Legislature. 1964. *Redevelopment plan*, In re 389 P2d 538, cert den 379 US 899.

———. 1996. *Health and safety code annotated*, 33333.2, 33334.1.

Colorado Governor's Office of Business Development, State of. 1997. Economic Development Discussion Paper. *WWW:* http://governor.state.co.us/ smartgrowth/econdev.htm.

Davidson, Jonathan M. 1979. Tax increment financing as a tool for community development. *Journal of Urban Law* 56 (Winter): 405–444.

Georgia State Legislature. 1996. *Official code annotated*, 36–44–9.

Hitchcock, David. 1995. CreaTIFity helps cities find development dollars. *American City & County* (May): 40–49.

Holupka, Scott C., and Anne B. Shlay. 1993. Political economy and urban development. In *Theories of local economic development: Perspectives from across the disciplines*, ed. Richard D. Bingham and Robert Mier. Newbury Park, CA: Sage Publications.

Huddleston, Jack R. 1982. A comparison of state tax increment financing laws. *State Government* (55): 29–33.

Illinois General Assembly. 1996. *Compiled statutes annotated*, 20 (620/3, 5).

Illinois State Supreme Court. 1963. In *Chicago v. R. Zwick Co*, 188 NE2d 489, app dismd 373 US 542.

Iowa State Supreme Court. 1975. In *Richards v. City of Muscatine*, 237 NW 2d 48.

Johnson, Craig L. 1997. *The national tax increment bond market: The mainstreaming of a fringe sector*. Bloomington, IN: Institute for Development Strategies.

Kansas State Legislature. 1996. *Statutes annotated*, 12–1771.

Klemanski, John S. 1987. Tax increment financing and urban redevelopment: States and cities as entrepreneurs. Paper delivered at the 1987 American Political Science Association meeting, September 3–6, Chicago. Cited in James R. Paetsch and Roger K. Dahlstrom, Tax increment financing: What it is and how it works. In *Financing Local Development*, ed. Richard D. Bingham, E. W. Hill, and S. B. White. (Newbury Park, CA: Sage Publications, 1990).

———. 1989. Tax increment financing: Public funding for private economic development projects. *Policy Studies Journal* 17 (Spring): 656–671.

———. 1990. Using tax increment financing for urban redevelopment projects. *Economic Development Quarterly* 4 (February): 23–28.

Massachusetts State Legislature. 1996. *Annotated laws*, 23A:3C, 40:59.

Michigan State Legislature. 1996. *Statutes annotated*, 3.540(213, 218, 220).

Minnesota State Legislature. 1996. *Statutes*, 469.176 subd. 2.

———. 1996. Local economic development. In *Statutes*, 469–175 subd. 3.

Missouri State Legislature. 1996. *Revised statutes of the state of Missouri*, 99.825.

Missouri State Supreme Court. 1989. In *Tax increment financing commission of Kansas City v. Dunn*, 781 SW 2d 70.

Nevada State Legislature. 1995. *Revised statutes annotated*, 361B.190.

New Hampshire State Legislature. 1996. *Revised statutes annotated*, 162–K:1 note 175:1.

New Jersey State Supreme Court. 1971. In *Levin v. Township Committee of Bridgewater*, 274 A2d 1, app dismd 404 US 803.

New Mexico State Legislature. 1996. *Statutes annotated*, 3–46–45.

New York State Legislature. 1996. *Consolidated law services general municipal law*, 970–h.

North Dakota State Legislature. 1995. *Century code*, 40–58–20.

Ohio State Legislature. 1997. *Revised code annotated*, 5709.73.

Oklahoma State Supreme Court. 1995. In *Muskogee Urban Renewal Authority v. Excise Board of Muskogee County*, 899 P 2d 624.

Oregon State Legislature. 1995. *Revised statutes*, 457.085.

Paetsch, James R., and Roger K. Dahlstrom. 1990. Tax increment financing: What it is and how it works. In *Financing local development*, ed. Richard D. Bingham, E. W. Hill, and S. B. White. Newbury Park, CA: Sage Publications.

Pennsylvania State Legislature. 1996. *Statutes*, 53:6930.5.

Purver, Jonathan M. 1996. What constitutes a blighted area within urban renewal and redevelopment statutes. *ALR* 3d (45): 1096.

Resnick, Amy B. 1996. West Virginia supreme court ruling bars use of tax increment financings. *The Bond Buyer* (July 31): 3.

South Carolina State Legislature. 1996. *Code*, 31–6–80.

South Carolina State Supreme Court. 1985. In *Wolper v. City Council of Charleston*, 336 SE 2d 871.

South Dakota State Supreme Court. 1984. In *Meierhenry v. City of Huro*, 354 NW 2d 171.

Texas State Legislature. 1997. *Statutes and codes*, 311.006–013.

United States Congress. 1949. Fair Housing Act of 1949. In *Statutes*, 63.413.

Washington State Legislature. 1996. *Annotated revised code*, 35.81.100.

Wisconsin State Legislature. 1996. *Statutes*, 66.46.

Wisconsin State Supreme Court. 1992. *City of Hartford v. Kirley*, 493 NW 2d 45.

Wyatt, Michael D. 1990. The TIF smorgasbord: A survey of state statutory provisions for tax incremental financing. *Assessment Digest* (November/December): 3–9.

CHAPTER 4

Nonproperty Tax Increment Programs for Economic Development: A Review of the Alternative Programs

John L. Mikesell

States authorizing tax increment financing for the support of development or redevelopment normally limit their programs to property taxes. In the typical arrangement, the additional property taxes produced by the new development are captured by a TIF district established in the area of the proposed new development or redevelopment to service debt issued to construct capital infrastructure important for the economic project. The TIF mechanism disperses the public cost of development to all governments that stand to benefit, eventually, from the higher tax base associated with the growth and economic revitalization generated by the TIF project. Without the TIF-supported infrastructure, there would have been no project, so the governments are, as a practical matter, not surrendering much when they allow the tax increment to be captured by the TIF district. The district receives tax revenue without any net increase in tax rate paid by economic activity in the district.

Overlapping jurisdictions and their citizens complain that TIFs take revenues from their basic operations without their permission and without normal budgetary control on how the money is spent. The revenue loss may even endanger the finance of customary local services provided as the district develops, but states continue the programs in their quest for economic development. In effect, the TIF district becomes a new jurisdiction for the delineation of property tax rates. From the base assessed value in the district, the proceeds of all assessed value increases go to TIF district finances, rather than to the traditional governments serving that area.

A small group of states include, or have included, other taxes, mostly sales and use, in TIF programs. These programs for major nonproperty taxes are the topic of this chapter. Much of what can be said about property tax TIFs also applies to these systems as well. However, there are features that differ considerably from those in typical property tax programs, and the several nonproperty tax programs are far from identical in format.

AN OVERVIEW OF THE NONPROPERTY TIF PROGRAMS

Several states now offer or at one time offered TIF programs for major taxes other than the property tax: California, Colorado, Illinois, Indiana, Kansas, Louisiana, Maine, Missouri, Wyoming, and the District of Columbia.[1] All programs but one recently adopted in Maine involve the sales tax (STIFs); some of them have also included narrow business taxes as well, but the sales tax revenue dominates each program.

California

Redevelopment agencies were allowed to levy sales and use taxes in 1981 as a mechanism to support redevelopment projects in blighted areas, defined to be areas that had become physical, social, or economic liabilities to the community (California State Legislature 1981). The program does not follow the pattern of property tax programs or of other true STIFs. Under the California legislation, the redevelopment agency can levy a sales tax rate up to 1 percent, provided the city or county reduces its rate in the redevelopment area by a corresponding amount. In other words, the redevelopment tax serves as a full credit against the other local rate. The redevelopment agency then uses that revenue to attract retail operations by capital development or by rebate of sales tax collections to project developers.

The redevelopment agency captures all revenue from its rate, not just the increments to a revenue base. However, while the redevelopment rate does not increase the combined sales tax rate applied in its area, it does divert revenue that would have otherwise gone to local government. From the view of a taxpayer, the program looks like a STIF: the redevelopment agency receives tax revenue, but the tax rate faced by the taxpayer does not increase. From the government side, all revenue, not just the increment, flows to redevelopment and away from traditional local governments.[2] Nineteen redevelopment agencies in California received sales tax revenue in 1994 and 1995.

Authority for redevelopment sales and use taxes was rescinded in January 1994 (California State Legislature 1993). The change was the result of concern that land use patterns in California were being driven heavily by fiscal impact, without adequate concern for other community issues and without particular interest in whether redevelopment areas were truly blighted. Communities were guiding land use with extraordinary attention to retail sales tax that might be generated. It had become common for agencies to rebate a portion of the tax to projects generating large amounts of sales tax. Retail development was simply being moved about by competition among communities, with automobile dealerships seen as a particular problem, although any high sales tax volume business (retail malls, hotels, etc.) was an attractive target. The 1993 act terminated the redevelopment agency sales tax authority, the ability of agencies to rebate sales tax to projects, and the seldom used authority to use that revenue to secure debt service, although debt issued before 1 January 1994 could be liquidated under a grandfather clause. Ending the program stopped bidding wars.

Colorado

Colorado authorizes local sales tax increment financing of bonds issued to redevelop blighted areas as designated by a city (Colorado State Legislature 1997). Redevelopment agencies (which may manage several TIF districts) that have issued sales tax increment district bonds have operated in Arvada, Boulder, Denver, Englewood, Estes Park, and Littleton; other agencies in the state limit their TIFs to the property tax.

These are conventional tax increment programs. The law establishes a base-year sales tax amount as tax collections from the renewal area in the twelve-month period ending on the last day of the month prior to the effective approval date of the development plan. Amounts collected above that are the increments. The TIF is limited to twenty-five years unless bonds issued from the proceeds are in default or are about to go into default. There are no constraints on the sorts of projects that may be financed, nor are there controls in regard to possible shifts in economic activity caused by such projects. Some districts have included the central business district (Estes Park); others have financed regional shopping malls (Boulder). The sales tax increment usually swamps the property tax increment.

District of Columbia

In 1998 the District of Columbia passed a tax increment finance law (D.C. Law 12–143) that included sales tax revenue along with property tax revenue. Within a defined downtown area, development projects can be supported by tax increments, and bonds can be supported by those tax increments. The sales tax increment is defined to be revenue above sales tax collections from locations in the tax increment area in the calendar year immediately preceding the year in which the increment area is established. There is no effort to adjust the calculated increment for any increase that might have resulted without the project. The District of Columbia Council was particularly interested in encouraging retailing and entertainment activity in the downtown area with the program. Therefore, inclusion of sales tax revenue in the increment was particularly important to that objective.

Illinois

The Illinois program, adopted in 1985 as the Tax Allocation Re-development Act, permits municipalities to include both state and local sales taxes (and utility taxes) in TIF programs in "conservation" or "blighted" areas (Illinois General Assembly 1985). Specifically, areas must be blighted, have shown no recent or current growth, and show no prospect for future growth "but for" the TIF. The conventional property tax increment, initiated in 1977, enticed few private developers to invest in the more seriously depressed urban portions of the state. The legislature made the redevelopment schemes more attractive by adding sales tax revenue to the plan. Municipalities creating or expanding TIF districts before 1 January 1987 could receive the increment in state sales tax revenue collected in the district above 1985 collections if they levied a 1 percent local sales tax and dedicated property tax increments to redevelopment. Adding the state sales tax was a powerful inducement: by the end of 1986, 137 TIF districts were eligible for state distribution, compared with only around 25 districts in 1984. However, the state sales tax increment had to be appropriated by the legislature; the increment was not automatic, and payments were to be prorated if STIF claims exceeded the total appropriated for payment, as they first did for fiscal 1988.

Concern for the long-run revenue impact on state finances induced the General Assembly to revise the program in 1988: STIF districts would receive 80 percent of sales tax increment up to one hundred thousand dollars, 60 percent of increment from one hundred thousand dollars to five hundred thousand dollars, and 40 percent of any increment above five hundred thousand dollars. From 1999, all increment payments are reduced by 10 percent per year until they are phased out in 2007 (Illinois General Assembly 1998). The 1993 state budget proposed by the governor included no such appropriation, raising severe concern about probable district defaults. A compromise in the middle of the fiscal year eventually provided an appropriation and prevented defaults. At that time, 110 bond issues totaling $300 million were supported by

STIFs (Pierog 1996). For the fiscal 1996 STIF distribution, eighty-seven districts shared in the distribution of more than $13 million. For most TIF projects, the sales tax flow is much larger than the property tax increment.

Although the motive behind the STIFs was recovery of older urban areas, districts now are likely to be specific development projects, commercial strips, or shopping malls. They have not corrected blight in older central city business districts (Pierog 1996). Cities drew district boundaries around so much commercial activity—to capture as much state sales tax revenue as possible for the city area—that state finances were stretched without much real development impact.

Indiana

Two different STIF programs have been available in Indiana, but neither has been used. The General Assembly first authorized them in 1987 (Indiana General Assembly 1987). The program was intended to support Circle Centre Mall in downtown Indianapolis but could have been used for other large retail developments. Because Indiana does not allow local sales taxes, only state sales tax increments were involved. Under the program, 75 percent of state sales tax revenue generated by the project would be placed in a STIF fund to be used as repayment of a loan from the Indiana Employment Development Commission. Projects had to entail private costs at least two and one-half times the amount spent by any public entity. The process required that the increment be estimated after allowing for growth in the base that would have occurred without the project and for shifts in purchase patterns resulting from the project. The state general fund received the remaining quarter of the increment, as well as the base sales tax revenue, natural growth, and transferred base. Money in the STIF would have had to be appropriated by the state legislature, and the legislature was under no obligation to make that appropriation. The complexities involved in attempting to limit STIF revenue to the definitely incremental discouraged investment banker interest in bonds backed by such revenue. Traditional property tax increment bonds were used for the Circle Centre Mall instead.

The second program, authorized in 1990 legislation, was to support an economic expansion project in Hammond, Indiana: a marina development. The legislation authorized the city to create STIF districts to (a) attract new business enterprise to the district or retain or expand existing business enterprises in the district; (b) benefit the public health and welfare and be of public utility and benefit; (c) protect and increase state and local tax bases or revenues; and (d) result in a substantial increase in temporary and permanent employment opportunities and private-sector investment in the district. However, a STIF could be created only if a property-tax-capturing TIF was also created for the district. The process required the state department of revenue to establish the base retail sales and use tax revenue from the district;[3] the district would then receive the net increment in the district. That net was defined to be the gross increase of revenue multiplied by an adjustment factor determined by the department of revenue to account for the portion of incremental retail sales and use tax revenue attributable to investment in the district and resulting from the development project. However, the district could receive, at a maximum, 80 percent of gross incremental revenue from its retailers.

Kansas

Kansas provided sales tax increment financing for certain historic theaters in 1999 (Kansas 76 1999). The eligible historic theaters must be in buildings built before 1940, must have been constructed for staging entertainment, must be operated by a nonprofit corporation, and must have appropriate historic designation. The increment is the amount collected from taxpayers doing business in the theater that exceeds collections prior to the designation of the building as a historic theater. Designation as a historic theater involves the municipality and the state secretary of commerce and housing as to the appropriate nature of the structure and that the designation will contribute significantly to the economic development of the city and surrounding area. Prior to this law, cities could pledge any or all city transient guest tax, sales and use tax, and utility franchise fee revenue collected within a redevelopment district for payment of redevelopment bonds, including those supported by property tax increment, but this was not a nonproperty tax TIF mechanism.

Louisiana

The Louisiana legislature has permitted STIFs since 1990. Under the law, a local government may establish nonprofit economic development corporations, subject to a finding that the "concerned jurisdiction is suffering from extreme conditions of unemployment, underemployment, or such other form of severe economic distress" (Louisiana State Legislature 1990). The corporation then devises an economic development plan that sets out the geographic location for economic development activities and specifies the types of activities "that may best achieve the purpose of increasing the aggregate income of the community, enabling income to be distributed to low and moderate income persons, and creating greater job diversity by attracting and retaining job producing establishments" (Louisiana State Legislature 1990).

Louisiana approved STIFs in two 1990 laws. Act 1082 defined a sales tax increment to be

> that portion of sales tax revenues for any or all taxing authorities collected each year . . . from taxpayers located within an economic development area which exceeds sales tax revenues that were collected for such taxing authority in the year immediately prior to the year in which the area was designated as an economic development area. (Louisiana State Legislature 1990)

Increments could be used only on approval of the Joint Legislative Committee on the Budget (JLCB). Act 96 provided local sales tax increment financing for Calcasieu Parish, using the same language to define the increment as did Act 1082, except excluding the state tax. JLCB approval was not required under this act because only the local tax was involved.

Legislation in 1995 removed the state tax from all STIFs (Louisiana State Legislature 1995). Only two programs—in the cities of Ruston and Monroe—had used the prior law, and the new law allowed them to continue in operation. Louisiana thus continues to allow STIFs, but only the local tax is now captured in the increment. Local governments may issue revenue bonds supported by the pledge of as much as the full amount of the increment in the development area. However, revenue previously dedicated to a specific purpose is excluded from the increment.

Maine

In 1996, Maine adopted an Employment Tax Increment Financing (ETIF) program (Maine State Legislature). The ETIF puts state individual income, employment, and payroll taxes into the increment. The program provides ten-year reimbursement of state tax withheld (the standard amount only) from qualified employees above a base employment level. That base is the greater of total employment of the business on the last day of the year prior to establishment of the plan or average employment in the three previous years. If market area unemployment is below or equal to the state rate, the reimbursement is 30 percent; if it is above that rate, the percentage is 50 percent. However, the increment is only for tax growth above the percentage change for all businesses in the state. The law limits total reimbursement for the state to $20 million, but the amount is inflation adjusted from 1996. The participation in the program requires a finding of no harm to existing business. The program is available to retail operations only under conditions designed to prevent competition with existing retail establishments. Applications have been made to Maine Department of Taxation, but none are yet in operation.

Missouri

Missouri includes (since 1982) local taxes on economic activity, mostly county sales taxes, in the TIF (Missouri State Legislature 1982).[4] There are around one hundred such districts, more than half of them being in St. Louis and Jackson (Kansas City) counties. Districts may be formed in blighted areas, for economic development, or for conservation; most have been formed to improve blighted areas. The Missouri system, however, does not establish a true increment for taxes on economic activity. Instead, the law provides that half of county sales tax collected within the redevelopment area has to be used to pay for costs of improvements in those areas.[5] This is far simpler than trying to determine the increment, especially if the intent is to exclude sales diverted from neighboring areas from the increment. Some county sales taxes have been adopted by referendum for the support of particular capital improvements. Nevertheless, these taxes, although previously dedicated to particular county purposes, are subject to capture by the redevelopment programs (Missouri Supreme Court 1995).

TIF district finances in Missouri normally are driven by property tax increments that support development bond issues. Sales tax revenue is seen as prospectively too volatile for debt service; districts include sales tax increments in the program to accelerate retirement of debt and to pay overlapping taxing jurisdictions that have lost property tax collections to the TIF.

Wyoming

Wyoming authorizes downtown development authorities to finance development of public facilities or other improvements to public or private property through property or municipal sales tax increments (Wyoming Statutes 1997). Under the system, the municipality receives base municipal sales tax revenue, an amount equal to sales tax collected within the development area in the twelve-month period ending on the last day of the month before the effective date of the development plan. Amounts collected above that go to the development authority. The authority receives no revenue until revenue exceeds that base amount. If the municipal sales tax rate changes (municipalities may choose rates of either one-half or 1 percent), the original base is adjusted proportionately. Increment capture is limited to twenty-five years. There are four such authorities in the state, but only the Cheyenne Downtown Development Authority uses the municipal sales tax increment option. Municipal sales taxes are adopted by counties, collected by the state, and distributed between county and city governments on the basis of population rather than where the revenue was collected. The increments are on the amounts of this county tax and do not include the state tax or county capital improvement sales taxes. County option rates range from 0 to 4 percent.

INSIGHTS FROM NONPROPERTY TIF PROGRAMS

The experience with nonproperty tax increment financing schemes provides several insights about their use, as well as what the government finance and developmental effects have been. Several STIF programs are not increment programs as traditionally defined. Instead, they involve dedication of some portion of the existing local sales tax to the TIF district. That removes the need to divide revenue between the base and the increment, but it can cause a significant loss of revenue to local governments dependent on sales tax revenue. There is considerable gain in system simplicity, accompanied by an excellent chance that the STIF will cause great fiscal challenge for local governments.

State to Local

Property tax increment financing involves a tax that is almost exclusively local. When nonproperty taxes are brought into the scheme, state tax bases usually will be involved as well, and state controls on that revenue transfer are likely. Bringing a state tax into the scheme is extremely attractive for a TIF district because it locks what would have otherwise been state revenue into the district, rather than letting it flow to the state treasury for allocation through the state budget. The money is free to the district and assures that sales tax revenue generated in the project district will be spent locally. If it goes to the general state budget, that is never guaranteed but depends on state priorities and the skill of local representatives in bringing funds into the district.

State legislatures are wary of giving away sales (or other state) tax revenue. They probably suspect that increased sales in the STIF district means lower sales in surrounding areas; there is considerable doubt about the net gain for the state. Therefore, the increments usually require state approval, sometimes budgetary appropriation, before revenue is available to the district. The total approved may be less than the total "earned" from the increments. Illinois went through a near crisis when the STIF appropriation was delayed in 1992 during a state budget struggle. Also, including state tax in STIF gets complicated when firms do consolidated filing: the system requires special administrative and processing operations to determine what sales tax revenue comes from stores within the STIF.

Revenue Potential

Sales tax increment programs have produced much revenue for their development districts. In many instances, the stream of nonproperty tax increment revenue is substantially larger than that from the property tax increment, and, in some instances, inclusion of sales tax increments has put life into moribund TIF programs—Illinois being the best example. For that state, adding the sales tax to the TIF package brought a huge increase in TIF districts in the state. However, STIF is particularly attractive for only certain sorts of projects, namely high sales volume retailers such as malls, automobile dealers, and hotels. These activities may do little for the regional economic base. Manufacturing or whole-saling development would not have much revenue potential under a STIF program.

Revenue Stability

The sales tax base is less stable than is the property tax base. Sales tax revenues are far more responsive to declines in economic activity than are property tax revenues. A national recession or a local economic slow down can have a major adverse impact on a local sales tax base. That negative economic impact, unless the problem is of depression dimensions, usually will not be seen in the property tax base. STIFs are therefore less attractive for support of debt service than are property tax TIFs. Nonproperty tax revenues can change dramatically from year to year, even with exactly the same complement of establishments (and real property base) operating within the TIF district. When change is an increase, that is no particular problem. However, when there is a decrease, the district can be hard pressed to meet commitments to the base governments, let alone satisfy the demands of developmental activity and debt service required for the infrastructure.

Districts and the Transferred Activity Problem

STIF financing is particularly attractive for projects that might not be so attractive for property tax increment financing. A regional shopping mall, for instance, would yield considerable STIF revenue, while its property tax increment, especially if it were in an otherwise rural area, could be relatively modest. This sort of development might add little to the local economic base and might well dislocate sales from local retailers just outside the district. In general, dislocation of economic activity is almost certainly a more difficult issue for nonproperty tax increment finance programs than for those involving only the property tax. Therefore, these other structures often have more complicated formulas and restrictions that define what is a true increment. Sales tax increments are especially attractive for retail activities, not for other sorts of economic activity. The sales tax collections in a retail development district may largely have been diverted from other nearby establishments, rather than from larger export markets. The district increment may not be much of an increment for the local jurisdictions involved and certainly would not be an increment for the wider region. The development may simply be moving business around, rather than stimulating net new activity. And a considerable portion of the increment may be from changing general economic conditions that have nothing to do with developments in the district.

CONCLUSION

Nonproperty taxes are less suited for use in tax increment finance programs than are property taxes. First, if the program truly seeks to include only the increment induced by the development program, the definitional controls become extremely complex. General changes in economic activity are more likely to increase nonproperty tax revenue. These general increases are difficult to remove if one seeks to limit captured funds to the true increment. Defining the base from which the increment is calculated can be difficult with the sales tax if the state wishes to prevent the TIF district from getting credit for economic activity transferred in from surrounding localities. That has caused several states to simply assign a portion of the local sales tax to the TIF, without worrying about what is increment and what is base. Where the TIF district is supporting the development of, say, a retail shopping mall on undeveloped land, there is no problem: all sales tax revenue collected is an increment to that district. It may not be an increment to the full city, the county, or the state; the sales in the new mall may be transferred from a nearby central business district.

Second, the most attractive areas for generating nonproperty tax increment flows are undeveloped tracts, not blighted urban areas, or areas with the potential for manufacturing or wholesaling development that will add to the regional export base. These projects stretch the logic of the normal requirement that development would not occur in the absence of the STIF designation. STIFs are particularly attractive for the development of retail projects—malls, hotels, automobile dealers, and so on. Such economic activity is far more likely to be transferred from some other nearby location than are the sorts of activity adding to the local export base (wholesaling, manufacturing, or business services). Struggles between neighboring localities have been a frequent part of STIF projects in several states (Missouri, California, Louisiana, and Illinois, in particular).

Third, retail sales tax flows in a mall or similar commercial development, the sort of project for which STIF financing appears most lucrative, fluctuates with the general economy as particular retail establishments in the development open and close. That increment base lacks the stability of property assessed value and suggests that this is not a good foundation upon which to service project debt. Bond raters are more interested in property tax pledges than in the sales tax. Accordingly, districts in some STIF states do not involve the sales tax in the basic service pledge, but they use the revenue for early retirement of any debt and for other development costs.

The case for tax increment finance based on nonproperty taxes is considerably weaker than is the case for such financing with property tax increments. Where STIF authority has been terminated, the reason has usually been concerns about damaging competition for economic activity between local governments. The state believes that the preferenced activities are not new, but rather are simply diverted from other nearby jurisdictions. The STIFs are thought to move business around, rather than to develop new business. STIFs have proven more productive in development rather than in the redevelopment of blighted areas.

NOTES

1. In Alabama, the state Industrial Development Authority at one time could arrange state tax increment finance districts. None were ever approved, and the law has been changed to end the authorization.

2. The program also had a state impact. Although the credit was against local tax, the state of California had to replace revenue lost by schools to the development agencies.

3. Indiana permits consolidated returns for multilocation retailers, so there is no easy link.

4. Indeed, all "economic activity taxes" may be part of the increment financing program. Along with the local sales taxes are included franchise taxes and, in Kansas City and St. Louis, earnings taxes. These latter do not, however, appear to have been included in TIF programs. Hotel and motel taxes are explicitly excluded from TIF schemes.

5. The finances are complicated in St. Louis County: about one-third of the municipalities keep their sales tax revenue ("point of sale" cities), while the remainder share their collections in a countywide pool with distribution back on a population-based formula. The STIF provides a way for the latter to keep the fruits of their economic activity; they literally have nothing to lose with the STIF.

REFERENCES

California State Legislature. 1981. *Senate bill 152.*

———. 1993. *Assembly Bill 1920.*

Colorado State Legislature. 1997. *Statutes,* 31–25–107.

District of Columbia. Law 12–143.

Illinois General Assembly. 1985. Tax Allocation Redevelopment Act. In *Compiled Statutes,* 5/11–74.4.

———. 1988. *Compiled statutes,* 5/11–74.4.

Indiana General Assembly. 1987. *Indiana code,* 36–7–27.

———. 1990. *Indiana code,* 36–7–26.

Kansas Senate Bill. 76–1999.

Louisiana State Legislature. 1990. *Revised statutes,* 33:9023–A, B.

———. 1995. Act 1118, Regular Session.

Maine State Legislature. 1996. *M. R. S. A.,* Chapter 917.

Missouri State Legislature. 1982. *R. S. Mo.,* 99.845.

Missouri Supreme Court. 1995. In *County of Jefferson, et al v. Quiktrip Corporation, et al.,* No. 78023. (December 19).

Pierog, Karen. 1996. Illinois passes compromise to save funding of TIF districts. *The Bond Buyer* (December 7): 1.

Redfield, Kent. 1995. *Tax increment financing in Illinois.* Springfield: Taxpayers Federation of Illinois.

Wyoming State Legislature. 1997. *Wyoming statutes,* 15–9–207.

CHAPTER 5

The Use of Debt in
Tax Increment Financing

Craig L. Johnson

INTRODUCTION

This chapter provides an analysis of tax increment debt finance in the
United States. Tax increment financing (TIF) is a method of generating
local own-source revenues to fund economic development projects. TIF
is implemented through the creation of tax increment districts and redevelopment authorities that are set up to provide financial and organiza-
tional support for the development or redevelopment of a specific geographical area.

In order to generate funds quickly and in large amounts, redevelopment authorities commonly sell tax increment debt secured primarily by
incremental tax revenues derived from property taxes levied within the
tax increment district. The incremental tax revenue does not represent a
new tax, but rather a reallocation of a portion of the municipality's general property tax revenues. Municipalities issue tax increment bonds, in
part, to circumvent constitutional and statutory debt limitations and
voter approval requirements on tax-supported debt. Unlike traditional
general obligation (GO) bonds, in most states, tax increment bonds are
not subject to municipal debt limits or public referendum requirements.
Moreover, since the redevelopment agencies are not legally a part of the
sponsoring general government, TIF is a way for general governmental
units to provide off-balance sheet capital asset financing.

Revenue to repay bonds is generated in TIF districts from the incremental taxes levied on the districts' new assessed valuation after a given
base year. The incremental portion of the tax base is derived solely from
the increase in assessed real estate valuation in the district. The financ-

ing structure is designed to capture new property tax revenues generated from increased property values expected to result from development. As a result, TIF districts must be located in areas capable of realizing significant (and sufficient) increases in assessed property value in order to meet their debt obligations in full and on time. If the tax base does not grow as projected or, worse, falls (as happened in numerous instances), debt repayments may be put in jeopardy.

Assessed property value growth is especially important for TIF districts since they are "passive" tax receivers. TIF districts lack independent revenue raising power; the tax base and tax rate are under the control of the general government, not the TIF district itself. The passive nature of the revenue stream is an inherent and significant risk common to all pure tax increment bonds that are not enhanced by some additional revenue source. In addition, redevelopment authorities have little expenditure flexibility because fixed debt service costs normally account for most of their annual expenditures.

In many states, TIF districts have become a fundamental part of the local revenue structure, exhibiting strong and sustained revenue base growth. In 1993, for example, tax increment districts (TIDs) in Minnesota captured 9 percent of the total property value of the cities and towns containing property tax increment districts (Legislative Audit Commission 1996). In some other states the captured value of TIF districts is extraordinarily large. The state of Wisconsin provides an extreme example where the value of the property tax increment is much larger than the frozen base value. As of 1992, the total amount of incremental value in TIDs was $3.4 billion, compared to a total frozen base of $1.5 billion (Wisconsin Department of Development 1993). A similar situation exists in California, where the statewide incremental assessed valuation ($160.6 billion) is significantly larger than the statewide frozen base assessed valuation ($69.4 billion) (California State Controller 1994). In these states the incremental value of the property tax base is more than double the base value. As a result, more annual revenue is generated from property incremental value than base value.

TIF was originally designed to provide money to finance redevelopment projects in blighted areas. It now appears, however, that TIF is used to finance capital projects—in blighted and nonblighted areas. Moreover, TIF bond proceeds are used for a variety of purposes, not just redevelopment (or development), including elementary and secondary education, roads, bridges, parking facilities, airports, water and wastewater facilities, recreational facilities, and electrical power plants.

This chapter continues with a discussion of the characteristics of the national market for tax increment financing debt. We then provide an analysis of the risks to bondholders and taxpayers, using illustrations of

TIF in selected states. We focus on the states with the most extensive and established local TIF structures: California and states in the Midwest-Great Lakes region. Finally, we end with policy implications and a conclusion.

THE NATIONAL TAX INCREMENT FINANCING (TIF) MARKET

The state and local (municipal) securities market is where state and local governments and their instrumentalities go to sell securities in return for cash proceeds. The market has served the financing needs of state and local governments since their inception by financing a diverse set of capital infrastructure and improvement needs, including education, environment, general government, health care, housing, transportation, utilities, and economic development. Some of the earliest occasions of economic development financing, that in the first decades of the nineteenth century, occurred with the building of canals and turnpikes.

Beginning with the enactment of the Federal Revenue and Expenditure Control Act in 1968, federal authorities have sought to restrict the ability of municipalities to issue economic development bonds. These efforts culminated in the Tax Reform Act of 1986, which defined all economic development bonds as "private-purpose" bonds and subjected them to state issuance volume constraints, unless otherwise specifically exempted by federal statute.

The interest income on redevelopment bonds may be taxable unless they meet the "qualified" redevelopment bond test (Section 144 of the 1986 IRS Code). This test includes one significant hurdle and several additional requirements. Generally, to qualify as a redevelopment bond entitled to tax exemption, 95 percent or more of the net proceeds must be used for redevelopment purposes in an area officially designated as blighted. Among some of the other requirements, the bond issue must be accompanied by a redevelopment plan, and the debt service must be primarily secured by general taxes imposed by a general purpose government or incremental taxes attributable to the financed improvement. Even when meeting the qualified redevelopment bond test, bond issuance is subject to state volume cap limits. The imposition of these constraints does not appear to have reduced redevelopment bond sales significantly.

Figure 5.1 illustrates TIF total (new issue and refunding) bond issuance from 1990 through 1995.[1] Over this period, 819 TIF securities were sold for a total outstanding dollar amount of $10.2 billion. National annual issuance peaked in 1993 at 213 issues for $3.7 billion, consisting of 112 new issues and 82 refundings. The total number of

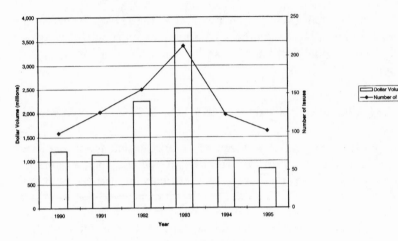

FIGURE 5.1
TIF Debt (millions) 1990–1995
Dollar Volume and Number of Issues

Source: *Munilris CD-ROM Database*, DPC Data

issues sold declined to 123 and 102 in 1994 and 1995, respectively. However, annual new issue volume remained steady at 75 in 1994 and 1995. Local governments in twenty-seven states issued TIF bonds, but seven states, California, Colorado, Florida, Michigan, Minnesota, Nevada, and Oregon, accounted for more than 96 percent of the total dollar amount of TIF bonds sold. California is, by far, the most prolific TIF-issuing state with 476 bond issues for $8.2 billion, more than 80 percent of the market. Minnesota is a frequent issuer of TIF bonds, with annual issuance peaking at more than $81 million in 1995. On the other end of TIF bond sales, many states have issued only a small number of TIF bonds and seem to be experimenting with the TIF concept.

Federal tax exemption constraints on economic development bonds have led to the sale of a disproportionate number of taxable TIF securities. From 1990 through 1995, 12 percent of TIF bonds were taxable, compared to only 3.6 percent for all municipal bonds over the same time period. The frequent sale of significantly more expensive taxable securities in the TIF market is a cause of concern, particularly if many of these bond issues are sold without electorate approval. A few states—California, Minnesota, and Iowa—account for most of the taxable issues. Indeed, in Iowa, more taxable TIF bonds were sold than tax-exempt TIF bonds.

Most TIF bond issues are relatively small, with the average issue size around $6 million, compared to $16 million for the entire municipal market. TIF bonds are expected to be relatively small since the money required to finance most development projects, while large in terms of a local government budget, is not large in terms of the municipal securities market; for example, a $5 million bond issue is considered a small issue in financial market terms. California and Colorado have a slightly larger average issue size than the market, which may indicate that in these states TIF revenues are being used to finance larger capital projects and may have supplanted the use of general obligation and some revenue bonds in several local communities. Moreover, the larger bond issues in California and Colorado may be the beginning of a trend. This is especially likely since TIF appears to have become a basic component of the local fiscal structure in many states, with incremental property tax bases growing unabated.

Often the maturity of the bond issue is directly related to the expected duration of the project being financed. Therefore, bond maturity may be viewed as a surrogate for the expected useful life of the project financed by bond proceeds. Most TIF bonds are long-term bonds sold to finance long-term projects. Figure 5.2 shows that more than 65 percent of TIF bond issues have a term-to-maturity greater than twenty years, and one-quarter of the issues have a maturity of thirty years. Moreover, twenty-eight issues have an even longer final maturity date, six of which stretch bond retirement out forty years.

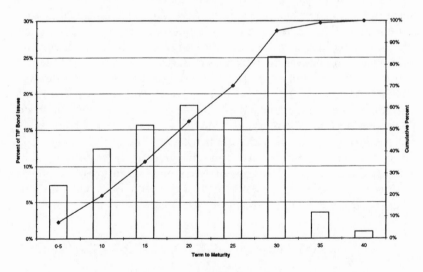

FIGURE 5.2
TIF Bond Issues by Term to Maturity

Source: *Munilris CD-ROM Database*, DPC Data

Issuers sell virtually all TIF bonds by negotiated offering or auction method (competitive bid). From 1990 through 1995, 71 percent of all TIF bonds were sold through negotiated offering, and 29 percent, by (competitive) auction bidding. These percentages are consistent with the broader municipal market. However, if most TIF bonds are viewed by investors as more "risky" than most municipal bonds, the use of auction bidding for 29 percent of TIF sales may not be the least costly means of selling TIF bonds. Research studies have indicated that the negotiated offering method should produce lower borrowing costs than the auction bid method for small, infrequent issuers of more risky bonds, primarily because such bonds receive an insufficient number of bids in auction sales (Leonard 1994). This wisdom is at least partially confirmed by the fact that, for our sample, 40 percent of all TIF auction bid sales received two bids or less, and one-quarter (forty-seven) received only one bid. Research indicates that issues sold by auction bid receive lower interest costs if they receive four or more bids (Simonsen and Robbins 1996). Therefore, TIF issues receiving less than three bids may have incurred higher interest costs than necessary; lower interest costs may have been achieved if such bonds had been sold by negotiated offering.

There appears to be a pattern in the method of sale used across certain states. Most local governments sell their TIF securities by negotiated offering, with Michigan and Minnesota being the exceptions; Minnesota and Michigan sold 80 percent and 59 percent of their TIF securities by auction bid, respectively. According to a municipal finance professional, this is the practice in Minnesota because most TIF bonds are viewed by local investors as GO bonds since most TIF bonds are sold by a general government and secondarily secured by a GO pledge.

A significant number of TIF bonds are insured. From 1990 through 1995, 30 percent of the TIF bonds sold were insured, compared to 35 percent for the entire municipal market. The closeness of these figures is surprising since the TIF market is viewed as an obscure and risky (high-yield) sector of the municipal bond market, and bond insurers are generally viewed as shying away from the more risky segments of the municipal market. The majority of states have no insured TIF bonds, but five states—Alabama, California, Florida, Montana, and South Carolina—had more than 40 percent of their bonds insured.

RISKS INHERENT IN TAX INCREMENT DEBT

This section analyzes the risks in tax increment debt financing from the perspectives of bondholders (investors) and taxpayers. We analyze certain risks inherent in TIF and some vehicles that have been developed for risk sharing. The primary point to keep in mind while reading this section is that tax increment debt finance, by its very nature, is subject to substantial uncertainty and risk.[2] The risks begin prior to the issuance of TIF debt and last throughout the life of the TIF project, and perhaps beyond. The trade-off between the risk characteristics of a TIF bond and the return required by bond buyers is directly related to the level of repayment security for TIF debt, which varies from state to state.

As a general relationship, we expect investors to demand a higher yield on TIF debt that is repaid solely from tax increment revenues. Such is the case in California, where TIF debt is a limited tax obligation, secured only by a pledge of incremental property tax revenues. Perhaps a slightly stronger limited tax security is found on some bond issues in Illinois and Colorado, where the limited tax obligation may be secured by a blended structure of property and sales tax increment revenues. States such as Michigan, Minnesota, Wisconsin, and sometimes Indiana provide greater repayment security and expect to pay lower yields, by providing a "double-barrel" source of repayment. TIF bonds in these instances are secured primarily by incremental tax revenues but also are frequently backed secondarily and ultimately by the full, faith, and credit pledge of the overlapping general taxing unit. Another way of viewing the decision of how much security to provide is to ask how much project risk taxpayers are willing to absorb. The greater the level of repayment security, the more taxpayer risk. Moreover, bond issuers must insure that any additional risk is fully compensated by investors in the form of marginally lower borrowing costs.

RISKS TO TAXPAYERS

This section covers three specific risks to taxpayers in selling TIF debt. The first area covers the events leading up to bond issuance, when government officials may bond out future taxpayer revenues without explicit permission. The second risk pertains to the loss of revenues by overlapping taxing entities during the life of the project. The final area concerns the potentially vulnerable position of the sponsoring general government's general obligation debt credit rating.

Issuance Risk

Issuance risk refers to the possibility that tax increment debt will be sold without the direct or indirect approval of the taxpayers responsible for repaying the debt. One reason tax increment debt has become so popular is because of the restrictions on local general obligation debt in many states. Such restrictions commonly limit outstanding GO debt to some percentage of aggregate property value and/or require some type of electorate approval in order to issue debt. As an illustration, in Indiana the total principal indebtedness of any political subdivision may not exceed 2 percent of the net assessed valuation of taxable property.[3] The issuance of general obligation bonds in Indiana is also subject to a petition and remonstrance process. Prior to selling GO bonds, if taxpayers opposed to the bond sale can gather more signatures than those for it— called the "process of remonstrance"—then the financing is defeated at least for one year. These limitations place restrictive constraints on GO debt issuance and have led to the proliferation of more costly special taxing districts and lease financing arrangements.

Since TIF debt is usually not subject to public referendum requirements or municipal debt limits, local governments in need of economic development funds commonly turn to TIF debt. The sale of TIF debt to avoid such limits, however, is a red flag that public officials are sidestepping direct public accountability—a basic tenet of prudent debt financing policy—and that the majority of the electorate may not support the debt issue. TIF debt policy should hold public officials accountable to taxpayers by requiring some form of voter approval or consent to establish the redevelopment district and voter approval of any debt issues. This is a way of ensuring that the ultimate repayers of the debt—taxpayers in the redevelopment district—have an effective voice in the debt issuance process. In order to sell TIF debt in California, local governments must file a plan with the state and hold a public hearing, but voter approval is not required to form a redevelopment district, and the district is not subject to an appropriation limit, as are most local agencies. Unlike local general obligation bonds repaid from property taxes, TIF bonded indebtedness is not subject to limit, nor must redevelopment agencies get voter approval prior to selling TIF bonds.

TIF debt is subject to debt limitations in some states. In Wisconsin, for example, TIF debt is not exempt from state debt limitations. On 16 December 1992, the Wisconsin Supreme Court ruled in *City of Hartford v. Dean T. Kirley and John C. Spielman* (No. 91–1390–OA), that tax increment finance bonds are subject to state constitutional limits on municipal indebtedness. Article XI, section 3(2) of the Wisconsin Constitution limits the indebtedness of counties, cities, villages, and towns to an amount not to exceed 5 percent of the equalized value of property within the local government boundaries. The court ruled that tax increment revenue is not distinct or special fund revenue. Rather, it represents a "carving out" from the city's general property tax revenues of a discrete source of revenue that is "absolutely obligated" for a significant period of time to the retirement of the city's TIF bond obligations and therefore creates debt within the meaning of Article XI, section 3, of the

Wisconsin Constitution (Wisconsin State Supreme Court 1992). The court's opinion in the Hartford case is reasonable, fiscally accurate, and encourages the prudent use of TIF debt.

Risks to Overlapping Taxing Districts

A unique aspect of property tax increment financing is the setting of the base assessed value. Once the base year and base assessed value are established as a point of reference, annual property taxes are levied only on the district's new assessed value after the base year. The incremental portion of the tax base is derived from the increase in assessed real estate valuation in the district. The revenues generated from the assessed valuation set at the base year remain with the overlapping taxing districts. In a pure tax increment scheme, the base value does not change for the entire life of the district. While this may result in more revenue for the redevelopment district, it can be disastrous for overlapping taxing entities. At a minimum, the base value should be regularly adjusted for inflationary and deflationary changes in the property value of parcels that constitute the base value.

In addition, mechanisms must be put in place to account for any assessment process changes that affect the property tax base, like periodic reassessment, because property values are determined through an administrative assessment process. An effective administrative base adjustment procedure is used in Indiana. Contrary to standard TIF theory and practice, in Indiana a TIFs base assessed valuation is not necessarily fixed for the life of the TIF. The tax base of each Indiana TIF district is protected from potential adverse changes in assessed valuation that can result from general property value reassessments. The State Board of Tax Commissioners is required to make a *one-time* adjustment to the base assessed value to neutralize any effect of a reassessment on the property tax proceeds allocated to a redevelopment district. The captured assessed value of the TIF is protected by adjusting the TIF's base assessed value. This adjustment, in turn, is based on a comparison of the changes in net assessed value between the *allocation area* and the *county* and can be viewed as a "hold harmless" adjustment. The procedure is designed to ensure that the new adjusted TIF base value will result in the production of a tax increment that equals or exceeds the amount that would have been produced without a reassessment.

The base adjustment assessment procedure is a locally based, state government supervised, flexible and effective, albeit somewhat messy to administer, procedure for making adjustments to TIF base assessed valuation. It is also effective for accomplishing at least two related things that are beneficial to TIF and overlapping taxing districts alike. First, the base adjustment mechanism enables the TIF base assessed value to be upwardly adjusted so that increases in the assessed valuation of overlapping taxing districts are not automatically, and inappropriately, captured by the TIF allocation area. Second, the hold harmless base adjustment also provides significant protection to bondholders by ensuring that the reassessment does not adversely impact TIF-captured assessed valuation. How assessed value is determined is potentially a vulnerable area for all financing mechanisms supported by the property tax base, but it is the Achilles heel of property tax increment financing.

Once a redevelopment district is operational, it siphons off revenues that would otherwise flow to overlapping governmental units that share the redevelopment agency's property tax base. For example, the portion of the revenue an overlapping taxing entity, like a school district, would normally receive from an incremental increase in the tax base (assuming the increase would have occurred without redevelopment agency activities) is reallocated to the redevelopment agency. Some states allow overlapping governments to withhold revenues from TIDs, while others have put institutional structures in place that encourage development cost sharing without overburdening the overlapping taxing districts.

Over the years, overlapping taxing entities in California suffered substantial revenue losses until they sued redevelopment agencies to get back a portion of their lost revenue base. Ultimately, they reached a negotiated settlement that called for instituting a mechanism for passing some captured incremental tax revenues to the overlapping taxing entities. "Pass-through" agreements between the redevelopment agency and its affected overlapping governmental units were initially developed on a negotiated case-by-case basis. In a well-designed pass-through arrangement, all taxing entities share proportionately in the gains and losses in assessed valuation. Some arrangements, however, had provisions that stepped up payments to underlying taxing entities once a certain threshold was reached. This resulted in a sudden and unexpected loss of TIF revenue, which adversely affected the financial condition of some redevelopment agencies and hurt the credit quality of their debt securities.

With the enactment of Assembly Bill 1290 in 1993, pass-through agreements are standardized revenue-sharing agreements for project areas adopted on or after 1 January 1994 and for territory added by plan amendment on or after the same date. For a TIFs first ten years (after a base year is determined), 25 percent of the gross tax increment (after deductions for low and moderate income housing) is passed through to the affected taxing entities, with payments allocated between them in proportion to their share of property taxes. In years eleven to thirty, the share drops to 21 percent, and 14 percent after year thirty.

Payments to local agencies may be subordinated to debt service payments upon consent of the affected taxing entities. But subordination of pass-through arrangements to debt service is not automatic after Assembly Bill 1290. This mechanism protects the revenue stream of overlapping taxing units from complete usurpation, while allocating to them a share of the costs of development from which they expect to derive future benefits.

Another forward-looking intergovernmental arrangement in California subjects redevelopment agencies to cumulative tax increment revenue limits, which cap the amount of tax increment they may receive from a project area. Once the cap is hit, collected property taxes go directly to the overlapping general government and bypass the redevelopment agency altogether. In addition, to ensure that some tax increment revenue goes toward improving the housing stock, 20 percent of the gross tax increment revenue allocated to redevelopment agencies established after 1976 must be set aside in a low and moderate income housing fund.

The Cost of the Moral Obligation

Local general governments establish redevelopment authorities that are legally separate and distinct entities and authorize them to issue limited tax obligation debt repaid from non-general government revenues. Such debt is usually viewed by the market as having the "implicit" moral backing of the government, but legally the government is not required to make debt service payments in the event of nonpayment by the redevelopment authority. Nevertheless, the nonrepayment of TIF debt can have an adverse impact on the general government's general obligation debt.

In Colorado, for example, redevelopment authorities are created and partially controlled by the city, and, in some cases, city administrators are involved in the official review and approval of the authority's budget. Despite substantial budgetary and management oversight by the authorizing city, most cities do not pledge their general tax revenues to pay TIF debt service. But when the Englewood Urban Renewal Authority defaulted on a $27 million bond issue, Moody's Investors Service downgraded the city's general obligation bond rating from A1 to A, citing the inextricable financial links among the city, the authority, and the city's unwillingness to follow through on its capital projects, regardless of how the debt that financed the project is ultimately secured (Moody's Public Finance Department 1991). This indicates that the wall between a municipality's TIF and general obligation debt is not fire proof, at least in terms of credit rating downgrades.

RISKS TO BONDHOLDERS

The circuitous structural arrangements that make TIF finance attractive to local issuers are offset by the structural disadvantages for investors. The risk to bondholders that actual returns may be less than expected returns on tax increment debt primarily evolve around the passive nature of the tax increment revenue stream.

The Passive Nature of the Revenue Stream

Redevelopment authorities are passive tax revenue receivers. The tax rate imposed on the property tax base is under the direct control of the municipal government, not the redevelopment agency; the agency has no independent authority to levy and collect property taxes. Therefore, while growing property values increase incremental tax revenues even if rates remain unchanged, property tax rates may not be raised by the redevelopment agency in the face of property value declines. Moreover, the determination of assessed value, base and incremental, is conducted by general government officials, usually at the county level, and not by the redevelopment authority. Assessed value may be vulnerable to significant devaluation from assessment appeals, especially from major commercial taxpayers, when real estate values fall. Consequently, when property tax revenues may be most vulnerable to decline, the local redevelopment agency (the agency responsible for making debt service payments) has no control over assessed property valuation and no legal authority to raise rates. The lack of independent revenue-raising authority in the face of plunging real estate values has led to systematic fiscal stress for redevelopment agencies recently, especially in southern California and several credit rating downgrades on tax increment debt (Standard and Poor's 1992).

Intergovernmental Fiscal Relations

Moreover, the state ultimately controls the tax increment and has shown in the past that it will use its authority to usurp tax increment revenue from local redevelopment agencies. Specifically, the state government of California shifted $205 million in redevelopment agency revenue to school districts in the FY92–93 State budget, approximately 16 percent of total redevelopment agency revenues, and then shifted $65 million the following fiscal year.

The 1994 property tax reform measure in the state of Michigan, Proposal A, illustrates the level of complexity and uncertainty associated with TIF intergovernmental relationships (Standard and Poor's 1994). Proposal A literally "took back" the operating school millage from TIF districts, adversely affecting debt service coverage on outstanding bonds. Proposal A capped the annual assessment base growth at 5 percent, or the rate of inflation, whichever is less, and significantly reduced the millage accessible to TIDs by prohibiting TIFs from capturing school mills. The state legislature subsequently passed legislation to allow TIFs created prior to Proposal A to capture all millage, including school millage rates. But since their assessed value was now subject to a state imposed cap, a debt service backstop in the form of an unlimited call on state appropriations for TIF districts had to be developed. This back-up call on state funds was exercised on more than one occasion.

In addition, many bond issues have exhibited lower debt service coverage levels after the reforms. Based on a review of a sample of official statements, TIF bonds did not have minimum debt service coverage requirements in Michigan prior to Proposal A. It is worth mentioning that the adverse legal changes that weakened the structure of TIF in Michigan were caused by the Michigan state government, not local TIDs or general governments. This illustrates that TIF debt service is very vulnerable to the actions of higher levels of government.

Project-Related Risks

A large percentage of tax increment districts are small areas carved out of the tax base of a larger jurisdiction. In such cases, debt repayment may be dependent on a few taxpayers—TIDs with substantial tax base concentration are considered riskier than TIDs with numerous taxpayers. In addition, larger TIDs are generally viewed as more creditworthy than smaller TIDs because of their usually broader economic base. Research indicates that a primary determinant of a TIF bond credit rating is the strength of the TIDs' incremental assessed valuation. Investor pricing decisions, however, are primarily based on the TIDs' debt-to-assessed value ratio (Johnson 1999).

Some states also back tax increment bonds with incremental sales tax revenues. In Colorado, TIDs are allowed to capture sales as well as property tax increments, and both sales and property tax revenue increments may back bond issues; indeed, many TID bond issues in Colorado are supported primarily by incremental sales taxes. Since sales tax revenue generated from the TID goes directly to the authority and is not shared by other taxing entities, bonds secured primarily by incremental sales tax revenues would appear to be more secure than bonds secured by incremental property tax revenues. This, however, has not proven to be the case.

There have been frequent debt service repayment problems with sales tax increment (STIF) bonds, mainly because many STIF bonds have financed risky start-up retail projects. Supporters of such projects apparently believe that if you build it, people will come, and business will follow; on several projects, however, the people did not come, the development did not materialize, and sufficient tax revenues did not flow.

SUMMARY

TIF has become a widely used, inextricable part of local government finance in California and many Midwestern-Great Lakes states. In practice, TIF is not limited to blighted geographical areas. TIF is used to fund traditional, project-related economic development and redevelopment expenditures, but it is also used to fund physical infrastructure projects traditionally undertaken by general governments. TIF bond issuance is stable, and TIF bonds are sold in many states throughout the nation. Moreover, bond buyers can expect to see more and larger issues in the future, as the use of TIDs grow and as their revenue structures mature.

Most states have chosen to bond out future TIF revenues by selling TIF debt repaid from incremental revenues. TIF bonds are mostly long-term bonds backed by local property taxes sold to finance long-term projects with long payback periods. Such a project financing profile implies that property taxpayers should be directly involved in the TIF debt issuance process. Some form of voter approval prior to issuance should be required, especially for taxable securities. Moreover, outstanding TIF bonds and debt service payments should count against legal debt limits. However, voter approval requirements and debt limitations should not unreasonably prohibit the sale of TIF debt for prudent capital improvements.

Sales tax increment financing (STIF) has been used in a few states but generally has not caught on because, as traditionally structured, STIFs have fatal structural weaknesses. In order to provide a minimum level of security, STIFs should be locally based and controlled and should have a history of revenue production prior to debt issuance. While STIFs as structured may be inherently more risky than property tax increment bonds, they are not without significant structural weaknesses also. Foremost among them is the passive nature of the property tax increment revenue stream. The issuer has no control over the tax rate, the determination of incremental assessed value, or incremental revenue. Moreover, the increment is ultimately controlled by the state government, which has chosen, in more than one state and on more than one occasion, to use its power to the detriment of redevelopment agencies and TIF bondholders.

In general, the nation's TID revenue base is solid and robust. In some states, incremental assessed values have become larger than base values. Property tax increments have grown rapidly. In the isolated and relatively few instances where incremental revenue growth has dangerously underperformed expectations, it is mostly because of poor project planning or state usurpation. However, TIDs may prosper to the detriment of overlapping taxing entities. Therefore, it is important to structure local oversight, revenue (pass-through) arrangements, and base valuation adjustment procedures that enable overlapping taxing entities to enjoy the benefits of TIF without hurting bondholders. To put a cap on excessive long-term revenue growth, cumulative revenue limits on the total amount of revenue a TID may collect over its life-span may be appropriate. To put a cap on the revenue downside, a bond covenant that puts a floor on increment declines may be appropriate, as well as moderate debt service coverage ratios mandated by the state.

NOTES

1. The data used to analyze the national TIF debt market comes from the MuniIris CD-ROM Database published by DPC Data.
2. According to a February 1996 Moody's Municipal Credit Report on California Tax Allocation Bonds, most California TIF bonds are rated Baa, barely investment grade. In 1991 Moody's Investors Service Incorporated conducted an analysis of eleven Colorado cities with TID debt outstanding. They reported a rating distribution for TIDs—AAA-insured (2), Baa1 (1), Baa (1), B (1), and Not Rated (5)—that illustrates the high-risk nature of most Colorado TID bonds. In the Moody's report, four of the TID bond issues had current debt service coverage levels below 1.00, and zero possessed coverage above 1.63. See Moody's Public Finance Department (1991).
3. Indiana uses the true tax value assessment method, which is a replacement cost assessment method. The true tax value of real property is its replacement cost minus depreciation, plus the value of land. Assessed value is one-third of true tax value. True tax value is commonly viewed as being equivalent to fair market value, but it is not and, in fact, underestimates aggregate fair market property value (see DeBoer et al. 1996).

REFERENCES

California State Controller. 1994. Financial transactions concerning cities of California: Annual report. Sacramento: State of California.
DeBoer, L., D. Good, C. Johnson, and J. Man. 1996. *Report of the Indiana fair market value study*. Indiana: State Board of Tax Commissioners.
Johnson, Craig L., 1996. Administering public debt. In *Handbook of public administration*, ed. James L. Perry. 2d ed. San Francisco: Jossey-Bass.

———. 1997. *The national tax increment bond market: The mainstreaming of a fringe sector*. Bloomington, IN: Institute for Development Strategies, Indiana University.

———. 1999. Tax increment debt finance: An analysis of the mainstreaming of a fringe sector. *Public Budgeting and Finance* 19(1) (Spring).

Legislative Audit Commission. 1996. *Tax increment financing*. St. Paul: Minnesota Office of the Legislative Auditor. (March).

Leonard, P. 1994. Negotiated versus competitive bond sales: A review of the literature. *Municipal Finance Journal* 15–2 (Summer).

Moody's Public Finance Department. 1991. *Moody's focus on Colorado tax increment district debt*. Moody's Investor Service. (November).

Simonsen, W., and M. Robbins. 1996. Does it make any difference anymore? Competitive versus negotiated municipal bond issuance. *Public Administration Review* 56–1 (January/ February).

Standard and Poor's. 1992. Tax increment bonds: Mixed picture. *Standard and Poor's Creditweek Municipal* (27 January).

———. 1994. Last call for Michigan tax increment bonds. *Standard and Poor's Creditweek Municipal* (28 November).

State of California. 1994. *Financial transactions concerning community redevelopment agencies of California: Annual report 1993–94 fiscal report*. Sacramento: Office of the State Controller, Accounting and Reporting Division, Local Government Reporting Section.

Wisconsin Department of Development. 1993. *1991–93 Biennial report on tax incremental financing (TIF)*. Madison: Division of Policy, Research, and Information Services, Bureau of Policy Development.

Wisconsin State Supreme Court. 1992. In *City of Hartford v. Dean T. Kirley and John C. Spielman* (16 December): No. 91–1390–OA.

CHAPTER 6

Determinants of the Municipal Decision to Adopt Tax Increment Financing

Joyce Y. Man

This chapter identifies the factors that may cause cities to adopt the tax increment financing (TIF) program and reviews the evidence on the determinants of the municipal TIF adoption decision. It explores the following important issues: Why do cities adopt TIF programs? Does a city adopt TIF because its neighboring cities have implemented such a program? Do fiscal pressures play a significant role in the municipal TIF adoption decision? Understanding the factors that increase the probability of adopting TIF programs may help in the selection process for local incentive programs and provide valuable information concerning economic development and TIF programs.

WHY DO CITIES ADOPT TIF?

Local governments use TIF to finance infrastructure investment and improvement in a specific geographical area as a means to attract private investment to the targeted area and thus encourage local economic growth. As Bartik (1991:1) observes, most policymakers use state and local economic development policies in expectation of creating more jobs, resulting in "lower unemployment, higher wages, greater property values, increased profits for local businesses, more tax revenues, and reelection for the politician who can take credit for those booms." As one of the most commonly used economic development policies, the TIF program is assumed to enhance property values and generate additional tax revenues for infrastructure financing. A review of the market failure approach, the median voter theory and the previous studies in the literature of public policies reveals that the following factors may influence the municipal TIF adoption decision.

Unemployment and Economic Decline in Large Cities

State and local governments may have adopted development policies like TIF in order to correct private market failures, such as involuntary unemployment and underemployment, and to restructure the local economy toward high-wage premium industries (Bartik 1990). As Bovaird (1992) suggests, the increasing use of development programs in the 1980s may have attributed to the rise in unemployment in certain localities in the 1970s and the early 1980s.

In the past two decades, unemployment has been a chronic urban problem, particularly in inner-city areas. Poverty is often related to unemployment and low wages. In the 1970s, a large number of cities were plagued with fiscal and economic problems. New York and several other cities were approaching the brink of bankruptcy. Although the economy improved at the end of the 1970s and grew in the 1980s, and some cities like New York City have recovered remarkably, not all U.S. cities have fared equally well. As demonstrated in the National League of Cities Report (Ledebur and Barnes 1992:4), "More than 5.5 million people lived in poverty at the end of the decade of the 1980s than 10 years previously. Over this period, poverty became increasingly concentrated in the nation's central cities. These trends result in systematic differentials among localities in income, wealth and poverty. These differences create fiscal stress in many central cities." In their study of the fiscal and economic performance of large cities through 1986, Ladd and Yinger (1989) conclude that the average improvement in city fiscal health in the 1980s was modest. The average city was in worse shape in 1986 than it had been in 1972, with cities in the Northeast and Midwest deteriorating the most. In the early 1990s, another recession began, leaving many cities very few options for dealing with chronic urban problems.

In order to reduce unemployment and poverty, elected state and local officials chose to use tax and financial incentives and/or provide improved infrastructure facilities to stimulate job creation out of a fear that they may be accused of inactivity in a declining economic environment in large cities.[1] One primary goal of TIF programs is to create jobs and increase the demand for labor by encouraging new businesses to locate in the targeted blight area, encouraging existing businesses to expand, or discouraging existing businesses from decreasing their local activities. Many state and local government officials believe that without government participation in the development or redevelopment of downtown areas, real estate developers and investors are more willing to choose outlying areas of the city as their location choices of investment because land in these areas is usually less expensive, and the infrastructure there is often in a better shape. To encourage redevelopment, municipal governments attempt to make the inner-city area more attractive to developers by improving infrastructure facilities in that area. To pay for such investments and/or improvements, many cities use TIF as a revenue source to finance renovation of blight and deteriorated areas of the city in an attempt to stop the erosion of the existing tax base, generate more tax revenues, and possibly reduce urban sprawls. To achieve this goal, most state TIF-enabling legislation requires the finding of a "blight" or "slum" condition as a prerequisite for the designation of an area as a TIF district (Kim, Forrest, and Przypyszny 1984).

Klemanski (1990) conducts a national survey in the mid-1980s and finds that 55 percent of those thirty-three states that had passed legislation authorizing local use of TIFs enacted such legislation between 1974 and 1979. He argues that the economic recession felt by cities and states during the mid-1970s led to the adoption of many state and local economic development initiatives, including TIF. His study also reveals that the heaviest use of TIF had occurred in the northern and western states, the larger central cities, and those jurisdictions with council-manager forms of government.

Based on his survey of 300 randomly selected municipalities, Forgey (1993) reports that among 189 cities that responded to the survey, 128 or about 68 percent of cities had created at least one TIF district. The primary goals for establishing a TIF district were to attract new businesses, promote downtown development or redevelopment, and retain or expand existing businesses. Their goals also include residential developments for low-income individuals and senior citizens and control of urban sprawl. According to Forgey, 70 percent of these municipalities surveyed had a population of less than fifty thousand. For the cities using TIF, 92 percent of those responding had a population above ten thousand. For the cities not using TIF, 48 percent of those responding had a population under ten thousand. His study suggests that cities with population of ten thousand and over are more likely than smaller cities to use TIF.

This finding is confirmed by Anderson (1990) in his empirical analysis of municipal TIF adoption decisions. By estimating a structural probit model of municipal TIF adoption decisions for a data set drawn from Michigan, Anderson finds that large cities are more likely to adopt TIF. Most important, his research seems to indicate that cities experiencing population growth are more likely to look to TIF to provide for infrastructure needs. If this finding can be generalized, it may suggest that TIF is not an economic development tool but a budget manipulating mechanism adopted by growing cities to use TIF to maximize their own revenues and budget at the expense of other jurisdictions whose tax boundaries overlap the TIF district. However, the positive effect of prior population growth on a city's likelihood of adopting TIF found by Anderson (1990) is not detected by Man (1999) in her study of the TIF adoption decision using data for Indiana cities. Instead, her research reveals that cities with higher per capita incomes are less inclined to adopt TIF than cities with lower incomes.[2] This empirical finding does not support the contention that public officials in growing cities, because of the wealth generated by past growth, are more inclined to adopt TIF. On the contrary, it suggests that financially strained and economically distressed cities are more likely to use TIF as an economic development tool. Dye's (1997) analysis of municipalities in northeastern Illinois also suggests that TIF-adopting municipalities are relatively larger, have lower per capita incomes, are slower-growing, and have a greater non-residential property tax base.

Fiscal Stresses

The municipal adoption of TIF may come in response to increasing fiscal strains prompted by reduced intergovernmental aid to large cities. Municipal governments finance service delivery through tax dollars generated by local taxes and user charges and intergovernmental aid. Throughout much of the 1980s, however, targeted federal programs for urban development were discontinued, and the aggregate flow of federal aid to state and local governments slowed markedly. For example, in 1980, federal aid accounted for 15.5 percent of federal expenditures and 26.3 percent of state and local government outlays, but in 1990, federal aid accounted for only 10.8 percent of federal government expenditures and 18.7 percent of total state and local government outlays (see table 6.1). Real federal aid per capita decreased from $487 per capita in 1980 to only $414 per capita in 1990, down by $73. The share of total federal aid going to local governments has declined from 28 percent in 1978 to about merely 12 percent in 1991 (U.S. Statistical Abstract 1980, 1989, and 1996).

During the 1980s, federal assistance for infrastructure development and maintenance has also been reduced. Man and Bell (1993) point out that federal policy shifted resources away from federal infrastructure grants that declined in relative importance and actual purchasing power during much of the 1980s. From 1983 to 1990, the purchasing power of these grants declined by 21 percent, and federal infrastructure grants

TABLE 6.1
Trends in Federal and State Grants-in-Aid in Selected Years

	1975	1980	1985	1990	1993	Change 1980–1990
Real Federal Aid						
Per Capita	$420	$487	$413	$414	$519	–$73
As % of Total						
Federal Spending	15.0%	15.5%	11.2%	10.8%	13.7%	–4.7
As % of S-L						
Government						
Spending	23.5%	26.3%	21.3%	18.7%	21.2%	–7.6
Real State Aid						
Per Capita	$439	$453	$475	$539	$574	+$86
As % of Total						
State Spending	32.7%	32.8%	31.1%	30.6%	28.8%	–2.2
As % of Total						
City Spending	21.5%	17.0%	16.5%	17.2%	17.2%	+0.2
Real Total Aid to						
Cities Per Capita	$166	$151	$140	$139	$136	–$12
As % of Total						
City Revenue	32.9%	29.8%	24.3%	22.4%	22.2%	–7.4

Source: U.S. Statistical Abstract, 1980, 1989, and 1996.
Note: The dollar value is deflated by the Consumer Price Index (CPI), 1982–1984 = 100.

as a share of total federal obligations declined by nearly one-third. Federal government aid for infrastructure financing declined from nearly 22 percent of total infrastructure spending in 1983 to 14 percent in 1990.

At the same time, state and local tax revenues have been increasingly committed to medical assistance expenditures and other current operating expenses, leaving little resource for capital improvements. Although the last two decades have witnessed an increased role for state governments in the federal system, grants to local governments have declined as a share of total state government expenditures. In 1980, state aid to local governments accounted for 32.8 percent of state expenditures but only 28.8 percent of its total outlays in 1993. If welfare and education grants are excluded, state aid to cities could have decreased in the 1980s and the early 1990s. As table 6.1 reveals, from 1975 through 1993, the total federal and state aid to cities in a real dollar value decreased from $166 per capita to $136 per capita, about $30 less per person. The relative importance of federal and state aid to cities as a revenue source has also declined from nearly 33 percent of total city revenue in 1975 to 22 percent in 1993. The trends clearly indicate that state and local governments, especially cities, have become less of a national priority in the 1980s and early 1990s.

The era of "fend for yourself federalism" (Shannon 1991) presented a fiscal challenge to large cities and forced state and local governments, especially city governments, to search for alternative means to finance infrastructure needs. In the presence of reduced intergovernmental aid for urban redevelopment and the deteriorating infrastructure, the method of financing necessary capital investment in urban areas through TIF becomes increasingly popular to many local governments.

The municipal adoption of TIF may also come in reaction to fiscal stresses as a result of taxpayers' resentment to tax increases and self-imposed tax and expenditure limits. The 1980s was a decade marked by widespread taxpayers' revolts. Since California passed Proposition 13 in 1978, which rolled back property taxes and significantly limited property tax increases, many state and local governments have faced voters' resistance to state and local governments' attempts to finance necessary capital improvements through tax increases. Taxpayers' resentment to tax increases also contributed to the passage of the tax and expenditure limitation legislation in many states. More taxpayers believe that the existing tax structure is inefficient and unfair and that public goods and services are not provided in a cost-effective way. As a result, in political elections, voters pushed for lower taxes and improved efficiency in government without lowering the level and quality of public services. In response to voters' resentment, forty-six states imposed tax and expenditure limitations on local government in an effort to control and reduce the property tax burden, to curb the growth of public spending, and to improve fiscal accountability of state and local governments (Mullins and Cox 1994).

Faced with voters' resistance to tax increases and pressured by the budgetary constraints resulting from the state-imposed limitations on tax and expenditure, city officials are compelled to look for innovative means to generate sufficient funds for infrastructure improvements without raising taxes. Because TIF is a borrowing technique that allows a city to substitute current borrowing for future revenue, it becomes especially appealing to the cities that have experienced fiscal stresses and are facing difficulty in further raising property taxes to meet infrastructure needs.

Chapman (1998 and this volume) asserts that fiscal stresses as a result of rapid population growth and self-imposed tax and expenditure limits played an important role in the use of TIF in California. After the passage of Proposition 13, local governments in California could not issue general obligation bonds between 1978 and 1986 because they did not have the ability to increase the property tax and thus failed to meet the full faith and credit pledge required for these bonds. Ease of issuing bonds backed by the tax increment makes the TIF mechanism increasingly attractive. Testing the effects of fiscal pressures on the municipal TIF adoption decision, Man (1999) finds that cities with declining real per capita state aid over the years prior to possible TIF adoption are more likely to adopt TIF, while the cities experiencing increases in per capita state aid are less likely to create a TIF district. A city's probability of adopting TIF is also increased if the city has experienced property tax increases during the period prior to possible TIF adoption. Her study suggests that fiscal stresses resulting from decreases in intergovernmental aid to cities have played a significant role in the municipal TIF adoption decisions. It also indicates that TIF has been used as an alternative to property tax increases to finance economic development in the presence of the voters' growing resistance to further property tax increases.

Political Attractiveness of TIF

TIF is politically popular because it is claimed to be a self-serving mechanism that finances development projects from increased tax revenues that the projects generate rather than from new taxes or tax increases. It is perceived that under TIF, property owners pay no more than the normal tax burden, and there is no real loss to the community from using the incremental tax dollars for infrastructure financing. In addition, most of the state TIF laws require that to qualify for TIF designation, an area usually must meet a state statutory definition of blighted status. Thus, the development or redevelopment financed through TIF in a distressed area is believed to produce larger tax revenues from that area than would have been produced had no development occurred. Therefore, for taxpayers, it seems reasonable to earmark a portion of the increased tax revenue for the purpose of paying some of the costs of that development (Klemanski 1990).

Many cities rely on a "pay-as-you-go" method in generating funds for TIF projects, which allow cities to spend money for projects only when enough revenue has accumulated in the TIF fund. This method is appealing and acceptable to voters who worry about municipal debt and prospect of local tax increases. If TIF bonds are issued for development projects, the issuance of such bonds normally does not require voter approval through a referendum and does not violate existing constitutional or statutory debt limitations of the city. It is very appealing to public officials who face a difficult task of generating funds for urban development in the era of taxpayers' revolt and "new federalism."

TIF is also viewed as preferable to many other tax incentive programs, the tax abatement program in particular, because many people believe that TIF programs stimulate economic activities in the targeted area without giving away tax breaks to businesses. Public investments in TIF districts are financed out of increased local tax revenues, predominantly from property taxes, instead of a direct subsidy in many earlier economic development incentive programs. Thus, the concept of TIF is acceptable to the ordinary taxpayers who are increasingly weary about government subsidies to businesses, commonly known as "corporate welfare."

Furthermore, the TIF mechanism allows cities or other enacting government authorities to recover certain expenditures they made for development activities in specially created districts from a portion of the property tax revenues realized by the county, school district, and other local taxing jurisdictions. City officials often consider it unfair that the cities undertake all the economic development activities and bear the cost of development alone, but counties, schools, and other local taxing jurisdictions share the benefits of resulting increases in tax revenue without paying for the cost of development. With TIF, all taxing jurisdictions in a targeted area share the cost of development in proportion to their relative property tax gain (Huddleston 1981). This way of capturing funds during the allocation process is justified on the grounds that the tax increments would not have occurred without the development project financed through TIF. Meanwhile, the city officials argue that the other overlapping taxing jurisdictions are not harmed by TIF, because they still receive the taxes derived from the property tax base at the time that the TIF district was established, and they would benefit from the enhanced tax base upon the completion of TIF projects and retirement of all debts.[3]

Interjurisdictional Competition

In recent years, state and local governments often find themselves being engaged in competition for businesses. They may adopt incentive programs to remain competitive with their neighbors with respect to business climate. Many jurisdictions fear that without local incentive programs, they would be at a competitive disadvantage compared with other jurisdictions that offer incentive programs such as TIF. The bidding war over the location of the General Motors Saturn plant is just one of the more visible examples of this competition.

Competition among jurisdictions for capital investment is driven by the perception that the offer of a local incentive package may have a significant effect on a firm's decision to relocate or to remain in a community.

It is also believed that the new investment will pay off in terms of more jobs and higher tax revenues. Therefore, local governments compete among themselves in offering financial or tax incentives to win a bidding war.

This competitive adoption hypothesis was offered by a number of researchers (Morgan and Hackbart 1974; Harrison and Kanter 1978) to answer the questions as to why state and local governments continue to adopt new incentive programs. Recently, there have been some empirical results to support this hypothesis. McHone (1987) reveals that a state's industrial development incentive decision is influenced by the recent adoption of similar incentives in neighboring states. Anderson and Wassmer (1995) also provide evidence that communities adopt property tax abatements simply in response to the fact that other communities had adopted abatements. Such "copy cat" behavior was also found in Man's (1999) study of the municipal TIF adoption decision. Her empirical results indicate that a city's probability of adopting TIF is increased if its neighboring cities have implemented a TIF program. Based upon the existing research, it may be safe to conclude that one of the factors influencing the municipal TIF adoption decision is a city's desire to win a bidding war by copying their neighbors' behavior in their competition for businesses.

Reorientation of Local Development Policies

The 1980s also experienced a change in urban renewal strategies from rehabilitation of residential areas to revitalizing downtown business districts and strengthening commercial and industrial tax bases. Clarke and Gaile (1992) point out that during the 1980s, as a response to the cuts in federal economic development programs, local governments shifted notably their policy away from conventional economic development orientations toward a market-based, or entrepreneurial, approach. This new approach focuses on public policies that encourage job creation and economic growth rather than respond to entitlement obligations.

TIF has emerged to be well suited to the redevelopment of central business districts because the predominant commercial and industrial tax base in a downtown area grows faster than in a residential area, which makes it possible for the TIF program to succeed as claimed. Thus, local governments use TIF to target some specific development activities, including business attraction and retention, downtown revitalization, commercial and industrial development, service and retail sector growth in areas with a large commercial and industrial tax base.

The national survey of cities by Forgey (1993) reveals that 53 percent of responding cities using TIF reported a predominant commercial and industrial economic base, while only 40 percent of responding cities that do not use TIF claim a predominant commercial and industrial economic base. Man (1999) also provides evidence that a city is more likely to adopt TIF if it has a higher than average proportion of service industry in its economy. These results may indicate that municipalities with a primarily commercial economic base may benefit more from using TIF than those whose economies depend on noncommercial activities.

Expected Gains

The increasing use of TIF as an economic development tool may be driven by the presumption that local incentives provided through TIF programs have significant influence on business location and expansion decisions. State and local officials and the general public share the belief that the TIF program will be effective in attracting firms to locate or expand their businesses in the targeted area, which in turn will result in increased economic activity.

This perception is further reinforced by the recent studies of the impact of state and local tax and expenditure policy on economic performance. Bartik (1991) reviews the recent studies of interjurisdictional business location decisions since 1979 and found that 70 percent of those studies reported evidence of state and local tax effects on state and local business activity.[4] Research (Munnell 1990; Duffy-Deno and Eberts 1991) has also found a positive relationship between public infrastructure investment and economic performance. These findings reinforce the belief that reducing business costs by offering tax incentives, financial subsidies, and new and improved infrastructure facilities will attract more businesses to locate and expand in their communities and stimulate economic growth in the entire community.

The research by Anderson (1990) and Man (1999) confirms that expected gains from the implementation of TIF influences the municipal adoption decision. Both of them find a statistically significant positive effect of the expected growth resulting from the use of TIF on the probability of a city's adoption of TIF. The empirical evidence supports the argument that city officials implement TIF programs with an expectation that local incentives provided through TIF stimulate economic development and lead to increases in property value beyond the level that would have been expected in the absence of TIF. This may explain TIF's continued proliferation in the absence of significant positive results of its effectiveness in the past decades.

CONCLUSIONS

Researchers have been trying to find answers to the question of why cities adopt TIF by either applying the market failure theory or the competitive adopting theory or surveying state and local government officials or estimating empirical models of municipal TIF adoption decisions. Recent studies have revealed that the increasing use of TIF as an economic development tool may have been influenced by a variety of factors such as (1) distressed economic conditions in large cities; (2) fiscal stresses on local government prompted by reduced intergovernmental aid and voters' resistance to tax increases; (3) interjurisdictional competition for business; (4) a shift in urban renewal strategy from rehabilitating residential areas to strengthening commercial and industrial tax base; (5) the availability of alternative economic development programs; (6) jurisdiction-specific characteristics; and (7) expected growth that may result from the implementation of TIF. From a policy perspective, local governments clearly utilize the TIF mechanism as an economic development and redevelopment tool geared toward stimulating local economic activities. Cities may also adopt TIF because of adoption of TIF by its neighbors. They mimic their neighbors' behavior in order to remain competitive in their bidding for private capital investment.

However, the existing studies only focus on the likelihood of the municipal adoption of TIF rather than the timing issue as it relates to first adoption. In light of the increasing popularity of TIF among state and local governments, we have more questions than answers with regard to the use of TIF as an economic development tool. Additional research is warranted to further examine factors in the adoption of TIF and address the current debates on issues concerning whether TIF is an effective tool in influencing the location of capital investment and whether the benefits of TIF exceed the costs associated with the administration and implementation of the TIF program.

NOTES

1. Generally speaking, tax increment financing programs have been primarily adopted by municipalities. However, some states such as California, Florida, Nevada, Utah, and Indiana also allow counties to establish TIF districts. TIF programs are used by some nonmetro communities as well (Stinson, 1992).

2. This finding is consistent with Anderson and Wassmer's (1995) study of property tax abatement, which demonstrated that higher-income communities wait longer, ceteris paribus, to grant manufacturing property tax abatements.

3. TIF is a popular tool when redevelopment is truly necessary and TIF is used in an appropriate manner. However, in some cases when TIF is misused, school and other affected jurisdictions often object to TIF on the grounds that they lose tax revenues from investments in the area unrelated to the TIF district and fear increased demand on their services without compensation (Davis 1989).

98   JOYCE Y. MAN

4. Based on his estimation, Bartik (1991) suggests that a 10 percent reduction in all state and local business taxes led to an increase in economic activities by between 1.5 percent and 8.5 percent. A reduction of a jurisdiction's business property tax rate by 10 percent would in the long run increase the level of business activity in the jurisdiction by 18 percent on average. These results imply that a jurisdiction that cuts business property tax rates could result in net fiscal benefits for the jurisdictions, ceteris paribus.

REFERENCES

Anderson, John E. 1990. Tax increment financing: Municipal adoption and growth. *National Tax Journal* 43(2): 155–163.

Anderson, John E., and R.W. Wassmer. 1995. The decision to 'bid for business': Municipal behavior in granting property tax abatement. *Regional Science and Urban Economics* 25(6): 739–57.

Bartik, Timothy J. 1990. The market failure approach to regional economic development policy. *Economic Development Quarterly* 4(4):361–70.

Bartik, T. J. 1991. *Who benefits from state and local economic development policies?* Kalamazoo, Michigan: W. E. Upjohn Institute for Employment Research.

Bovaird, Tont. 1992. Local economic development and the city. *Urban Studies* 29(3/4):343–368.

Chapman, Jeffrey, I. Tax increment financing as a tool of redevelopment. In *Local government tax and land use policies in the United States,* ed. Helen F. Ladd. Northampton, MA: Edward Elgar.

Clarke, Susan E., and Gary L. Gaile. 1992. The next wave: Postfederal local economic development strategies. *Economic Development Quarterly* 6(2): 187–198.

Davis, Don. 1989. Tax increment financing. *Public Budgeting & Finance* (Spring): 63–73.

Duffy-Deno, Kevin, and Randall W. Eberts. 1991. Public infrastructure and regional economic development: A simultaneous equation approach. *Journal of Urban Economics* 30: 329–343.

Dye, Richard F. 1997. A comparative analysis of tax increment financing in northeastern Illinois. In *Assessing the impact of tax increment financing in northeastern Illinois. An empirical analysis and case studies,* ed. R. Calia. Chicago: The Civic Federation.

Forgey, Fred A. 1993. Tax increment financing: Equity, effectiveness, and efficiency. *The Municipal Yearbook,* 1993. Washington, D.C., International City Management Association: 25–33.

Harrison, B., and Kanter, S. 1978. The political economy of states' job-creation business incentives. *Journal of the American Institute of Planners* 44:424–35.

Huddleston, Jack R. 1981. Variations in development subsidies under tax increment financing. *Land Economics* 57(3): 373–384.

Kim, T. John, Clyde W. Forrest, and Karen A. Przypyszny. 1984. Determining potential gains and losses of TIF. American Planning Association, Planning Advisory Service, Report number 389.

Klemanski, John S. 1990. Using tax increment financing for urban redevelopment projects. *Economic Development Quarterly* 4(1): 23–28.

Ladd, Helen, and John Yinger. 1989. *America's ailing cities: Fiscal health and the design of urban policy*. Baltimore: Johns Hopkins University Press.

Lawrence, D. B., and S. Stephenson. 1995. The economics and politics of tax increment financing. *Growth and Change* 26:105–137.

Ledebur, Larry, and William Barnes. 1992. Metropolitan disparities and economic growth. Paper prepared for the National League of Cities.

Man, Joyce Y. 1999. Fiscal pressure, tax competition and the adoption of tax increment financing. *Urban Studies* 36(7): 1151–1167

Man, Joyce Y., and Michael E. Bell. 1993. Federal infrastructure grants-in-aid: An ad hoc infrastructure strategy. *Public Budgeting & Financing* 13(3) (Fall): 9–22.

McHone, W. W. 1987. Factors in the adoption of industrial development incentives by states. *Applied Economics* 23:17–29.

Morgan, W. E., and Hackbart, M. M. 1974. An analysis of state and local industrial tax exemption programs. *Southern Economic Journal* 41:200–205.

Mullins, Daniel R., and Kimberly A. Cox. 1994. A profile of tax and expenditure limitations in the fifty states. Center for Urban Policy and the Environment, School of Public and Environmental Affairs, Indiana University, Indianapolis, Indiana.

Munnell, A. H. 1990. Why has productivity growth declined? Productivity and public investment. *New England Economic Review* 3–22.

Stinson, Thomas F. 1992. Subsidizing local economic development through tax increment financing: Costs in nonmetro communities in southern Minnesota. *Policy Studies Journal* 20(2):241–248.

Shannon, John. 1991. Federalism's 'invisible regulator'—Interjurisdictional competition. In *Competition among states and local governments*, by The Urban Institute, Washington, DC: The Urban Institute.

CHAPTER 7

Effects of Tax Increment Financing on Economic Development

Joyce Y. Man

An issue of great interest to state and local officials is the effectiveness of tax increment financing (TIF) programs in stimulating economic development. Because of its location-specific nature, the TIF program may serve as a valuable tool for evaluating the effectiveness of state and local economic development policies. Therefore, a thorough understanding of TIF will contribute to the longstanding debate over the impact of state and local tax and expenditure policies upon the location of capital investment.

This chapter reviews the current debate over the effectiveness of state and local economic development policies and discusses the evidence on the effects of TIF programs on economic development. The following issues will be addressed: Should State and Local economic development policies matter? Do TIF programs raise property values in a community beyond the level that would have been expected had the TIF district not been created? Is the TIF mechanism an effective tool in stimulating economic growth? Could TIF generate sufficient tax revenues over time to offset the costs of TIF to contributor governments?

SHOULD STATE AND LOCAL ECONOMIC DEVELOPMENT POLICIES MATTER?

The effectiveness, or lack thereof, of state and local government tax and expenditure policies to influence business location and investment decisions has received considerable attention from economists as well as policymakers. Economic theory predicts that variations in tax rates across jurisdictions affect the location and investment decisions of firms. If tax differentials are not perfectly correlated with service differentials, the high-tax jurisdiction may raise the costs of production and thereby reduce profits and induce firms to locate in the low-tax jurisdiction (Mieszkowski 1972).

However, for many years, the consensus among researchers was that state and local taxes had little effect on economic activity of either states or metropolitan areas. They believed that state and local taxes represent such a small percentage of total costs that tax effects cannot be of major importance. Consistent with their opinions, most pre-1980s studies (Due 1961; Oakland 1978; Wasylenko 1981) found no significant statistical relationship between state and local taxes and economic growth. Based upon this argument, many researchers believe that the state and local policies to promote economic development through either a tax or expenditure tool are ineffective and inefficient in influencing firm location or expansion decisions and stimulating economic development (Cummings 1988).

However, research in the 1980s and 1990s has found that state and local taxes and expenditures exert statistically significant influences on the level of economic activity. In his review of fifty-seven studies produced after 1979 on interjurisdictional business location decisions, Bartik (1991) found that forty of these studies (about 70 percent) reported evidence of state and local tax effects on state and local business activity. Recent research (Plaut and Pluta 1983; Helms 1985; Bartik 1989; Munnell 1990; and Duffy-Deno and Eberts 1991) has also found a statistically significant positive effect of public expenditure on economic development. This research suggests that government investment and improvement in infrastructure may actually raise the number of small business start-ups and stimulate growth in state personal income and state private employment. Voith (1993) and Haughwout (1997) also provide evidence that public investment on infrastructure, especially transportation, has a positive effect on land values, and the benefits of the central city's infrastructure even spill over to suburban residents. The new consensus that taxes and public expenditures affect location decisions indicates that state and local incentive policies designed to promote economic development may be effective.

DOES TIF STIMULATE ECONOMIC DEVELOPMENT?

TIF is one explicit attempt by state and local governments to promote economic development through tax or expenditure policy instruments. Since TIF is primarily a mechanism of financing infrastructure investment and improvement, many government officials believe that the new or improved infrastructure facilities provided through TIF reduce private firms' production costs and increase business profits and thereby may influence business location or expansion decisions. Under TIF, local governments pledge to use all increases in property tax revenues generated from new development to finance the public infrastructure and development expenditures that directly benefit businesses located in the TIF district. Thus, TIF may act as a geographically targeted tax, expenditure, and regulatory inducement to attract firms to a specific location in an attempt to generate higher property values, more jobs, higher wages, more tax revenues, and thereby economic growth.

The critics of TIF claim that the TIF program is ineffective and inefficient because incentives provided through TIF usually account for only a small portion of a firm's production cost so that they are unlikely to affect business location choice or expansion decisions. In addition, as the use of TIF by one city is likely to lead other cities to adopt it as a defensive policy, TIF is likely to become increasingly ineffective over time. Some critics even charge that TIF is little more than a budget-manipulating tool adopted by growing cities to capture property tax revenues that would otherwise have gone to school districts, townships, or other overlapping jurisdictions.

In the past, researchers usually relied on national surveys and site-specific case studies to find answers to the question of the effectiveness of TIF. For example, Forgey (1993) surveyed 300 randomly selected municipalities. He found that among 128 cities that reported the use of a TIF program, 78 percent of them experienced increases in property values, and only 2 percent of the respondents actually experienced a decline in property taxes after the establishment of the TIF district. This result strongly supports the proposition that the use of TIF is highly associated with the property value growth within the district itself and the surrounding communities as well. The case studies in Illinois (Davis 1989; Ritter and Oldfield 1990), Wisconsin (Huddleston 1984) and Minnesota (Stinson 1992) demonstrate that TIF projects do stimulate economic development.

Recently, there is a growing interest among researchers to evaluate the effectiveness of TIF using econometric models. Anderson (1990) investigates the fundamental issue of whether the TIF adoption decision and the growth of the city's property value are related using a data set drawn from Michigan cities. He jointly estimates the change in the aggregate city property value and the TIF adoption decision in a structural probit model. After taking into account the sample selection bias, he reveals that TIF-adopting cities experience greater property value increases than non-TIF-adopting cities. However, his study did not address the issue of growth induced or caused by the creation of a TIF program.

Wassmer (1994) conducts a regression investigation of whether various local incentives exert the desired additive effect on a community's economic development. Using a data set drawn from cities in the Detroit metropolitan area, he examines the economic impact of four local programs, industrial development bonds, commercial property tax abatements, the establishment of a downtown development authority, and a tax increment financing authority district. He finds that only the variable for the tax increment financing exerts a positive effect on real retail sales.

Man and Rosentraub (1998) investigate the fundamental issues of whether TIF programs raise property values in a community beyond the level that would have been expected had the TIF district not been created. They estimate the net additive effect of TIF on property value growth for a data set drawn from Indiana cities by comparing pre-TIF to post-TIF property value changes in a first-difference regression model. There empirical results reveal that the municipal adoption of TIF has a statistically significant positive effect on property value growth in the entire host city. Their study shows that Indiana TIF programs have increased the median owner-occupied housing value by 11.4 percent in the TIF-adopting cities relative to what it would have been without the program. That is equivalent to about a $4,900 increase in the median real value of owner-occupied houses in the entire community that implements a TIF program. Their regression analysis also reveals that the TIF program has no effect on the property value in the initial first two years after its adoption but has strong positive effects thereafter. Their results indicate that the adoption of a TIF program does stimulate property value growth in the TIF district and surrounding communities. This finding suggests that the infrastructure investment and improvements in a targeted area financed through TIF has a substantial spillover effect on the host community's real estate market. If increasing property values reflect an expanding economy, then their results provide empirical evidence on a positive impact and effectiveness of TIF programs on local economic activities.

Man (1999) also investigates the impact of TIF programs on local employment. She estimates a local employment determination equation with TIF as one of the independent variables using a cross-section time-series regression model. After controlling for a series of other variables, including tax and expenditure, labor market characteristics, local specific amenities and agglomeration forces, social economic conditions and time effects, her study reveals that TIF programs have a statistically significant positive effect on local employment. Based upon the empirical evidence, she concludes that the targeted public investment in a TIF district yields a substantial positive impact on economic activity, and

TIF is an effective local economic development tool.

By contrast, Dye and Merriman (1999) do not find a statistically positive effect of TIF adoption on the city's post-TIF annualized growth rate of property values using a data set drawn from cities in the Chicago metropolitan area. Based upon their empirical results, they conclude that the adoption of TIF reduces assessed property value growth rates in the entire city and that municipalities that elect to adopt TIF stimulate the growth of blighted areas targeted by TIF at the expense of nontargeted areas. However, their empirical results should be interpreted with caution. First, their empirical model evaluates the association between the TIF adoption and the equalized assessed value growth in the post-TIF period instead of the net effect of TIF. The negative relationship between the municipal TIF adoption and the city's property value growth does not necessarily indicate that the use of TIF causes a decline in the city's property value growth. It only suggests a correlation between the adoption of TIF and the city's tax base growth. Second, the lack of evidence on a statistically significant positive effect of TIF projects on the entire TIF-adopting city does not preclude the effectiveness of TIF as an economic development tool. It may well be that the use of TIF stimulates higher property value growth in the TIF district, but these positive effects may not be big enough to offset the declines in other non-TIF areas. As a result, the tax base of the city as a whole may have not yet shown any positive growth. It merely indicates that the development in TIF districts may not necessarily yield immediate positive spillover effects to the surrounding areas and the entire host communities.[1] Finally, Dye and Merriman's empirical results show that the coefficient estimate of the variable on the TIF district's share of the city's total equalized assessed property value is positive and statistically significant.[2] This could be interpreted as evidence suggesting that TIF programs yield substantial spillovers of benefits to the host community's real estate market, a conclusion different from the one drawn by the two researchers.

Given the conflicting views with respect to the effectiveness of TIF, more research needs to be done before we can reach a consensus, if any, on the issue of whether TIF programs have achieved their goals of stimulating economic development.

COST-REVENUE ANALYSIS OF TIF

Effectiveness of TIF as an economic development tool is a necessary but not a sufficient condition for the policy adoption because the effectiveness criterion does not address the issue concerning whether the benefits of such policies outweigh the costs to taxpayers.

Huddleston (1982) develops a conceptual framework that measures the costs and revenues associated with a TIF project over time. He conducts a present value comparison of the taxpayers' funding of the project with the future flow of subsidies that would derive from the TIF-induced property value increases and the additional excess increments the sponsor governments release. He demonstrates that TIF projects have a positive fiscal impact on both sponsor and contributor governments, but the expected financial gains to contributor governments must be considered extremely long run under TIF programs in Wisconsin.

Huddleston's finding is supported by the evidence presented by Lawrence and Stephenson (1995). They reveal that the taxpayers in the entire metropolitan area of Des Moines, Iowa, subsidized the downtown activities in the early years of the TIF program, but later they enjoyed lower property tax rates due to the urban economic revitalization program funded by the TIF mechanism.

CONCLUSIONS

Recently, economists have reached a consensus that state and local tax and expenditure policies may have influence on business location and economic activity. But empirical studies have yielded conflicting conclusions about the effectiveness of TIF programs. There is evidence suggesting that the TIF-adopting cities in Michigan experienced faster property value growth than non-TIF cities, and TIF programs in Indiana raised property value and employment level in a city beyond the level that would have been expected had the TIF district not been created. But such positive spillover effects of TIF on property value in the entire TIF-adopting city are not found in the study using data drawn from municipalities in the Chicago metropolitan area. Clearly there is room for additional research on the effects of TIF using data from other states and jurisdictions. The existing studies often use dummy variables as proxies for TIF programs that take the value one if a jurisdiction creates a TIF district or zero if it does not. This way of measuring local incentives provided through TIF has major limitations. It can't quantify the extent to which local governments use TIF-financed incentives. It also ignores the differential effects of variations in the size and use of TIF programs. According to Klacik (this volume), the size of TIF districts and the type of projects financed through TIF may differ considerably among jurisdictions. For example, some cities use TIF for redevelopment or revitalization of a depressed area, but others may use it to allure business to a growing area for the purpose of economic development. TIF may be used to finance expansion of roads and streets or to pay for residential developments for low-income households. It is likely that differences in uses and structures of TIF programs among jurisdictions and different types of projects financed through TIF may have differential effects on economic activity. Given diversity of geographic sizes of TIF districts and types of projects funded through TIF, future research needs to focus on a microlevel analysis of costs, revenues, success, and failure of individual TIF programs.

Recent studies of the efficiency aspect of TIF programs using the benefit-cost analysis demonstrate that a TIF project may have a positive fiscal impact on both sponsor and contributor governments, but the expected financial gains to contributor governments may not occur until sometime in the future. In general, the benefit of TIF programs will outweigh the costs to taxpayers, especially in the long run.

NOTES

1. The authors measure the TIF programs in three ways, a dummy variable for the TIF adoption, a variable measuring the size of the TIF district, and a variable describing the number of years of TIF adoption. However, these variables are very likely to be highly correlated with one another. Including variables on different measures of TIF programs simultaneously in the estimation of the property value growth equation may lead to biased and inconsistent coefficient estimates of these variables, the TIF dummy variable in particular. The opposite signs of the TIF dummy variable and the TIF size variable may indicate a problem of multicollinearity.

2. Measuring TIF-financed incentives with a dummy variable has major limitations. It is unable to quantify the extent to which local governments have used TIF. Estimation with an alternative measure of the size of the targeted TIF area relative to the municipality may yield a more accurate analysis of policy effects.

REFERENCES

Anderson, John E., 1990. Tax increment financing: Municipal adoption and growth. *National Tax Journal* 43(2): 155–163.
Bartik, T. J. 1989. Small business start-ups in the United States: Estimates of the effects of characteristics of states. *Southern Economic Journal* 55:1004–1018.
———. 1991. *Who benefits from state and local economic development policies?* Kalamazoo, MI: W. E. Upjohn Institute for Employment Research.
Cummings, S., editor. 1988. *Business elites and urban development.* Albany: State University of New York Press.
Davis, Don. 1989. Tax increment financing. *Public Budgeting & Finance* (Spring): 63–73.

Due, John F. 1961. Studies of state-local tax influences in location of industry. *National Tax Journal* 14:163–173.

Duffy-Deno, Kevin, and Randall W. Eberts. 1991. Public infrastructure and regional economic development: A simultaneous equation approach. *Journal of Urban Economics* 30: 329–343.

Dye, Richard F., and Merriman David F. 1999. The effects of tax increment financing on economic development. Working Paper #75, Institute of Government and Public Affairs, University of Illinois, Chicago.

Forgey, F. A. 1993. Tax increment financing: Equity, effectiveness, and efficiency. *The Municipal Yearbook.* Washington, DC: International City Management Association, 25–33.

Haughwout, A. F. 1997. Central city infrastructure investment and suburban house values. *Regional Science and Urban Economics* 27: 199–215.

Helms, J. L. 1985. The effect of state and local taxes on economic growth: A time series-cross section approach. *The Review of Economics and Statistics* 67(4):574–582.

Huddleston, Jack R. 1982. Local financial dimensions of tax increment financing: A cost-revenue analysis. *Public Budgeting and Finance* 2: 40–49.

———. 1984. Tax increment financing as a state development policy. *Growth and Change* 15(2):11–17.

Lawrence, D. B., and S. Stephenson. 1995. The economics and politics of tax increment financing. *Growth and Change* 26:105–137.

Man, Joyce Y. 1999. The impact of tax increment financing programs on local economic development. *Journal of Public Budgeting, Accounting and Financial Management* 11(3): 417–430.

Man, Joyce Y., and Mark S. Rosentraub. 1998. Tax increment financing: Municipal adoption and effects on property value growth. *Public Finance Review* 26, 523–547.

Mieszkowski, P. M. 1972. The property tax: An excise tax or a profit tax? *Journal of Public Economics* 1, 73–96.

Munnell, A. H. 1990. Why has productivity growth declined? Productivity and public investment. *New England Economic Review* 3–22.

Oakland, William. 1978. Local taxes and intra-urban industrial location: A survey. In *Metropolitan Finance and Growth Management Policies,* ed. G. Break. Madison: University of Wisconsin Press.

Plaut, Thomas R., and Joseph E. Pluta. 1983. Business climate, taxes and expenditures, and state industrial growth in the United States. *Southern Economic Journal* 50,1:99–119.

Ritter, Kevin, and Kenneth Oldfield. 1990. Testing the effects of tax increment financing in Springfield, Illinois: The assessor's role in determining policy outcomes. *Property Tax Journal* 9(2):141–147.

Stinson, Thomas F. 1992. Subsidizing local economic development through tax increment financing: Costs in nonmetro communities in southern Minnesota. *Policy Studies Journal* 20(2):241–248.

U.S. Department of Commerce. Bureau of the Census. Statistical Abstract of the United States. U.S. Government Printing Office. Washington, D.C. (1980, 1989, and 1996).

Voith, R. 1993. Changing capitalization of CBD-oriented transportation systems. *Journal of Urban Economics* 33:361–376.

Wassmer, R. W. 1994. Can local incentives alter a metropolitan city's economic development? *Urban Studies* 31:1251–1278.

Wasylenko, Michael. 1981. The location of firms: the role of taxes and fiscal incentives. *Urban Affairs Annual Reviews* 20:155–89.

PART II

CHAPTER 8

Tax Increment Financing
and Fiscal Stress:
The California Genesis

Jeff Chapman

Tax increment financing in California is a redevelopment financing technique that raises revenues that are then used to ameliorate blight. It is also a technique used to encourage economic development and finance low-cost housing. But what is not mentioned, at least in the public descriptions of its use, is the utilization of tax increment financing to effect the fiscal condition of the jurisdiction.

There are secondary benefits for the implementing jurisdiction that are recognized when blight is eliminated and economic development occurs. These benefits not only include the physical and social amenities that occur when blight disappears (for example, cleaner streets and less crime) but also the increased net fiscal benefits that flow to the jurisdiction's coffers. Under tax increment financed development, an increase in sales tax revenues, construction of new infrastructure that might be difficult to finance under general obligation (GO) or revenue bonds but can be more easily financed through tax allocation debt, and the reduction of social welfare expenditures all might occur.

Although blight elimination, economic development, and the bettering of the jurisdiction's financial characteristics are separate phenomena, they can be closely related. However, the former two reasons are usually the only ones mentioned. The purpose of this chapter is to examine the third reason—the role of tax increment financing in California over the last two decades as used as a response to the fiscal stresses that localities within the state have faced. After a brief discussion of the history of tax increment financing in California, there will be an analysis of the fiscal

113

stresses faced by California jurisdictions and then an analysis of the use
of tax increment financing as a potential response to these stresses. The
chapter will then draw some tentative conclusions.

HISTORY[1]

Urban blight has existed since the beginning of the republic. However,
no federal programs were developed to ameliorate this problem until the
Great Depression forced the national government to address the problems of a country that was not adequately housed. The Industrial Recovery Act of 1933 included a federal housing component, and the Federal
Housing Authority, the Federal Savings and Loan Insurance Corporation, and the Federal National Mortgage Authority were all New Deal
Programs. In 1941, the state of New York enacted the first statutory
authority to allow the use of eminent domain by public entities to
acquire slum property for the purpose of providing new housing.

After World War II, public officials at all levels of government continued to be concerned about the general condition of the urban arena.
A deteriorated housing stock faced returning soldiers. In 1945, California was the first state to enact a Community Redevelopment Act that
gave cities and counties the ability to establish redevelopment agencies.
In most cases, the Redevelopment Agency's board consisted of the city
council or board of supervisors of the respective jurisdiction, and concurrent meetings were sometimes held. These agencies had the authority
to undertake a variety of activities: to buy real property using the power
of eminent domain; to develop the property (but not to construct buildings); to sell the property without bidding; to relocate persons who have
an interest in the acquired property; to finance this operation by borrowing from the federal or state government and by selling bonds; and,
to impose land use controls in order to implement a comprehensive
development plan. Other states followed California's lead, but because
of inadequate financing arrangements, all of the state programs were
initially ineffective.

Because the states failed to make much progress, Congress came to
believe that only federal aid could make a difference, and the Housing
Act of 1949 (whose slum clearance provisions become known as urban
renewal) was passed, principally through the lobbying efforts of housing advocates for low-income persons and real-estate developers
(Frieden and Sagalyn 1989). This act provided the first major source of
federal money for redevelopment, and although the state had the
authority to plan and regulate land use, it was the federal money with
its restrictions that shaped the programs.

California was responding to the same post-World War II pressures that faced the national government when the state enacted the 1945 legislation. Because this act initially provided no money or local financing method to implement projects, the first activities occurred in cities that used the funds available under the federal housing acts. The cities were expected to contribute between one-fourth and one-third of the costs after the land sale proceeds were realized. Projects were often undertaken without any knowledge of private demand (Beatty et al. 1995).

In 1951 the Community Redevelopment Act was codified (into the Health and Safety Code—not the Tax Code) and renamed the "Community Redevelopment Law." Included in this codification was the ability to undertake tax increment financing.[2] The incentive for this approval occurred when several cities failed to approve the local matching share that was necessary to obtain the federal money. Tax increment financing (TIF) was intended to provide the match. This original financing method, which has now been adopted by over forty states, was designed to allow redevelopment agencies to finance projects without any dependence on federal funds. Although only 34 redevelopment projects had begun by 1966, by 1976 there were 204 projects adopted in addition to the 31 then in the process of adoption.[3]

Perhaps the most controversial element of TIF-financed redevelopment in California has been its mandated use to eliminate blight. However, from its enactment in 1945 until 1993, blight was never defined by statute, although there were nine separate court decisions that attempted to define what blight was and wasn't (California State Legislature 1995). This is an important conceit, since under some definitions of blight, TIF redevelopment could be a major revenue-producing instrument.

The redevelopment law has been changed several times since its enactment, both by the courts and by the state legislature. The current statute now more clearly defines blight, regulates the provision of low and moderate-income housing, mandates the sharing of the increment between jurisdictions, and more carefully defines the life of the project.

FISCAL STRESS IN CALIFORNIA[4]

Fiscal stress in local California jurisdictions originates from four different sources: natural disasters; exogenous influences; voter initiatives; and, with particular respect to redevelopment, the changing state and local tax structure. The importance of these reasons varies by jurisdiction, but nearly all localities experienced some form of fiscal constraint that originated from each of these sources.

Natural Disasters

Natural disasters have always been part of the California environment. Droughts, earthquakes, and forest fires have been part of the state's culture since its history has been recorded. While many of these disasters are ameliorated by state or federal disaster aid or by private insurance, they still put fiscal pressure on localities, both directly and indirectly. In the first half of the 1990s, drought cost California farmers about $3 billion, the Loma Prieta and Northridge earthquakes resulted in about $12 billion worth of damage, and fires (including the urban Oakland fire in 1991) cost about $4 billion. These disasters led to a decline in sales and property tax revenues and a short-run increase in public expenditures. Both of these forces caused fiscal stress in specific areas.

Exogenous Influences

There are at least three principal exogenous influences on the state and local economies. Although California has a large and robust economy, it is still subject to national business cycles. The recessions in the mid-1970s, the early 1980s, and the early to mid-1990s were all serious, and the last long-lived. All areas of the state were affected, and all sectors of the economy contracted. Unfortunately, the use of TIF as a stress-reducing mechanism is unlikely to work well during a recession since there is very likely to be little or no developer interest.

A second exogenous influence on the local economy was military expenditures. California prospered during the military build-ups of the late 1970s and the decade of the 1980s. Not only were the military bases well supported, but there were a multitude of defense contracts to California industries as well. During this time period, these military expenditures helped to mitigate local fiscal stress. However, beginning in the early 1990s, the base closure process began. Just as California benefited more than most areas from the buildup, it was disproportionately hurt by the shut down. Twenty-nine bases were shut, with a direct loss of over ninety-seven thousand jobs.[5] By September, 1996, as a direct result of this process, four redevelopment projects had been started, and fourteen more were probable (Office of Planning and Research 1996).

The third exogenous influence on local fiscal stress was the illegal immigration that surged in the last half of the 1980s, but that seems to have slightly moderated during the most recent recession (Johnson 1996). There is still uncertainty about the number and net cost of the illegal immigrants, although a strong argument can be made that local governments principally see only sales tax revenues from this population, with the bulk of the taxes paid going to the state or national government. TIF-financed redevelopment would have been influenced by the illegal immigrant surge, since there is a mandate for the provision of housing that would be affordable by low and moderate-income families. The TIF reforms of 1983 and 1993 directly addressed the housing issue by stiffening the penalties on redevelopment agencies that did not meet the mandated housing requirement. This chapter will later present a discussion of the housing controversy.

Initiatives

Voter initiatives also lead to California fiscal stress. Proposition 13, passed in June 1978, eliminated the ability of local governments to raise property taxes for General Fund revenues (and for nearly a decade, made it nearly impossible to issue GO debt based on the property tax). For most jurisdictions, this increased the importance of the sales tax and made the extension and improvement of capital facilities very difficult. Spending limits on local governments were also imposed (Proposition 4 in 1978), which sometimes led to an increase in public-private partnerships (Kirlin and Kirlin 1982). In the 1980s, voters passed a series of initiatives (Proposition 98 in 1988 and Proposition 111 in 1989) that mandated a formula-driven contribution for state aid to K-14 schools. These two propositions would ultimately have the effect of constraining the state's ability to aid local government.

The most recent initiative that will impact the fiscal well-being of local government in California is Proposition 218, passed in November 1996. This initiative ensures that all taxes and most charges on property owners are subject to voter approval in an attempt to curb some perceived abuses in the use of assessments and property-related fees to pay for general governmental services. The Legislative Analyst's Office (LAO) believes that it is highly unlikely that there would be a more than 5 percent decline in aggregate local revenues because of this initiative, although the impact on some jurisdictions could be substantial (Legislative Analyst's Office 1996). Further, in the tradition of many California initiatives, much of the initiative is not clear as to intent—the LAO lists nineteen questions that must be legislatively answered before the full impact of the proposition can be calculated.

Revenue Flow Structures

The final cause of local fiscal stress is the state/local revenue flow structure in the state. In the years after Proposition 13, the state/local tax relationship became extraordinarily convoluted and understandable only to those who make a career of analyzing it. The state allocated the remaining property taxes collected based on previous tax collections; developments in these allocation formulas became an important variable; realignment of some revenues and services occurred at the county level; and in the early 1990s, the state took billions of dollars of property taxes away from cities, counties, and redevelopment agencies and reallocated them to school districts in order to meet the Proposition 98 mandates. Coming in the midst of a recession, this was another fiscal shock to local governments.

Compounding these intricate relationships was the way the tax increment generated by redevelopment was shared. Before the 1994 reform, the increment was allocated based on a fiscal review committee, in which the redevelopment agency, the school districts, the county, and other affected jurisdictions would negotiate for a share. Schools realized that if they did not get any money from the increment, the state would backfill their loss; counties, over time, realized that they could threaten a lawsuit and thereby increase their share of the allocation. Cities further usually controlled the RDA, so they were willing to settle for less money. Table 8.1 illustrates this changing pattern of increment allocations.

These four sets of reasons for local fiscal stress often have interdependencies. An earthquake destroys property, leading to a lowering of the reassessment under the Proposition 13 rules, which then could lead to a lower level of funding for schools, which could then lead to the state changing the property tax allocation formula. The next sections of this chapter, through both case studies and broader portraits, will examine a few examples of these fiscal stress-tax increment relationships in more detail.

TABLE 8.1
Tax Increment Allocation

Year	Percent to County	Percent to Cities	Percent to Schools	Percent to Other	Percent to RDA
1984–85	2.46	0.02	0.36	0.61	96.55
1985–86	3.41	0.08	0.64	1.17	94.70
1986–87	3.81	0.16	0.64	1.53	93.86
1987–88	4.24	0.08	0.60	1.90	93.18
1988–89	4.67	0.11	0.62	2.24	92.36
1988–90	5.58	0.12	0.87	2.61	90.82
1990–91	6.14	0.14	1.29	3.21	89.22
1991–92	6.70	0.19	1.45	3.08	88.58
1992–93	8.17	0.09	1.58	3.27	86.89
1993–94	9.00	0.08	2.23	2.70	85.99
1994–95	9.08	0.08	2.00	2.76	86.08
1995–96	9.72	0.07	2.34	2.62	85.25

Source: Controller's Reports

VOTER INITIATIVE EXAMPLES

Prior to Proposition 13, TIF was seldom mentioned as a response to local fiscal stress. By the decade following Proposition 13, many cities assumed that the use of this tool could be an effective response to financial pressures.

Proposition 13 dramatically lowered the importance of property taxes as a revenue source for local jurisdictions. It set the rate at 1 percent of market value and then defined market value on an acquisition basis with a 2 percent growth cap (or the rate of inflation, whichever was lower). Prior to any sale, property values were rolled back to their 1975–76 levels, which were then subjected to the 2 percent cap. Property taxes could not be increased, which essentially eliminated the use of general obligation debt financing at the local level. The state legislature reacted to this property tax cut through a series of complex "bail-out" and "buy-out" measures that enabled localities to continue to have some financial strength, although they were forced to give up some discretion (Chapman 1981; Kirlin and Kirlin 1982). Later, however, as the state drew down and then exhausted its surplus, the state aid lessened, and cities and counties faced an increase in fiscal stress.[6]

The initial predictions concerning the future of TIF were quite negative. It was assumed that the growth in the property taxes within any district would be far smaller than in the past, and thus fewer tax allocation bonds could be sustained. And although a major underwriting firm predicted the demise of TIF (Merrill Lynch 1979), this did not occur. One reason was that TIF became part of a large series of measures designed to legally circumvent the draconian implications of Proposition 13. Public administrators developed new instruments for debt and new ways of financing operations and new methods for providing infrastructure. Since the legal structure of TIF was already in place, it could be immediately utilized to help solve this new fiscal stress problem.

Table 8.2 illustrates the rapid growth of TIF and a corresponding number of agencies. The size of the increment grew, and the expenditures of the agencies also grew. It is interesting to recognize that in real terms, the increment per agency peaked during the 1991–94 period—a time of significant state fiscal crises.[7]

This growth occurred for at least three reasons. Jurisdictions discovered that redevelopment could be used to entice sales tax generators into the jurisdiction, that TIF financing could be used more extensively for infrastructure finance, and that redevelopment activities could be used as a weapon in interstate competition for new businesses.

Because of the decline in property tax revenues, local jurisdictions have become more aware of the importance of the sales tax. Since the

TABLE 8.2
TIF Growth by Year

Year	Apportioned Tax Increment	Total Expenditures	Total Agencies	Increment/Agency in 1978 Dollars
1977–78	$179,140,831	$558,897,443	127	$1,410,558
1978–79	$91,175,585	$592,560,676	130	$643,884
1979–80	$149,318,208	$805,862,848	142	$868,354
1980–81	$205,140,085	$667,705,212	151	$1,020,979
1981–82	$271,280,972	$886,898,507	160	$1,195,829
1982–83	$323,706,802	$1,069,555,820	188	$1,159,658
1983–84	$382,527,107	$1,094,839,359	204	$1,210,001
1984–85	$431,119,207	$1,340,264,107	299	$894,141
1985–86	$557,978,597	$1,133,676,382	322	$1,046,932
1986–87	$687,429,663	$2,757,084,400	333	$1,197,325
1987–88	$806,986,672	$2,453,508,573	344	$1,321,742
1988–89	$936,708,222	$2,269,873,738	349	$1,462,101
1989–90	$1,100,436,321	$2,570,698,302	364	$1,570,523
1990–91	$1,283,781,741	$2,878,229,672	375	$1,723,948
1991–92	$1,471,469,538	$3,109,861,541	381	$1,904,028
1992–93	$1,541,109,568	$3,723,317,860	385	$1,932,831
1993–94	$1,577,507,098	$3,484,751,946	388	$1,934,758
1994–95	$1,544,815,000	$3,306,010,000	390	$1,830,182
1995–96	$1,451,094,000	$3,250,663,000	399	$1,423,206

Source: Controller's Reports

mid-1950s, the sales tax in California has been a joint state-local tax. For much of the time, the state rate was 4 percent, and the city (or county) rate was 1 percent. This 1 percent was subvened back to the jurisdiction in which the sale occurred.[8] Thus, even before Proposition 13, there were clear benefits for jurisdictions to have commercial development. These benefits increased since the proposition's passage. In 1977 and 1978, 15.4 percent of city revenue came from sales taxes and 21.9 percent came from property taxes. By 1993 and 1994, the numbers were 9.5 percent and 7.2 percent, respectively (California State Controller 1995). Particularly desired developments were car dealerships and big-box development, such as Wal-Marts or Price Clubs. These would generate a good deal of sales tax revenue from a relatively small geographic area. Of course, retail malls were always welcome. Anecdotally, there were many instances in which redevelopment agencies used their power of eminent domain to assemble property for the building or expansion of these types of commercial projects, regardless of whether blight existed (California State Legislature 1995).

This emphasis on commercial development benefited both the agency and the city or county. The agency recognized that property values would increase more rapidly when commercial (as opposed to residential) redevelopment occurred. This larger increase in property value would give an extra margin of safety to the tax allocation bond holders and likely make the debt cheaper to sell. The city or county gained because it was the recipient of the additional sales taxes generated because of the redevelopment. Shortly after the passage of Proposition 13, redevelopment agencies were given the power to include a portion of the sales tax increment as part of their revenues, which further encouraged redevelopment activities.[9] In addition, for most of this time period, California was relatively recession free or only lightly touched by economic downturns. This encouraged even more emphasis on the importance of sales taxes. It was not surprising, however, to see a decline in the growth rate of TIF during the recession of the early 1990s since all development within the state stagnated.

The most recent initiative, Proposition 218, may cause fiscal stress to increase for some jurisdictions. The Legislative Analyst's Office believes that redevelopment agencies are not directly affected by this proposition. It may be that this will be an added incentive for the increased use of redevelopment to generate additional resources for at least some cities. As earlier noted, much of Proposition 218 needs legislative clarification, so the ultimate results are still unknown.

Noted previously as well, Proposition 13 essentially eliminated GO financing until 1986, when voters approved the possibility of a property tax override for GO financing. Even after 1986, however, GO financing was still difficult to use since a two-thirds vote for approval was necessary. Although several new financial tools were developed to help in financing capital infrastructure, TIF financing continued to be used.[10] Unfortunately, data is not available to measure directly the extent of capital financing undertaken by RDAs using TIF. However, this might be indirectly measured by the size of the projects. Table 8.3 shows the distribution of projects by size since 1984. Since that time, projects greater than one hundred acres have slowly increased as a percentage of total projects from about 75 percent to 80 percent. Because of their size, these projects are likely to include large amounts of vacant land and therefore imply a need for new infrastructure.[11]

An additional reason for the increase in the financing of infrastructure through TIF redevelopment is that the tax allocation debt can be issued without a vote of a jurisdiction's residents. A majority vote of the Redevelopment Agency's Board of Directors is sufficient authorization. In fact, residents are often unaware of the magnitude of the debt issued and the size of the tax increment, although California property tax

TABLE 8.3
Project Distribution

Year	Total Projects	1–50 Acres	Percent	51–100 Acres	Percent	101–500 Acres	Percent	501–2500 Acres	Percent	>2500 Acres	Percent
1984–85	503	94	0.19	57	0.11	185	0.37	134	0.27	33	0.07
1985–86	526	95	0.18	54	0.10	195	0.37	144	0.27	38	0.07
1986–87	529	88	0.17	55	0.10	198	0.37	151	0.29	37	0.07
1987–88	559	86	0.15	58	0.10	200	0.36	173	0.31	42	0.08
1988–89	578	86	0.15	57	0.10	209	0.36	186	0.32	40	0.07
1989–90	603	84	0.14	58	0.10	210	0.35	203	0.34	48	0.08
1990–91	633	85	0.13	61	0.10	215	0.34	219	0.35	53	0.08
1991–92	643	84	0.13	62	0.10	218	0.34	226	0.35	53	0.08
1992–93	658	83	0.13	58	0.09	226	0.34	236	0.36	55	0.08
1993–94	676	83	0.12	62	0.09	224	0.33	252	0.37	55	0.08
1994–95	675	83	0.12	57	0.08	223	0.33	254	0.38	58	0.09
1995–96	676	85	0.13	55	0.08	233	0.34	244	0.36	59	0.09

Note: Projects that did not report size are excluded from the table.
Source: Controller's Reports

assessors often insert a statement describing the magnitude of the tax increment into the property tax bill mailing. This method of gaining approval for capital finance may not be as disturbing as it appears since the Redevelopment Agency's Board has more knowledge than the voters about the state of redevelopment and city/county finances.

There is also some fungibility associated with TIF debt. It would not be surprising to discover that the city might declare that an area with low quality infrastructure is blighted so that tax allocation bonds could be used, thus increasing the amount of available resources to repair or add infrastructure in other areas of the city.

For good or evil, TIF development activities have also been used as a weapon in interjurisdictional economic competition. For example, the city of Sacramento was able to entice a major computer manufacturer to move from a city in southern California partially through the use of TIF infrastructure improvements. Although perhaps a positive sum game from Sacramento's view, from the view of the state it would have to be considered at best a zero sum transaction, prior to the counting of the transaction costs.

Economic incentives such as TIF are also used as part of interstate competition for industrial location. Although the state cannot provide TIF improvements, the state can provide other incentives such that TIF, the local incentive, can make a difference. Interstate competition using incentives has become quite controversial, and strong concerns about the appropriate use of these incentives have been raised (Burnstein and Rolnick 1995).

A NATURAL DISASTER EXAMPLE:
THE LOMA-PRIETA EARTHQUAKE

The Loma-Prieta earthquake occurred in October 1989. Centered in Santa Cruz County, approximately seventy-five miles south of San Francisco, this 7.1 magnitude quake struck at the height of the rush hour and caused over $7 billion worth of property damage. In terms of relative damage, the city of Santa Cruz was significantly affected: over two-thirds of the commercial buildings downtown were either destroyed or immediately demolished following the earthquake, two thousand jobs were lost overnight (about 60 percent of the jobs in the downtown area), and five hundred homes were lost (Kennedy 1996). Six people were killed, three hundred people were injured, and three thousand people were left homeless (Santa Cruz Sentinel 1989). Total property damage was over $112 million with a loss of assessed value in the city of about $40 million.[12] The Santa Cruz finance department estimated a sales tax loss of $750,000 to $1 million for the 1989–90 fiscal year, with an on-going loss of $500,000, due largely to losses of $300,000 in parking citations and $200,000 in parking meter collections.

The Santa Cruz Redevelopment Agency had originally been formed in 1956, following the December 1955 floods.[13] The initial charge of the agency was to develop a project to assist the city in recovering from the devastation in both commercial and residential neighborhoods along the San Lorenzo River. A new urban core was developed from 1957 to 1982, but the redevelopment activities associated with the project ended in 1978. At that time, the Redevelopment Agency was phased out as an independent agency, and the city council acted as the RDA's legislative body. The city manager acted as the agency's executive director, and other agency financing and planning activities were assumed by various city departments. Most of the agency's activities since that time revolved around flood control projects.

After the Loma-Prieta earthquake, the Santa Cruz City Council established a Redevelopment Department as a separate city administrative entity, with the director of redevelopment acting as the executive director of the Redevelopment Agency. The newly revitalized agency immediately undertook a number of simultaneous projects:

1. State legislation, which allowed for streamlining the process involved with new and expanded redevelopment projects, was passed in July 1990. This legislation enabled the RDA to merge its flood projects with a public improvement process to deal with rebuilding needs. The new merged project encompassed 807 acres and provided a mechanism with which to address post-earthquake reconstruction. This project was designed to provide $4 million in funds;[14]

2. A thirty-six-member public-private partnership was created. This advisory body was able to develop a plan quickly and lay the framework for downtown rebuilding. This plan, which included land use standards, circulation, parking, and streetscape improvements, was adopted by the city council in September 1991;

3. A series of other projects were implemented that were connected to the earthquake recovery plan. In particular, a business improvement project was established to improve parking, traffic circulation, and other blighted conditions. The Redevelopment Agency appointed a twelve-member advisory committee and held neighborhood workshops to help develop the plan, which was accepted in March 1994.

The project area of the Earthquake Recovery and Reconstruction Project was in an urban area and, after the earthquake, was clearly blighted. The Redevelopment Agency was able to successfully stimulate major repairs and new development. Nearly five hundred thousand square feet of commercial and office space has been repaired, constructed, or is under construction. This is a classic example of how redevelopment was intended to be used.

Interjurisdictional Relationship Examples

Any piece of property in California constitutes part of the tax base of a multitude of overlapping jurisdictions. For property taxes, there is often a city component, a county component, a school district component, and a nonenterprise special district component (there are usually several of these) to this overlap. If a redevelopment project is instituted, it will overlay these individual components, and any tax increment that occurs will go to the redevelopment agency.

These overlapping jurisdictions recognized that they may have a legitimate claim to a portion of the increment. Their argument would revolve around how much development would have occurred in the absence of redevelopment activity. One polar case would be that no development would have occurred without the intervention of the redevelopment agency. If this no-naturally-occurring-development case existed, then there would have been no property tax increment during the previous time period. In this situation the overlapping jurisdictions should get none of the increment that actually did occur, since the increment's existence is entirely due to the intervention of the agency. The other polar case concerns the imposition of a redevelopment project area on top of an area that is currently growing. In this case, the redevelopment agency could not claim that the increment was due to their intervention and that none of the increment should go to the agency.[15] It is unlikely that either of these polar cases exists. This gives rise to the practice that existed prior to 1994—the establishment and utilization of a fiscal review committee consisting of representatives of the affected jurisdictions. This committee would negotiate the split of the increment. The results of this negotiation were presented earlier in table 8.1. In large part, these results reflected both the accurate interpretation of how much growth would have occurred and the negotiation skills of the participants. As Table 8.1 illustrated, the negotiation skills of the nonredevelopment agency participants have been increasing, which results in a decrease of the share of the increment going to the RDA.

There is also a relationship between the state and the RDA. Beginning in 1991–92 and 1992–93, the state needed additional funds to finance its budgetary goals. One way of obtaining these funds was through the indirect use of the property taxes that other jurisdictions were receiving. The state, through a complex series of moves, transferred part of the property tax base of cities, counties, nonenterprise special districts, and redevelopment agencies to school districts. This allowed the state more leeway in its budget since it reduced the state's commitment to school finance. For redevelopment agencies, there was an aggregate loss of about $265 million from 1991 through 1995 (Yee 1995). A survey of RDAs in 1993 discovered that a large number were undertaking, or planning to undertake, cutbacks in a variety of areas, with especially large numbers planning cutbacks in infrastructure (76 percent), downtown renovation (57 percent), business retention (65 percent), and business attraction (59 percent) (Carlson 1993).[16] This shift appears to be a permanent transfer.

The state also has concerns that are similar to those expressed by the overlapping jurisdictions, although the state's interests are more complex. As part of the Proposition 13 buy-out process, the state became responsible for the vast majority of school district finance.[17] To the extent that school districts did not raise enough money through the property tax base that remained accessible to them, the state would back-fill until the districts reached their appropriate educational foundation level. If the entire increment would have occurred without the intervention of the RDA, then the school district should have received their share as calculated under the first polar case described above. In 1993–94, because about fifty-one cents of every property tax dollar collected went to schools, about 51 percent of the increment should have gone to the school districts in this extreme case. Since the total statewide increment was approximately $1.6 billion, this case implies an approximate state payout of nearly $800 million to schools that did not need to occur. If this were true, the net result of this process would be an indirect state subsidy to TIF redevelopment of nearly $800 million—an astounding figure.

Redevelopment agencies argue strenuously against the underlying assumption that the entire increment would have taken place without their intervention. If the RDAs are correct, then the state redevelopment subsidy is zero. Unfortunately, there is no data to substantiate either claim.

A by-product of these events is the lack of energy that school districts put into the fiscal review bargaining process. They knew that if they did not receive enough of the property tax increment, they would receive state funds to hold them harmless. Although state law entitled them to a minimum 2 percent of the property tax growth, even within the area, schools rarely utilized this opportunity.

HOUSING, FISCAL STRESS,
AND REDEVELOPMENT FINANCING

There also exist situations in which redevelopment is slowly being forced to deal with the fiscal stress of individuals as opposed to the types of governmental fiscal stress described above. The reason why so little housing services are produced under redevelopment, despite the continuing toughening of statute and the constant law suits, may be that the agencies are more concerned with governmental fiscal stress.

California is a high-cost housing state for a variety of reasons. There are a large number of land use regulations that restrict the supply of land and court decisions upholding them (Fischel 1995) and other additional requirements, such as earthquake standards, that add to the costs of construction. California's population has rapidly grown, and there are many two-income families. The high costs of housing, along with rigid property tax assessment and collection procedures, led to the high property taxes that were instrumental in the voter outrage that stimulated the passage of Proposition 13 in 1978. Although the recession of the early 1990s stopped the immediate rise in housing prices, and in some cases led to a transitory decline in housing values, housing prices are still considerably above the national average.

From their beginning, RDAs were expected to provide affordable housing for moderate and low-income families. In California they met part of this goal, although with a great deal of controversy that continues even today. Apparently, redevelopment agencies replace more housing than is torn down by their redevelopment activities; however, the larger question remains as to whether they are providing enough, with enough often being defined differently by builders, housing advocates, RDAs and the state legislature.[18] In 1976, in the middle of the first major increase of housing prices, the legislature mandated that, with few exceptions, 20 percent of the increment must be set aside for affordable moderate- and low-income housing.

The definition of affordable housing for moderate- and low-income residents is complex. For example, its current definition of eligibility for assistance for owner-occupied housing reads:

1. Very low income assistance is 30 percent of 50 percent of the area median income;

2. Lower income assistance is 30 percent of 70 percent of the area median income;

3. Moderate income assistance is 35 percent of 110 percent of the area median income.[19]

Nearly twenty years later, the California Research Bureau found that agency set asides had been averaging only 18.5 percent for the five-year period from 1990–91 through 1994–95. Those agencies that receive a large amount of tax-increment deposit more money in their housing funds than other redevelopment agencies. Reasons for this 1.5 percent shortfall in the required set-aside range from using set-aside money in the project include paying debt service, using net (after pass-throughs) as the base increment,[20] utilizing the permitted exemptions, or refusing, as some agencies do, to explain their reluctance (California State Legislature 1996). Further, even with these quibbles, RDAs have added more dollars to the low and moderate income housing fund each year than they have spent since 1991 (California Research Bureau 1996); the low and moderate fund balances had reached $979 million by June 1995, with more than half of the money, $462.1 million, unencumbered and available for housing activities (California State Legislature 1996).

RDAs did spend $442 million from their housing funds in 1994–95, constructing or rehabilitating over 8,700 units.[21] However, this reflects a somewhat skewed distribution, since 39 percent of the residential units and 56 percent of the rehabilitated units come from the top 30 RDAs (as measured by total increment). Even within this range, the data is again somewhat skewed—the city of San Jose constructed about one-fifth of all units developed in 1994–95, and Los Angeles rehabilitated about one-third of all of the units done that same year.[22]

In 1988, the legislature realized that some redevelopment agencies were collecting the 20 percent set-aside, but not spending it on affordable housing. It therefore passed legislation that required RDAs to identify the excess surplus in the low and moderate funds and spend it on affordable housing, or face transfers of the fund balances to the county housing authority. The agencies had a December, 1993, deadline to do this. But before this deadline was reached, another redevelopment reform was passed that revised the excess surplus definition and toughened the penalties for not spending money.

The 1993 act defined excess surplus to exist when the unexpended and unencumbered amount in the low and moderate income housing fund is greater than either $1 million or the total amount of property tax increment revenues placed in this fund in the preceding four years. If these funds are not spent within a legislatively set deadline, the death penalty provision applies. This provision essentially prohibits the agency from spending any money on new redevelopment projects (although it can still finance outstanding debts and make its pass-through payments to other local governments). Once the agency spends or encumbers its excess surplus, it must spend even more money on housing (California

State Legislature 1996). The amount of excess surplus is not large: the total excess surplus of the top ten agencies with excess surplus was only $29.1 million in 1994–95 (California Research Bureau 1996).

SOME STATE REFORMS

As the above discussion indicates, TIF redevelopment must be carefully monitored by public-sector decision makers. There is a good deal of money involved in the process, and there are often conflicting pressures on the RDA. These pressures come from the jurisdiction that initiated the redevelopment agency, developers, advocates for low-income residents, citizens, and overlapping jurisdictions. Gradually, the California law has been tightened to ensure that redevelopment activity is in response to blight, not in response to fiscal stress or arcane state revenue distribution formulas. The most recent reform enacted in 1993, which took effect in 1994, attempted to address many of these concerns so can serve as a template for other states as they regulate TIF redevelopment.[23]

Perhaps the most important reform was the enactment of a formal definition of what constitutes blight. If accurately followed, the use of TIF to avoid fiscal stress would be more difficult. Although the statutory language is complex, it can be paraphrased as follows: "A blighted area must be *predominantly urbanized* with a combination of conditions that are so *prevalent and substantial* that they cause a *serious physical or economic burden* which can't be helped without redevelopment. A blighted area must have at least one of four *physical conditions* and at least one of five *economic* conditions (emphasis in original)" (California State Legislature 1995). The physical and economic conditions are specified in the Health and Safety Code. "This new definition created three major changes from the prior statutes. First, it eliminated the lack of a public infrastructure as even a partial basis for the finding of blight; second, it did not recognize social blight; and third, the tighter language helped all parties by reducing the law's former ambiguities" (California State Legislature 1995).

A second important change that was implemented in the new statute was the replacement of the fiscal review committee's role in negotiating the sharing of the increment with a set of complex formulas that mandated specific amounts that must be shared with counties, special districts, and school districts. This gave somewhat more certainty to the process in that negotiation skills became less important but decreased flexibility in the use of the increment.

Merely a sample of the other legislated changes indicates the myriad of problems that have been associated with TIF development that was not always blight-related.[24] These changes were as follows:

1. Agencies were forced to adopt public implementation plans that linked their planned expenditures to the elimination of blight in the project areas;

2. Statutory time limits were adopted. Old plans were given up to thirty years to incur new debt and up to forty years to carry out other activities. New plans were given only thirty years;

3. The authority to provide financial assistance to automobile dealerships and large volume retailers proposing to locate on previously undeveloped land was eliminated;

4. Agencies were given more flexibility to achieve the inclusionary housing percentage requirements, but the penalties for failing to use the 20 percent set-aside moneys were increased (now referred to as the use-it or die penalty).

In the year in which the law was completing the legislative process, perhaps in anticipation of its more stringent requirements, redevelopment agencies placed about three times more land into project areas than they had in the year before (Legislative Analyst's Office 1994).

A BRIEF NOTE ON CALIFORNIA'S USE OF TAX INCREMENT FINANCING COMPARED TO OTHER STATES

As Johnson and Kriz (this volume) note, there was little use of tax increment financing techniques prior to the mid-1970s in most other states. It is probably not a coincidence that the growth of this technique roughly coincides with the advent of the fiscal limitation movement. California had provided the necessary template and was demonstrating that the technique could be worthwhile to confront fiscal stress. Further, the recession of the early 1980s put additional fiscal pressure on local governments to find alternative methods of financing infrastructure.

Financing public education is always complex, with a great deal of variation among states. TIF increases this complexity. Prior to the 1994 California reforms, school districts would negotiate with the redevelopment agencies for a share of the tax revenue, with a minimum share guaranteed by the state. However, the districts had no incentive to be tough bargainers since the state would backfill any lost revenues. The state still backfills, but California districts now receive a share of the increment by a mandated formula. Indiana school districts are partially treated in the same manner as the pre-1994 California districts. Indiana backfills the school districts general fund, so this amount of revenue is protected. However, for a variety of technical reasons, Indiana's school districts' capital projects, debt service, and transportation funds are negatively impacted.

Both Indiana (see Klacik, this volume) and Texas (see Cole, Arvidson, and Hissong, this volume) demonstrate similarities and differences when compared to California.[25] The differences are the most interesting since they revolve around the explicit elimination of blight as a necessary condition for the implementation of the technique. There are two types of tax increment districts in Indiana—a redevelopment district in which a finding of blight is necessary and an economic development district, which is principally established as an infrastructure-financing mechanism and which does not need a finding of blight. Available since 1993, the economic development districts have become far more used than the redevelopment use of TIF. In Texas, there is also no minimum requirement for blight to exist, but rather only a requirement that redevelopment or development would not occur solely through the mechanism of private investment.

The other principal differences are that Indiana jurisdictions explicitly use local option income taxes to reduce the risk in the tax increment debt, leading to a reduction in interest rates. Texas law is far more flexible in that property owners can petition to be a tax increment district, overlapping jurisdictions can negotiate with the city forming the district as to what proportion of the tax increment they will contribute to, and the project and financing plan must be adopted prior to the adoption of the TIF ordinance.

SOME CONCLUSIONS

There are two principal questions that surround the use of TIF redevelopment in California. The first is, how much is redevelopment needed in a particular area? The second is, how responsive is the use of redevelopment to fiscal stress?

If development is occurring in a particular area, or if that area is situated in a location in which development is highly likely to occur in the future (e.g., a vacant area close to an expanding subdivision), then a property tax increment will be generated. If a redevelopment agency decides to consider this area as blighted, it will unjustly appropriate the increment, the overlapping jurisdictions will not receive their fair share, and it is likely that the redevelopment project is being formed for reasons other than blight. Neutral analysis of the candidate project area must be obtained before it is considered a redevelopment designed to eliminate blight.

The California experience indicates that local fiscal stress might influence the degree of TIF redevelopment that occurs. In a case of local fiscal stress, blight might be loosely defined in order to ease the implementation of redevelopment projects, and interjurisdictional increment sharing and state backfilling might well hide from the public what is occurring in the interactions between the RDA and the local jurisdiction. In the short run, this might be efficacious, but in the long run citizens might not understand the underlying extent of the fiscal stress in their jurisdiction and may also begin to believe that their local government is only loosely following the redevelopment laws. This could heighten the current distrust of government. When the housing component is ignored or minimized during times of fiscal stress, this only exacerbates the situation.

Over the past fifteen years, California has enacted a complex series of laws that have attempted to ensure that TIF development is used appropriately. This illustrates that continual monitoring is necessary in order to convince the agencies, developers, and public that TIF is being used to eliminate blight—the purpose for which it was justified. But even under these continuing legal constraints, redevelopment agencies are likely to continue to search for exceptions (the declaration of disaster seems to be currently popular).

TIF can be a useful tool. Projects can generate revenue streams that can be turned into a self-financing instrument. But it only works correctly if it is carefully planned, monitored, and implemented under the light of public scrutiny.

NOTES

1. For a far more detailed history, see David F. Beatty et al., 1995.

2. This codification was ultimately approved in 1952 when a constitutional amendment was passed that allowed TIF to occur.

3. Only three project areas were formed prior to 1955 (Controller's Report 1994–95).

4. For more detail on recent fiscal stress, using the state as the level of aggregation, see Jeffrey I. Chapman, 1995.

5. This was nearly 60 percent of the total direct job loss in the United States.

6. Actually, in terms of real, per capita revenues, the jurisdictions were recognizing increases compared to FY 1977–78. However, society was also changing, and voters were demanding that elected officials respond to these changes. There were increases in incarceration rates, the exogenous effects described above were occurring, and education was taking more money out of the state budget.

7. See Chapman 1995.

8. If the city charges 1 percent, the county does not get any revenue. County sales tax revenues come from sales in unincorporated areas.

9. The ability to use this sales tax increment was taken away in 1993 by SB 1290.

10. Examples of these other types of capital financing are Mello-Roos Bonds and Certificates of Participation (Horler 1987).

11. The state controller separated data for redevelopment districts from other special districts beginning in 1984–85.

12. Property loss included public property such as bridges, reservoirs, sewers, streets, sidewalks, and levies.

13. This next section is based on the City of Santa Cruz Redevelopment Agency, n.d., *Report on implementation plan.*

14. In addition to the $4 million, approximately $12 million was scheduled to be raised through the imposition of a one-half cent sales tax override and approximately $8 million was received through state and federal grants. An approximate $3 million shortfall was to be eliminated through increased property taxes and sales taxes. See city of Santa Cruz Redevelopment Agency, n.d., *Earthquake recovery plan.*

15. Technically, the sharing of the sales taxes generated from the project area by overlapping jurisdictions is not allowed by state law. However, there have been isolated instances in which indirect sharing has occurred, typically through splitting some of the development expenditures.

16. The total property tax shift for 1992–94 was approximately $3.6 billion.

17. In part this was forced upon them by the *Serrano* decision, which mandated closer per-pupil expenditure levels within the state. See William A. Fischel, 1995.

18. By 1984, RDAs constructed at least twenty-five thousand more housing units than they destroyed. See Beatty et al., 1995.

19. These amounts are adjusted for family size. Assistance for rental housing is the same or slightly more generous. See Beatty et al., 1995.

20. The attorney general formally opined in 1993 that the gross increment must be used to calculate the low- and moderate-income set asides.

21. Total housing construction in 1994 was 101,200 units, of which 84,900 were single-family residents. See United States Department of Commerce, 1995.

22. Redevelopment agencies do not have to replace the housing they destroyed in the project area with new housing in that area. As long as the new housing is within the city, then it is an acceptable use of the funds.

23. It is interesting to note that this reform measure was strongly endorsed by the lobby group that represents the RDAs.

24. Although these are California changes, many of the studies of other states indicate that similar types of problems appear whenever TIF is used.

25. The similarities include the rapid growth in the use of the technique once it was understood and its use as a tool to increase the tax base.

REFERENCES

Beatty, David F., Joseph E. Coomes Jr., T. Brent Hawkins, Edward J. Quinn Jr., and Iris P. Yang. 1995. *Redevelopment in California.* 2nd ed. Point Arena, CA: Solano Press Books.

134   JEFF CHAPMAN

Burnstein, Melvin L., and Arthur J. Rolnick. 1995. Congress should end the economic war among the states. *Federal Reserve Bank of Minneapolis: 1994
annual report* 9(1) (March).

California Research Bureau. 1996. *Testimony for Senate committee on housing
and land use.*

California State Controller. 1980. *Financial transactions concerning cities of
California: 1978–79 Annual Report.* Sacramento: State of California.

———. 1995. *Financial transactions concerning cities of California: 1993–94
Annual Report.* Sacramento: State of California.

———. 1984–1994. *Financial transactions concerning redevelopment agencies
of California: Annual Report.* Sacramento: State of California.

California State Legislature. Senate Committee on Housing and Land Use and
the Senate Select Committee on Redevelopment. 1995. *Redevelopment and
blight.* (November). Sacramento: California State Legislature.

———. Senate Committee on Housing and Land Use. 1996. *End or means?
Redevelopment agencies' housing programs.* (13 November). Sacramento:
California State Legislature.

Carlson, William A. 1993. Killing the goose that lays the golden eggs. *Western
City* (June): 3–7, 31–32.

Chapman, Jeffrey I. 1981. *Proposition 13 and land use.* Lexington, MA: DC Heath.

———. 1995. California: The enduring crises. In *The Fiscal crises of the states,*
ed. Steven D. Gold. Washington DC: Georgetown University Press.

Fischel, William A. 1995. *Regulatory takings.* Cambridge: Harvard University
Press.

Frieden, Bernard J., and Lynn B. Sagalyn. 1989. *Downtown Inc.* Cambridge:
MIT Press.

Horler, Virginia. 1987. *Guide to public debt financing in California.* San Francisco: Packard Press.

Johnson, Hans. 1996. *Undocumented immigration to California: 1980–1993.*
San Francisco: Public Policy Institute of California.

Kennedy, Scott. 1996. Earthquake disaster reconstruction planning. Speech (12
January). Santa Cruz.

Kirlin, John J., and Anne M. Kirlin. 1982. *Public choices—Private resources.*
Sacramento: California Tax Foundation.

Legislative Analyst's Office. 1994. *Redevelopment after reform: A preliminary
look.* (29 December). Sacramento: Legislative Analyst's Office.

———. 1996. *Understanding Proposition 218.* (December). Sacramento: Legislative Analyst's Office.

Merrill Lynch, Pierce Fenner, and Smith. 1979. *California's tax allocation
bonds: Victims of Proposition 13.* New York: Merrill Lynch, Pierce Fenner,
and Smith, Inc.

Office of Planning and Research. 1996. *Fact sheet* (25 September). Sacramento:
Office of Planning and Research.

Santa Cruz, City of. n.d. *Earthquake recovery plan.*

Santa Cruz Redevelopment Agency. n.d. *Report on implementation plan.*

Santa Cruz Sentinel Publishers Co. 1989. *5:04 P.M.: The great quake of 1989.*
Santa Cruz: Santa Cruz Sentinel Publishers.

Tax Increment Financing and Fiscal Stress   135

United States Department of Commerce.1995. *Statistical abstract of the United States: 1995.* Washington DC: USGPO.

Yee, Betty. 1995. Background report prepared for the Assembly Budget Committee on the SB 756 conference committee. (August). Sacramento: California State Legislature.

CHAPTER 9

The Impact of Tax Increment Financing on School Districts: An Indiana Case Study

Robert G. Lehnen
and
Carlyn E. Johnson

INTRODUCTION

Financing public education in the 1990s poses significant policy issues for state and local governments. In many states, such as Indiana, the local property tax was the principle source of revenue for public elementary and secondary education for many years, but this revenue stream has come into increasing disfavor among taxpayers and has received increasing scrutiny from policymakers. Policymakers throughout the country historically have attempted to limit or reduce the share of education funding coming from the local property tax and have enjoyed some degree of success in this endeavor. In the 1959–60 school year 57 percent of public school revenue nationwide came from local sources, primarily the property tax, while 39 percent came from state sources, and the remainder, from the federal government. By 1990–91, the split had become almost even, with local source funding declining to 47 percent as the state share climbed to 47 percent and the federal share grew to 6 percent (Picus and Wattenbarger 1995).

In Indiana a similar shift away from the property tax occurred. In 1973 about 66 percent of instructional dollars, called the "general fund," came from local taxes, again primarily the property tax, while the 34 percent that came from the state with the federal share proved negligible. The state share increased steadily so that by 1998, the shares are projected to be essentially reversed. The state share will reach 66 percent of the total, and the local share will decrease to 34 percent.

The trend toward an increasing state share of education funding is similar for funding capital projects and transportation. Indiana makes essentially no effort to equalize funding for these expenditures. Most capital project costs as well as most transportation costs continue to be borne by the property tax. In 1998, the state and local shares of total school costs will be 55 percent from state funds and 45 percent from local sources (Indiana Fiscal Policy Institute 1997).

Together with its efforts to lessen reliance on the property tax, the Indiana General Assembly in 1993 adopted a new "reward for effort" formula for distribution of state monies to public schools. It was intended to equalize the revenues derived from the property tax—that is, equal property tax rates should produce equal dollars per pupil to spend regardless of local property tax wealth. The formula was to be phased in over a period of six years. Expenditures were limited by statute, and the level of expenditures per pupil dictated the property tax rate that school boards had to impose. This mandated expenditure/tax rate relationship was abandoned in 1997 and replaced with a qualifying property tax rate, a foundation level, and some equalization of revenues produced by rates above the qualifying rate. The short-term goal now is to reduce the disparity in General Fund property tax *rates* and ultimately to bring per pupil expenditures for similar pupils together. The new formula then raises tax rates in some school districts, lowers them in others, while simultaneously increasing the state share of the education dollar. It is in this changing context that the impact of tax increment financing must be examined.

SOME FACTS ABOUT TIF DISTRICTS AND PUBLIC EDUCATION

Considerable variation abounds in how states use TIF and how TIF districts affect public education, but very little current information is available (Huddleston 1981; Kemp 1986; Klemanski 1990; Wickert 1985). In order to understand these differences in policy and practice, we take a closer look at TIF districts in seven midwestern states: Illinois, Indiana, Iowa, Michigan, Minnesota, Ohio, and Wisconsin. Telephone interviews with officials in each of these states were conducted during the spring and summer of 1997, and state reports on TIF, where available, were examined to learn about how the current use of TIF districts impacts public education.

Table 9.1 presents information regarding the prevalence of TIF in the seven states showing the percentage of school districts affected by

TABLE 9.1
The Use of Tax Increment Financing Districts in Seven Midwestern States

State	Year	School Districts with 1+ TIFs	% of School Districts with TIF	Number of School Districts
Illinois	1997	NA	NA	904
Indiana[1]	1995	67	23%	294
Iowa	1997	221	58%	379
Michigan	1997	NA	NA	555
Minnesota	1997	243	68%	358
Ohio	1997	NA	NA	611
Wisconsin	1996	426	99%	428

Source: Telephone interviews (May and June, 1997)

TIF. Wisconsin has TIFs in nearly all of its school districts, whereas Indiana has such designation in only 23 percent of its school districts. With 68 percent and 58 percent of their districts so declared, Minnesota and Iowa respectively use TIF less than Wisconsin and Minnesota but more than does Indiana.

One unanticipated outcome of this limited survey was the finding that many states do not monitor their TIFs from a public education perspective, nor do they have information systems designed to access the impact of TIF on school districts. Illinois and Michigan were unable to provide the most basic information about how many school districts are affected by TIFs. Indiana's data were produced by the authors, but these data are not readily available to the public. Only Iowa, Minnesota, and Wisconsin maintain records that make it possible to show the effects of TIF districts on public education. At the time of this publication, the appropriate officials in Ohio had not been reached. Thus, information on whether and how TIF affects public education varies significantly among these surveyed states.

VARIATIONS IN TIF POLICIES IN THE MIDWESTERN STATES

Eleven states allow overlying school districts some form of choice concerning participation in the TIF district. All states surveyed, with the exception of Wisconsin, require participation from school districts. When a municipality proposes a TIF district in Wisconsin, representatives from overlying districts, including school districts, vote whether or not to approve the district, and a majority vote of these local officials binds all participating districts.

Michigan requires school district participation only in TIF districts established prior to 1994. From 1994 on, new TIF projects can no longer capture school district revenues. However, 1996 Michigan legislation allows TIF for environmental cleanup, and school district revenues can be captured for this purpose. The seven states surveyed reported considerable variation in the use of TIFs, and some have broadened the use of TIF beyond economic development. For example, Minnesota and Wisconsin use TIF for housing, as well as for soil conditioning, renovation, and erosion control. Table 9.2 illustrates that TIF is playing a role beyond economic development. Although TIF use in these seven states is usually reserved for development, many variations exist in the policies to achieve these ends. First, there is variation regarding which project costs are eligible for TIF. Second, there is considerable variation concerning the time limits placed on TIF life. A third difference is whether or not the state allows "inactive" districts. Finally, in an effort to reduce the overall impact on school districts, most states have attempted to reimburse school districts for lost revenues by means of a "hold harmless" provision.

Allowable Costs

Eligible TIF costs vary from state to state (National Conference of State Legislatures 1996). Illinois allows TIF for any public or private development project that is in furtherance of a development plan, including training. Iowa limits TIF to renewal projects, and Ohio limits the use to construction or repair of public infrastructure. Indiana uses TIF to make

TABLE 9.2
The Varying Uses of TIFs in Seven Midwestern States

State	Varying Uses of TIF Districts
Illinois	blight, underdeveloped, and undeveloped areas
Indiana	urban renewal, neighborhood development programs, redevelopment
Iowa	urban renewal projects
Michigan	redevelopment and new development
Minnesota	housing, soil conditioning, renewal, and renovation
Ohio	redevelopment
Wisconsin	redevelopment of blighted and eroded areas

Source: Telephone interviews (May and June 1997)

payments on leases, to reimburse local development costs associated with infrastructure, and, like Illinois, to fund training costs. Michigan employs TIF only for public facilities for manufacturing, agricultural processing, or high technology facilities, except for certain industrial parks. Minnesota expands TIF use further by allowing TIF for removal of blight, provision of housing for low-income families, acquisition and assembly of land, investment in public infrastructure, administrative costs, and write down of interest costs to the developer. More expansive than any of the other seven states, Wisconsin allows TIF for construction of public works, new buildings, demolition, alteration, repair, or reconstruction of existing buildings. Wisconsin also uses TIF for buying equipment, clearing and acquisition of land, financing costs, assembly costs, professional services, administration, and relocation costs, except for public buildings.

Time Limits on TIF

Table 9.3 shows the maximum time limit a TIF district can "capture" incremental value from the overlying taxing districts. The assumption here is that eventually school districts and other local taxing authorities will receive a "windfall" when the TIF expires. Clearly, the opportunity for school districts to realize windfall revenues, where it exists, is far in the future, and in Michigan, perhaps never.

Inactive TIF Districts

Indiana, unique among the seven states, permits "inactive" TIF districts. It allows TIF districts to operate such that a municipality may designate a district, but redevelopment does not have to begin immediately. TIF dis-

TABLE 9.3
The Life Span of TIF Districts in Seven Midwestern States

State	Maximum Life Span of TIF District
Illinois	23 years
Indiana	50 years
Iowa	10 years
Michigan	no time limit
Minnesota	8, 25, 30 years (by type)
Ohio	20–30 years
Wisconsin	20 years

Source: Wyatt (1990)

tricts may be declared, but it could be months or even years before development begins. This practice opens the door for abuse in the sense that a municipality may declare an area a TIF district simply to attract developers. However, when the time comes for financing a chosen project, TIF may no longer be the most suitable financing mechanism for the project. Indiana then creates the possibility that the method of financing (TIF) is established before the use of public monies is established.

Holding School Districts Harmless

At least four states have attempted to compensate foregone revenue to school districts by employing some form of reimbursement process. Illinois, Michigan, Minnesota, and Wisconsin all have such measures in place. Illinois employs a state aid formula that uses the lower assessed valuation prior to redevelopment to compute state assistance. This approach may be problematic because in Illinois it results in some districts (with TIF) receiving more aid than others because of varying tax levies in each district. Michigan and Wisconsin, meanwhile, have a state school aid fund/general aid fund, which serves to replace sacrificed revenues. Minnesota has taken steps to make TIF a more costly choice for municipalities. If a municipality chooses TIF, the state automatically reduces its state aid allowance because the state also receives less revenue as a result of a TIF district. In addition, prior to 1988, all levies in Minnesota were not equalized, and TIF had created a need for higher local tax rates. Since 1988, anything not based on a local tax rate gets a levy adjustment for school districts. Indiana's hold harmless policy will be discussed below.

The research presented above suggests some broad patterns:

1. TIF is common among the states, but there is considerable variation in how TIF is actually applied;
2. The variations in TIF policies among the states, including the uses of TIF, the requirements for school districts to participate, the length of time that a TIF district may be operational, and differences in allowable costs, make cross-state comparisons problematic;
3. Efforts are being made to minimize the impact of TIF on school districts, but the effects of these efforts are not documented.

TAX INCREMENT FINANCING DISTRICTS
AND INDIANA'S SCHOOL FINANCE FORMULA

State law in Indiana requires public schools to account for their revenue in five separate funds—the general, debt service, capital projects, transportation, and preschool special education funds. Annual increases in all but the Debt Service fund are controlled by state law, either by limiting the dollar amount by which the expenditures from the fund may increase or by imposing a fixed tax rate that the fund may not exceed. The capital projects and the preschool special education funds have a fixed property tax rate set either by statute or by action of the Indiana State Board of Tax Commissioners. Rates for the debt service and transportation funds are dependent on assessed valuation—and thus are adversely affected by TIF districts. A smaller assessed valuation means that a higher tax rate must be imposed.

In Indiana, from 1994 through 1996, annual increases in the general fund were limited by statute, and each school district computed a statutorily mandated target tax rate, which depended on its allowable level of expenditures. The state then distributed to each school district the difference between what the target tax rate produced and its allowable expenditures. A lesser-assessed valuation simply meant that more of the school's revenue came from the state and less from the property tax. For purposes of a school district's general fund, a TIF district did not harm the school or the taxpayers that reside in the school district. It simply caused more of the district's expenditures to be paid for by the state, thus shifting a portion of economic development costs in a given area to all of the taxpayers in the state. We will examine below the magnitude of this shift.

The preschool special education fund is designed as a foundation program. To the extent that assessed valuations produce smaller revenues from the fourteen mandatory rate, the state distribution will increase. For purposes of all of the other funds, however, the picture is quite different. In the case of the capital projects fund, the rate for each school corporation is fixed by the State Board of Tax Commissioners for a period of three years. A freeze on assessed valuations in part of the district simply means that the school may collect less money for its capital projects fund than it had anticipated when its rate was established.

The rate for the debt service fund is established annually by the school corporation to cover its obligations to repay principal and interest on all outstanding debt, be it general obligation bonds or lease-rental payments. To the extent that the school district's assessed valuation increases, the debt service rate can be set lower. If part of the district's assessed valuation is frozen, however, as would be the case if a TIF district were created within the school district, the debt service rate will be commensurately higher. This means that all taxpayers in the district will be paying more for debt service than they would if the school could tax the new increases in assessed value in the TIF district.

The same effect will be felt in paying for transportation. In Indiana, transportation is paid for with both state and local funds. The amount received from the state is based on the number of children transported, the student population density, and the number of miles driven by the school buses. The remainder of the cost is borne by the property tax. Like the debt service fund, the higher the assessed valuation of property in the district, the lower the required tax rate. A frozen assessed valuation in part of the school district means a higher property tax rate imposed on the remaining property in the district. For each of these funds, with the exception of the general fund and the preschool special education fund, TIF means either less revenue or an annual added tax burden on the taxpayers in the district for the life of the TIF district and considerable added pressure on members of the local school board and school administrators, who must face the wrath of taxpayers when new and higher tax rates are announced.

THE USE OF TIF IN INDIANA

To report on the current status of tax increment financing in Indiana, the authors assembled data for 1995 on TIF districts and Indiana school corporations into a special database. The information on the TIF district incremental assessed valuation came from the local government database maintained by the State Budget Agency. Data regarding school district assessed valuations, tax rates, and levies are from the school finance database maintained by the Indiana Department of Education. The data are correct as of May 1997 and represent the most current year for which data from each source was available. Since the state of Indiana has a policy of continuously updating these databases, the information reported here is correct as of May 1997 only.

The data assembled for this study show that the use of TIF in Indiana affects the 294 school districts differently. Less than one-quarter (23 percent) of school districts in 1995 had one or more TIFs. Forty-eight of these sixty-seven districts had only one TIF, and nineteen had two or more. Elkhart Community Schools in Elkhart County had the highest number (five) of TIFs. Thus, for most Indiana school districts TIF is not a major issue directly affecting their revenues.

In 1995, the sixty-seven school corporations with TIFs had a total of $21.1 billion in assessed valuations and another $502 million set aside in TIF districts, comprising 2.3 percent of total assessed valuation in these districts. The size of the incremental assessed valuation set aside for development varies widely among the sixty-seven districts with one or more TIFs. At one extreme is New Prairie United School Corporation in Laporte and St. Joseph Counties, where nearly one-third (31.8 percent) of its assessed valuation is set aside for economic development purposes (see table 9.4). Other districts with relatively large incremental assessed valuations are Tippecanoe School Corporation in Tippecanoe county (10.1 percent); South Bend Community School Corporation in St. Joseph County (5.9 percent); Westfield-Washington Schools in Hamilton County (5.7 percent); and Indianapolis Public Schools in Marion County (5.6 percent). Each of these five school districts has incremental assessed valuations exceeding 5 percent of total assessments. For thirty-five of the sixty-seven school districts with TIFs, incremental assessed values are less than 1 percent of total assessments. Harrison-Washington Community School Corporation in Delaware county had the smallest TIF district with $360 in incremental assessed valuation.

An alternative way to look at TIF financing in Indiana is to consider which districts account for most of the $502 million in incremental assessed valuations statewide. From this perspective only five of the sixty-seven school districts account for two-thirds of the incremental assessed valuations statewide. Indianapolis Public Schools accounts for 27 percent of all incremental assessed valuations; its incremental assessed valuation of $135.8 million far exceeded the next largest TIF assessed valuation (See table 9.4 and figure 9.1).

As a percentage of total statewide incremental assessed valuation, the next largest school district is South Bend Community School Corporation (12.4 percent), Tippecanoe School Corporation (10.2 percent), New Prairie United School Corporation (9.2 percent), and Fort Wayne Community Schools (5.6 percent). The remaining sixty-two school districts account for 35 percent of total incremental assessed valuation.

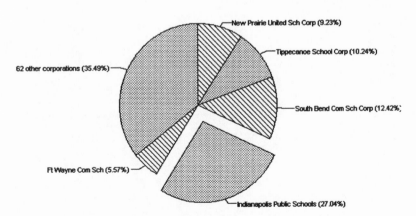

FIGURE 9.1
School District Percentages of Total Statewide Incremental Assessed Valuations

TABLE 9.4
Assessed Valuations of Sixty-Seven Indiana School Corporations with Tax Increment Financing Districts, 1995

County	School Corporation	Number of TIFs	School District Assessed Valuation	Incremental Assessed Valuation	Total Assessed Valuation[i]	TIF as % of Total Assessed Valuation[ii]	% of Total Incremental Assessed Valuation[iii]
Laporte	New Prairie United School Corp	1	99,664,568	46,375,669	146,040,237	31.8	9.2
Tippecanoe	Tippecanoe School Corp	3	458,162,765	51,445,470	509,608,235	10.1	10.2
St. Joseph	South Bend Community School Corp	3	998,498,000	62,400,822	1,060,898,822	5.9	12.4
Hamilton	Westfield-Washington Schools	1	124,145,460	7,573,430	131,718,890	5.7	1.5
Marion	Indianapolis Public Schools	1	2,311,877,460	135,856,920	2,447,734,380	5.6	27.0
Monroe	Richland-Bean Blossom CSC	1	101,218,161	4,686,833	105,904,994	4.4	0.9
Clark	Greater Clark County Schools	3	323,155,000	14,068,940	337,223,940	4.2	2.8
St. Joseph	Penn-Harris-Madison School Corp	2	322,595,000	12,379,935	334,974,935	3.7	2.5
Noble	West Noble School Corp	1	78,897,890	2,969,290	81,867,180	3.6	0.6
Hancock	Greenfield-Central Community Schools	1	145,732,090	5,047,150	150,779,240	3.3	1.0
Carroll	Delphi Community School Corp	1	69,822,534	2,251,590	72,074,124	3.1	0.4
Tippecanoe	Lafayette School Corp	2	415,648,485	13,110,635	428,759,120	3.1	2.6
Dubois	Southwest Dubois County School Corp	1	71,694,527	1,954,235	73,648,762	2.7	0.4
Hamilton	Noblesville Schools	1	230,103,440	4,981,640	235,085,080	2.1	1.0
Lake	Merrillville Community School	2	288,653,963	6,169,336	294,823,299	2.1	1.2

(continued on next page)

TABLE 9.4 (continued)

County	School Corporation	Number of TIFs	School District Assessed Valuation	Incremental Assessed Valuation	Total Assessed Valuation[i]	TIF as % of Total Assessed Valuation[ii]	% of Total Incremental Assessed Valuation[iii]
Marshall	Bremen Public Schools	1	66,572,060	1,344,493	67,916,553	2.0	0.3
Scott	Scott County School District 2	1	85,686,160	1,689,680	87,375,840	1.9	0.3
Tippecanoe	West Lafayette Community School Corp	1	149,431,910	2,853,340	152,285,250	1.9	0.6
Jasper	Rensselaer Central School Corp	1	91,146,210	1,731,710	92,877,920	1.9	0.3
Laporte	Michigan City Area Schools	1	323,560,846	6,128,730	329,689,576	1.9	1.2
Marion	MSD Wayne Township	2	646,369,860	12,035,360	658,405,220	1.8	2.4
Elkhart	Concord Community Schools	2	208,952,080	3,855,420	212,807,500	1.8	0.8
Elkhart	Elkhart Community Schools	5	670,724,000	12,274,970	682,998,970	1.8	2.4
Allen	Fort Wayne Community Schools	3	1,593,898,725	28,003,870	1,621,902,595	1.7	5.6
Madison	Anderson Community School Corp	1	432,063,676	7,366,670	439,430,346	1.7	1.5
St. Joseph	School City of Mishawaka	1	136,067,000	1,967,879	138,034,879	1.4	0.4
Whitley	Whitley County Consolidated Schools	2	157,991,469	2,237,830	160,229,299	1.4	0.4
Clark	Clarksville Community School Corp	1	101,146,620	1,372,750	102,519,370	1.3	0.3
Porter	Portage Township Schools	1	296,688,810	3,901,520	300,590,330	1.3	0.8
Fountain	Southeast Fountain School Corp	1	54,038,650	648,480	54,687,130	1.2	0.1
Hendricks	Danville Community School Corp	1	69,194,070	828,360	70,022,430	1.2	0.2

(continued on next page)

TABLE 9.4 *(continued)*

County	School Corporation	Number of TIFs	School District Assessed Valuation	Incremental Assessed Valuation	Total Assessed Valuation[i]	TIF as % of Total Assessed Valuation[ii]	% of Total Incremental Assessed Valuation[iii]
Morgan	Mooresville Consolidated School Corp	1	110,073,340	1,314,050	111,387,390	1.2	0.3
Fulton	Rochester Community School Corp	1	77,041,570	806,118	77,847,688	1.0	0.2
Marion	MSD Decatur Township	1	134,821,690	1,351,630	136,173,320	1.0	0.3
Marion	MSD Pike Township	1	915,596,480	7,118,500	922,714,980	0.8	1.4
Noble	Central Noble Community School Corp	2	50,257,630	371,960	50,629,590	0.7	0.1
Hendricks	Plainfield Community School Corp	1	142,177,700	1,041,440	143,219,140	0.7	0.2
Lagrange	Westview School Corp	2	108,978,210	685,785	109,663,995	0.6	0.1
Vigo	Vigo County School Corp	1	667,541,960	4,141,620	671,683,580	0.6	0.8
Kosciusko	Warsaw Community Schools	1	342,807,485	2,055,474	344,862,959	0.6	0.4
Laporte	Laporte Community School Corp	1	254,938,720	1,511,790	256,450,510	0.6	0.3
Marion	MSD Warren Township	1	647,242,580	3,739,190	650,981,770	0.6	0.7
Hamilton	Carmel City Schools	1	658,145,900	3,710,170	661,856,070	0.6	0.7
Monroe	Monroe County Community School Corp	2	592,737,331	3,196,306	595,933,637	0.5	0.6
Porter	Duneland School Corp	2	456,691,930	2,401,940	459,093,870	0.5	0.5

(continued on next page)

TABLE 9.4 (continued)

County	School Corporation	Number of TIFs	School District Assessed Valuation	Incremental Assessed Valuation	Total Assessed Valuation[i]	TIF as % of Total Assessed Valuation[ii]	% of Total Incremental Assessed Valuation[iii]
Huntington	Huntington County Community School Corp	1	251,560,255	1,167,440	252,727,695	0.5	0.2
Marshall	Plymouth Community School Corp	1	149,131,582	611,531	149,743,113	0.4	0.1
Dekalb	Dekalb County Central United School Dist	1	169,592,033	599,970	170,192,003	0.4	0.1
Delaware	Mt Pleasant Twp Community School Corp	1	84,443,455	286,830	84,730,285	0.3	0.1
Jefferson	Madison Consolidated Schools	1	161,024,490	498,100	161,522,590	0.3	0.1
Noble	East Noble School Corp	2	153,899,130	450,520	154,349,650	0.3	0.1
Lake	Hammond City Schools	1	275,833,101	769,860	276,602,961	0.3	0.2
Henry	New Castle Community School Corp	1	133,520,125	342,280	133,862,405	0.3	0.1
Lake	Crown Point Community School Corp	1	162,135,828	377,302	162,513,130	0.2	0.1
Vanderburg	Evansville-Vanderburgh School Corp	1	1,113,173,330	2,580,000	1,115,753,330	0.2	0.5
Wayne	Richmond Community School Corp	1	291,946,225	634,645	292,580,870	0.2	0.1
Scott	Scott County School District 1	1	29,049,315	60,390	29,109,705	0.2	0.0

(continued on next page)

TABLE 9.4 (continued)

County	School Corporation	Number of TIFs	School District Assessed Valuation	Incremental Assessed Valuation	Total Assessed Valuation[i]	TIF as % of Total Assessed Valuation[ii]	% of Total Incremental Assessed Valuation[iii]
Jennings	Jennings County School Corp	1	128,410,421	211,760	128,622,181	0.2	0.0
Perry	Tell City-Troy Twp School Corp	2	63,014,815	83,060	63,097,875	0.1	0.0
Hendricks	Brownsburg Community School Corp	2	155,779,820	174,060	155,953,880	0.1	0.0
Floyd	New Albany-Floyd County Consolidated Schools	1	429,824,220	347,320	430,171,540	0.1	0.1
Delaware	Daleville Community Schools	1	21,705,495	12,115	21,717,610	0.1	0.0
Delaware	Delaware Community School Corp	1	88,910,705	41,920	88,952,625	0.0	0.0
Delaware	Muncie Community Schools	1	367,396,575	94,830	367,491,405	0.0	0.0
Lake	Lake Central School Corp	1	337,086,475	69,500	337,155,975	0.0	0.0
Elkhart	Wa-Nee Community Schools	2	175,340,960	8,210	175,349,170	0.0	0.0
Delaware	Harrison-Wash Community School Corp	1	28,926,607	360	28,926,967	0.0	0.0

Source: Local Government database, State Budget Agency, and School Finance database, Indiana Department of Education.

i. Total SD Assessed Valuation = School District Assessed Valuation + Incremental Assessed Valuation

ii. TIF as % of Total Assessed Valuation shows the percent that the Incremental Assessed Valuation is of Total School District Assessed Valuation.

iii. School District % of Total Incremental Assessed Valuation is the school district's percent of the statewide Total Incremental Assessed Valuations.

From this perspective, it appears that TIF is a significant issue in five school districts alone.

The financial impact of TIF in Indiana is substantial. In 1995 the state's contribution to economic development through the school finance formula was nearly $27 million and averaged 2.4 percent of 1995 levies in these sixty-seven school districts (See table 9.5). This funding of local economic development projects through public education funding impacted taxpayers in different ways, depending on the fund. In the case of the general fund, $15.4 million was transferred to the TIFs, but these dollars were replaced through the school funding formula. Thus, taxpayers statewide funded these local projects through general revenues, principally the sales and income taxes. In effect, over $15 million represented to the public as "school funding" went, in fact, to economic development.

The remaining $11.4 million was paid for by local taxpayers through the local property tax. In the case of the debt service and transportation funds, local taxpayers in these sixty-seven districts paid for $6.2 million in economic development costs. This occurred because school districts had to impose higher property tax rates for these two funds in order to recover revenue lost to economic development. Hoosier taxpayers in these sixty-seven districts saw their local property tax rates for public education increase to fund economic development.

The capital projects fund poses a different issue than the other funds. The rate for this fund is fixed for a three-year period by the State Board of Tax Commissioners, and it cannot be increased by the school board to compensate for assessed valuations lost to the TIF. Thus, should a TIF district be established once a capital projects fund tax rate has been approved, the school district simply loses the additional revenue from the incremental assessed valuation until it can seek a rate increase again. In 1995, this amounted to $5.2 million in tax revenues, but it could not be determined what proportion of this amount was lost to TIF districts and how much was simply made up by raising the local property tax rates.

CONCLUSION

This analysis of tax increment financing in Indiana suggests the conclusion that, for most Indiana school corporations, TIF is not a major revenue drain. For a small number of school districts, however, the consequences of TIF are not trivial. In these districts, local property tax rates must be increased to maintain revenues diverted to economic development.

Indiana has experienced a thirty-year struggle over reducing reliance on the property tax. Since public education receives the lion's share of

TABLE 9.5
Financial Impact of Ninety-Three TIF Districts on
Sixty-Seven Indiana School Corporations, 1995

	Debt	General	Capital Projects	Transportation	Total
Levies, 1995[i]	$134,477,561	$667,429,226	$205,619,213	$124,359,339	$1,131,885,339
Levies on TIFs[ii]	$2,674,961	$15,449,759	$5,204,263	$3,549,493	$26,878,477
TIF % of levies	2.0%	2.3%	2.5%	2.9%	2.4%

i. Levies, 1995, are the sum of the levies for each fund for the 67 school corporations with TIFs.
ii. The levies on TIFs are computed by multiplying the 1995 rate for each fund times the Incremental Assessed Value (• 100).

these revenues, school districts have been consistently blamed for "excessive" property taxes. Thus, any policy that raises property tax rates in the name of education simply compounds the problem for local school boards and administrators. In 1995 school officials were in the position of raising local property tax rates for as much as $11.4 million for noneducation reasons.

At the state level a similar pattern holds. Biennial sessions of the legislature argue at length over the school funding formula. Differences in total school funding of one-tenth of one percent (0.1 percent) often deadlock the legislative session. In 1995 receipts for all funds totaled $5.0 billion; thus, increasing public education revenues by 0.1 percent amounts to a policy debate about $5 million. Since nearly $27 million of education funding went to economic development, the portion of total education funding redirected toward economic development amounts to five-tenths of 1 percent (0.5 percent) of total K–12 funding for 1995. This is not a politically insignificant amount.

TIF policies in Indiana raise fundamental questions of fairness and honesty with regard to informing Indiana's taxpayers about the use of public funds. If taxpayers statewide were told that over $15 million in general revenues was spent, not on education but on economic development projects in a few local areas, would Hoosiers support such expenditures? If taxpayers in these sixty-seven districts were told that the local school board raised property taxes to pay for local economic development, would they support these projects? These questions have never been posed to Indiana's taxpayers, but it is appropriate that a more honest public debate about how public moneys are spent be initiated. Open discussion on the amounts of economic development spending hidden in Indiana's school finance formula and in local property tax increases would benefit everyone since policy choices about the proper level of education funding could then be made in a more informed context.

ACKNOWLEDGMENTS

The authors wish to acknowledge the helpful assistance of Stephen Baker, Dale Drake, and Drew Klacik for their generous assistance in assembling the data for this study.

REFERENCES

Davidson, Jonathan M. 1979. Tax increment financing as a tool for community development. *University of Detroit Journal of Urban Law* 56-2 (Winter): 405–444.

Huddleston, Jack R. 1981. Variations in development subsidies under tax increment financing. *Land Economics* 57(3): 373–384.

Indiana Fiscal Policy Institute. 1997. *A guide to Indiana school finance: 1997–1999.* (September). Indianapolis: Indiana University.

Kemp, Roger L. 1986. Economic development: Revenues without taxes. *Journal of Housing* (November/December): 258–260.

Klemanski, John S. 1990. Using tax increment financing for urban redevelopment projects *Economic Development Quarterly* (February): 23–28.

Lemov, Penelope. 1994. Tough times for TIF. *Governing* (February): 18–19.

National Conference of State Legislatures. 1997. *Summary of tax increment financing.* Document Received by Fax (20 May).

Picus, Lawrence O., and James Wattenbarger. 1995. Where does the money go? In *Sixteenth yearbook of the American education finance association*, ed. Lawrence O. Picus and James Wattenbarger.

Wickert, Donald M. 1985. An entrepreneurial approach to participation in community redevelopment activities. *Journal of Education Finance* 10 (Winter): 327–338.

Wyatt, Michael D. 1990. The TIF smorgasbord: A survey of state statutory provisions for tax incremental financing. *Assessment Digest* (November/December): 2–9.

CHAPTER 10

Tax Increment Financing in Texas: Survey and Assessment

Enid Arvidson, Rod Hissong, and Richard L. Cole

INTRODUCTION

The Texas State Legislature recently issued a report acknowledging that tax increment financing has become one of the three most popular local economic development incentives in the state, alongside property tax abatement and the economic development sales tax (Texas Senate Economic Development Committee 1996). At least fourteen cities across Texas, some more than once, have used tax increment financing since legislation was first approved in 1981.[1]

The legislative report also recognizes the widespread debate over the effectiveness and fairness of incentives. On the one hand, incentives are seen as a helpful, competitive edge in today's decentralized and global environment. Without such governmental ability to effect attractive investment climates, it is argued, localities would be at the mercy of unpredictable global forces. The fairness of tax increment financing (particularly when compared with other types of incentives) lies in the sharing of project costs among all taxing jurisdictions ultimately benefiting from the improvements and growing tax base. Without such sharing of costs, other taxing agencies would free ride, reaping higher tax revenues from city-financed redevelopment projects without contributing to their costs. In addition, cities alone would not undertake needed improvements if they had to bear the cost burden by themselves (Texas Senate Economic Development Committee 1996).

On the other hand, others view incentives as an unfortunate but necessary scheme in today's economic development game where the only

156   ENID ARVIDSON, ROD HISSONG, AND RICHARD L. COLE

winners often are the direct private investors. In particular, the inter-governmental and interpersonal (or interclass) tax shifting under tax increment financing is seen as unfair, particularly if a city uses TIF to finance improvements in areas that would (re)develop anyway. In these cases, property tax revenues that would otherwise go to taxing agencies are diverted into a TIF fund to pay for improvements that may have happened without the TIF. Citizens thus can bear a real opportunity cost by needlessly helping fund projects that buoy private return while financially strapping taxing units and limiting service provision, until the project runs its course (Texas Senate Economic Development Committee 1996; Huddleston 1986; Davis 1982).

As if in response to these debates, auspicious rhetoric flows through much Texas talk of local development incentives. In their annual report, next to a picture of a pot of gold, is the city of El Paso's description of tax increment financing: "Tax Increment Financing (TIF) is a tool used by local governments to finance redevelopment while increasing future capacity through a strengthened tax base" (City of El Paso 1996: 1). The State Attorney General's Office similarly describes TIF as "a tool that local governments can use to publicly finance needed structural improvements and enhanced infrastructure . . . to promote the viability of existing businesses and to attract new commercial enterprises" (Attorney General's Municipal Advisory Committee 1996: 38).

One consequence of such rhetoric is to persuade public policymak-ers, the general public, and the media of the continued importance of local development incentives amid doubts about fairness or effective-ness.[2] TIF, as represented in these discussions, is a neutral, technical "tool" that can "strengthen," "increase," and "enhance" through "improvements" a city's "viability" and "future capacity." Such lan-guage invokes images of fairness, progress, hope—and of course, who could contest these things? As one critical commentator on local eco-nomic development observes, "Who can argue with an endeavor that attempts to . . . make our lives more enjoyable and fulfilling?" This observer adds, however: "Uncritical admiration . . . hides ideological biases and suppresses the inevitable tensions and disagreements that arise in a multiethnic society of tenacious inequalities, precarious demo-cratic practices, and deeply ingrained capitalist values" (Beauregard 1993: 267).

These issues appear throughout studies of tax increment financing and of local economic development in general. Many researchers agree, first, that in the past fifteen years there has been a dramatic increase in the level and types of state and local economic development incentives. This growing local involvement in economic development is due largely to the increased mobility of capital in search of profitable locations coupled with federal devolution of management and responsibility for economic health to states, cities, and local "growth machine" coalitions (Cole, Taebel, and Hissong 1994; Klemanski 1989; Logan and Molotch 1987). Second, there is widespread concern about the effectiveness as well as fairness of local development incentives, particularly whether "bidding wars" between municipalities for private investment yields public benefit, and, in a diverse society, *who* indeed does benefit from these deals (Cole, Taebel, and Hissong 1994; Huddleston 1986; Goodman 1979). The third issue concerns the rhetoric or ideology of local economic development, through which local incentives are framed in the hard-to-argue-against, "commonsense" language of local economic health. In effect, however, this rhetoric often condones very specific actions and ideas (e.g., public facilitation of privately profitable capital investment) while disqualifying or obscuring others, such as a focus on traditionally marginalized groups and classes, or cooperative rather than capitalist forms of enterprise (Squires 1996; Beauregard 1993).

Our findings from a review of TIF history in Texas and telephone survey of fourteen cities across the state that use TIF confirm these general issues. TIF, as a particular type of economic development incentive, is seen as an increasingly useful tool by local development officials, but its uses in some cases have disproportionately benefited those directly involved in the program, particularly private development interests, while making no specific effort to address concerns of traditionally marginalized enterprises or populations. Before discussing survey findings, we briefly outline tax increment financing's legislative history in the state, highlighting some unusual aspects of the Texas law. We then discuss and interpret findings from the survey, including a closer look at one city's use of TIF that has gained attention in the local press. We conclude with a critical assessment of the use of tax increment financing in Texas in light of the findings.

LEGISLATIVE OVERVIEW IN TEXAS

Interest in tax increment financing began in earnest in Texas in the mid 1970s, as it did in many other states, as federal funds for urban redevelopment began to decline. In 1977, TIF legislation was introduced in the Texas legislature, along with a constitutional amendment designed to permit tax increment financing as a legal redevelopment tool for Texas cities. The bill required TIF zones created by cities to be at least 60 percent developed and at least 25 percent blighted. This bill, as well as subsequent TIF bills introduced in the Texas legislature, was strongly supported by local growth-machine coalitions—local officials, local land

developers, bankers, as well as many local governments and their lobbying organizations, such as the Texas Municipal League. Although the
1977 bill was approved by the legislature, the constitutional amendment
was eventually defeated by skeptical voters.

Enabling legislation was again introduced in the 1979 session of the
Texas legislature. Three features of this bill distinguished it from earlier
legislation: it required that only city tax revenues could be diverted into
a tax increment fund; it limited the amount of private residential property in a tax increment zone to 10 percent; and it eliminated any requirement that a percentage of the zone be previously developed. This bill
also received legislative approval, however, in 1981 the Texas attorney
general ruled the statute unconstitutional because it violated the Texas
constitutional provision of "equal and uniform" taxation policies.

The tax increment financing bill that finally was passed and
approved by voters was introduced in a special session of the Texas legislature meeting in the summer of 1981. Again, local growth-machine
coalitions came out in support of the bill, while voices of school districts,
local property tax payers, and organized labor were practically unheard.
No witnesses testified in opposition to the bill during the special summer
session, although the state AFL-CIO was reported to have objected to the
bill, and almost immediately after its passage, school boards, counties,
hospital boards, and junior college districts organized to protest its use,
charging that it was unfair and fiscally ruinous for other taxing entities
to have their tax revenues garnered by cities (Davis 1982).

One outcome of these local political circumstances is that the Texas TIF
law is more "flexible" than that of many other states. Three features of the
Texas law distinguish it from those of other states. First is a provision permitting property owners to directly petition to have an area designated a TIF
zone. This provision, enabled by a 1989 amendment to the original 1981
law, met with no public opposition and was passed to accommodate a particular project about which property owners were organized. The law
requires the petition to be submitted by property owners constituting at least
50 percent of the appraised value of property within the zone.

A second unique feature is a provision permitting taxing units
within a designated zone to negotiate with the city as to what portion of
the tax increment they will contribute to the fund. A taxing unit may
decide to contribute anywhere from 0 to 100 percent of its incremental
tax revenue to the TIF fund. This feature, also a 1989 amendment to the
original 1981 law, intends to address charges of unfairness and avoid
lawsuits by school districts and other taxing units, by allowing each of
these units to decide, case by case, how much, if any, of their tax increment to contribute to the fund.

A third feature, common to a few other states, is the absence of any

minimum requirement for blight within a zone, with relatively few overall restrictions on what types of property can be included in a TIF district. Some critics of the Texas law, and of TIF use more broadly, argue
that it is an abuse of the intent of TIF to create TIF districts in areas that
are neither blighted nor underdeveloped, and especially that are increasing in value via market forces (Davis 1982). Some states, including
Texas, have addressed this criticism by including a "but for" clause in
their TIF legislation (see Johnson and Kriz, this volume). According to
Texas law, for an area to be considered eligible for tax increment financing, it must be shown simply that present conditions "substantially
impair or arrest the sound growth of the municipality" and that development or redevelopment of the area would not occur "solely through
private investment in the reasonably foreseeable future." These criteria
apply equally to open land on the city's edge, as well as older, developed
land in the center. As we attempt to make clear in the analysis of survey
findings, this rather weak but for clause has allowed Texas cities to
establish TIF districts practically anywhere political consensus allows.

There are two other features of the Texas law worth noting. Both
these features were enabled by 1989 amendments to the original law, and
both are considered "equity concerns," concerns that usually appear in the
TIF laws of more populated and urbanized states, such as Texas, California, Florida, and Illinois (see Johnson and Kriz, this volume). First, Texas
TIF boards of directors are empowered with the ability to dedicate revenue from the tax increment fund to pay the costs of replacement housing
in or outside the zone. The language *allows* but does not *require* this
expenditure, nor does the law permit more than 10 percent of property
within the zone to be used for residential purposes, which greatly restricts
the amount of replacement housing within the zone. Second, zones created
by petition in counties of 2.1 million people or more[3] are required to dedicate at least one-third of the surface area of the zone to residential housing and one-third of the tax increment of the zone to low-income housing.
The absence of stronger equity concerns has produced some unintended
and, from our perspective, undesirable outcomes, as shown below.

A few Texas cities reacted immediately to the newly approved legislation. By 31 December 1981 the city of Port Arthur had created three
TIF districts and Galveston had created two districts.[4] A TIF seminar
conducted by the Texas Municipal League in January 1982 attracted
about 250 people representing fifty Texas cities.

Initiation, Eligibility, and Procedure

As provided in the state legislation, tax increment financing can be initiated in one of two ways: by petition of property owners in a proposed

zone or by action of city council. Figure 10.1 describes the process through which cities can qualify for and implement a tax increment financing zone. The procedure in Texas corresponds with the typical TIF process, with a couple of notable exceptions (Paetsch and Dahlstrom 1990). Typically, it is considered *optional* to meet with other taxing units during the implementation stages. In Texas, however, it is *required*, early in the process, to meet with other taxing units and provide them with a formal presentation (figure 10.1, steps 3 and 4). Since

---

Qualifying for a Tax Increment Financing Zone

1. If the area is developed, its present condition must substantially impair the city's growth, retard the provision of housing, or constitute an economic or social liability to the public health, safety, morals, or welfare; *or*

2. If the area is not developed, it is predominantly open and substantially impairs the growth of the city because of obsolete platting, deteriorating structures or site improvements, or other factors; *or*

3. The area is adjacent to a "Federally assisted new community" (a provision applying to one specific area in Texas), *and*

4. No more than ten percent of the property within the zone may be used for residential purposes, *and*

5. A zone may not contain property that cumulatively would exceed 15 percent of the total appraised value within the city and its industrial districts.

Implementing a Tax Increment Financing Zone

1. The city council prepares a preliminary tax increment financing plan.

2. The city must provide 60 days' written notice of its intent to designate a Reinvestment Zone [an area created for the purpose of granting tax abatement or tax increment financing], and of a hearing.

3. Other affected taxing units are provided 15 days to designate representatives to meet with the city.

4. Following such meetings, the city must provide a formal presentation to each county and school district that levies property taxes within the proposed zone.

5. After formal presentation, the city must hold a public hearing on the zone creation.

6. City then adopts ordinance designating a Reinvestment Zone for Tax Increment Financing purposes.

7. The board of directors must then prepare both a "project plan" and a "financing plan."

8. The other taxing units within the zone must then contract with the city regarding what percentage, if any, of their tax revenues will be dedicated to the tax increment fund.

9. The board of directors recommends steps for implementation of the financing plan subject to council approval.

10. The city must submit an annual report to the chief executive officer of each taxing unit that leview taxes within the zone.

FIGURE 10.1
Qualifying For and Implementing a Texas TIF Zone

Texas TIF law leaves it up to each taxing unit to decide whether, and how much, to contribute to each TIF fund, this requirement is not truly an equity provision, where affected taxing units must "sign on" for the project to succeed. Cities in Texas can still legally adopt TIF ordinances even for projects "vetoed" by other taxing units. Rather, this provision results from a desire to provide both regulatory flexibility and also regulatory guidelines through which political goodwill can be instilled among the various affected taxing units.

Second, the typical process involves the preparation and adoption of project and financing plans *prior to* council's adoption of the TIF ordinance, thus holding the planning process politically accountable. In Texas, preparation and adoption of project and financing plans occur *after* council's adoption of the ordinance creating the zone. This provision results from Texas' strong pro-private interest lobby and is intended to allow greater "flexibility" in the planning process. Since there is no legal limit on the time lag between creation of a district and adoption of a plan, a city could conceivably create a TIF zone and, assuming market forces are pushing up property values, collect the incremental tax revenue without ever specifying how that revenue will be spent.

SURVEY FINDINGS

To further assess the use of TIF in Texas, we administered a telephone survey to fourteen cities across the state that use tax increment financing. The survey addresses three broad themes: participation, expectations, and results. *Participation* includes such issues as a description of the cities using TIF, the TIF districts themselves, and the boards of directors. It also includes the extent to which nonmunicipal taxing units are involved in TIF efforts, the nature of any opposition to the project, and the financial commitment of the public sector. *Expectation* issues include such items as the original condition of the land, intended goals of districts, and implementation policies. Issues connected with *results* include the extent to which intended goals are accomplished, the extent and types of unintended outcomes, and the city's own evaluation of their TIF experience.

Our initial list of cities using TIF, received from the State Attorney General's Office, included twenty-one cities. Upon interviewing, however, we learned that, for various reasons, seven of the twenty-one cities never actually used TIF. Two of these cities formed TIF districts but never used them due to political opposition; one city intended to use TIF but ended up using other incentives instead; and four cities formed TIF districts in the mid-1980s but then, due to the oil slump, experienced continuously declining property values, leading them to abandon the TIF process. A total of thirty-one TIF districts have been formed in the fourteen cities that have used TIF—twenty-three of these thirty-one are still active, and the other eight have been completed and closed.

The 1990 populations of the participating cities range from 10,555 to 1,630,553 and average 615,465 people. Participating cities are located across seven of the ten economic regions as defined by the Texas state comptroller. The Metroplex region, which includes Dallas-Fort Worth, has the most cities using TIF, while the Gulf Coast region, which includes Houston, has fewer cities using TIF but as many active TIF districts as the Metroplex. Districts range in size from nine blocks to just over one square mile (750 acres). The districts can thus be seen as rather small geographically. Table 10.1 lists the fourteen cities that contain the twenty-three active TIF districts.

Participation

Profile of TIF Users   Because the intent of TIF is to help cities revitalize blighted areas—or, more generally as in Texas, to confront impairment of sound city growth—we anticipated that larger cities would outnumber smaller and suburban cities in their use of TIF since we expected

TABLE 10.1
Texas Cities Using Tax Increment Financing

City	Region	1990 Population	Year of First TIF Ordinance (# of districts)
Abilene	Northwest	106,654	1983 (1)
Beaumont	Southeast	114,323	1982 (1)
Beeville	South	13,547	1987 (1)
College Station	Central	52,456	1988 (1)
Dallas	Metroplex	1,006,877	1989 (5)
El Paso	Upper Rio Grande	515,342	1982 (1)
Fort Worth	Metroplex	447,619	1995 (1)
Galveston	Gulf Coast	59,072	1981 (1 active; 8 complete)
Grapevine	Metroplex	29,202	1996 (1)
Houston	Gulf Coast	1,630,553	1990 (6)
Killeen	Central	63,535	1982 (1)
La Marque	Gulf Coast	14,120	1983 (1)
Schertz	Central	10,555	1994 (1)
Wichita Falls	Northwest	96,259	1988 (1)

Source: 1994 County and City Data Book

larger cities to have a greater need for revitalization. Contrary to expectation, however, we found that 75 percent of the projects adopted before 1990 were in small cities, and 85 percent of the projects adopted after 1990 were in large cities. El Paso was the only large city that quickly took advantage of TIF, passing its first and only ordinance in 1982. Dallas, Fort Worth, and Houston passed all of their TIF ordinances after 1989. Texas' smaller cities thus took advantage of TIF long before its larger cities.

In fact, Texas' large cities, with the exception of El Paso, did not use TIF at all until it became legally possible to form TIF districts through property owner petition. Of the thirteen TIF districts formed after 1989, three-quarters have been initiated by property owner petition. All of Dallas' five districts, four of Houston's six districts, and Fort Worth's only district are owner initiated. The legal sanction and use of owner-initiated districts coincides with recovery from the Texas slump of the late 1980s/early 1990s. As property owners have become more confident about the future of land values, more owner-initiated districts have been formed. The Texas experience with TIF thus seems to be one of early support by city government in small to midsized cities but more recently one of private-sector initiative in large cities.

We also found, as might be expected, a greater number of TIF zones in central urban areas than in suburban and edge areas—less than 20 percent of all active districts are located outside the central urban area. Central districts are typically older and perhaps more dilapidated than edge areas, and planners might thus more easily "find" that they impair city growth. In fact, over 80 percent of all active districts are located in areas that can be considered economically poor. Those few districts located in relatively prosperous areas are also located outside the central city. Half the districts in prosperous areas are owner initiated and half are city initiated. Table 10.2 compares the location of each district to the economic health of the area. The exceptions of College Station, home to Texas A&M University, and City Place in Dallas are districts adjacent to rather wealthy central city neighborhoods. The consequences of these locational patterns are further explored below.

Of the fourteen cities across the state using TIF, three—Dallas, Galveston, and Houston—have used it more than once. No other city in the survey has had more than one TIF district. Houston, with six, has the greatest number of active TIF districts, and Dallas, with five, the second greatest. Galveston has only one active district, having completed and closed its other eight. Dallas and Houston are Texas' largest cities, both with increasingly diverse economies. Neither city took advantage of the TIF legislation until the late 1980s when Dallas passed its first TIF ordinance, passing its other four in the '90s. Houston did not approve

TABLE 10.2
Location and Economic Health of TIF Districts

District	Location	Median HH Y*
Abilene	Central	0.68
Beaumont	Central	0.55
Beeville	Central	0.97
College Station	Central	2.37
Dallas		
state thomas	Central	0.72
oak cliff gateway	Central	0.47
city center	Central	0.52
city place	Central	1.51
cedars	Central	0.32
El Paso	Central	0.29
Fort Worth	Central	0.22
Galveston-downtown	Central	0.81
Grapevine	Sub/Edge	1.24
Houston		
st george's place	Sub/Edge	1.59
midtown	Central	0.75
market square	Central	0.98
village enclave	Sub/Edge	1.98
memorial hgts	Central	0.80
eastside	Central	0.91
Killeen	Central	na
La Marque	Sub/Edge	0.96
Schertz	Central	1.23
Wichita Falls	Central	0.63

*Median household income for zipcode in which TIF district is located as percent of median household income of entire city.
Source: 1990 U.S. Census of Population

any TIF ordinances until the '90s. Galveston, however, with a population of only sixty thousand and by no means among Texas' largest cities, is an older industrial and port city and quickly took advantage of the TIF legislation, passing all of its TIF ordinances in the early '80s.

Boards of Directors   Tax increment financing legislation in Texas requires a board of directors of at least five but not more than fifteen members if initiated by a municipality and a nine-member board if initiated by property owners. One might thus expect to see a difference in the size of boards between districts initiated by property owners versus those initiated by cities. But a comparison of board size across initiation method found no difference in the size of boards. Boards for districts initiated by property owners had an average of 9.6 members, while boards for districts initiated by municipalities had an average of 10.4 members. Overall, boards had an average of ten members. The nearly equal size of boards might be explained by the requirement that each participating taxing unit other than the municipality that created the district can appoint one member to the board.

We did find a difference in the ethnic and gender composition of boards between owner-initiated and city-initiated districts. Although Texas TIF legislation contains no language addressing the composition of boards with respect to ethnicity and gender, we were interested in their diversity because of growing politicization of these issues. If TIF boards were truly to reflect the ethnic and gender composition of Texas' population, they would be roughly 50 percent female and 40 percent minority (including peoples of Hispanic origin). We found, however, that boards, on average, consist of only about one-fifth women and one-quarter minorities. Owner-initiated boards (which tend to be the newer boards), as well as larger boards, all are more likely to have higher female and minority representation. One explanation for these correlations is that minorities and women own more property than serve on, or are appointed by, city councils and are thus more likely to serve on the boards of districts initiated by property owners than by cities. They may also reflect changing awareness about diversity or changes in the racial and gender composition of municipal government and other taxing units represented on the board.

Nonmunicipal Participation and Opposition Another aspect of participation is the rate of contribution by other taxing jurisdictions of their incremental tax revenue to the TIF fund. Given that some of the strongest initial opposition to the original state legislation came from school districts, counties, and other nonmunicipal taxing jurisdictions, we expected these jurisdictions to choose, given the opportunity, not to contribute to TIF projects. But we found, to the contrary, that of all nonmunicipal taxing units, counties and school districts contribute most frequently and at the highest rates to TIF project funds. Counties and school districts contribute to all the projects responding to this question and mostly at identical rates. Contribution information is unavailable for two TIF districts. The respective county and school district each contributes at the rate of 100 percent to fifteen of the TIF projects. The respective county and school districts contribute between 50 and 85 percent of their incremental tax revenues to five of the TIF projects. And in one TIF district, the county and school district each contributes 33 percent of their incremental tax revenues. Eight hospital districts and nine

ENID ARVIDSON, ROD HISSONG, AND RICHARD L. COLE

community college districts also contribute at the 100 percent rate. A tenth college district contributes at the 85 percent rate. Other districts (e.g. flood control, drainage, navigation, and water supply) also contribute to TIF funds, at rates varying between 85 and 100 percent.

Our finding that nonmunicipal taxing jurisdictions tend to contribute voluntarily to TIF funds at or near 100 percent, despite the legal option to contribute at lower rates or not at all, appears to contradict the notion that these governmental units are participating involuntarily. To further understand the participation decision of nonmunicipal taxing units, we asked cities to describe the nature of any expressed opposition to activities or plans of the TIF district. We found that two-thirds of the state's twenty-three TIF districts, including all owner-initiated districts, experienced *no* opposition whatsoever. Of those districts that experienced opposition, *all* were city-initiated. Most of these were initially opposed by only the local school district, but two also experienced public opposition along with the school district. And two of the state's twenty-three districts experienced public opposition but no opposition by any taxing unit.

Of the districts that enjoy 100 percent participation rates by nonmunicipal taxing units, most experienced no opposition whatsoever to the project. Of the districts that receive less than 100 percent of nonmunicipal incremental tax revenues, most experienced some school district and/or public opposition. These findings are summarized in table 10.3. It appears that state law provides an easy out, skirting bothersome lawsuits, for those nonmunicipal taxing units that oppose a TIF plan.

TABLE 10.3
Contribution Rates of Nonmunicipal Taxing Units

	Contribution Rates (number of TIF districts)					
	100%		*50–85%*		*49%*	
Taxing Unit	*opposed*	*not opposed*	*opposed*	*not opposed*	*opposed*	*not opposed*
County	0	15	2	3	1	0
School District	2	13	3	2	1	0
Hospital	0	8	0	1	0	0
Community College	1	8	1	0	0	0
Other	0	3	0	1	0	0

This "easy out" nonetheless begs the question: why would any taxing unit participate at 100 percent when the option to participate at a lower rate, if at all, is legally available? Politics probably plays an important role. State law requires any city undertaking TIF to meet early in the process with other taxing units to discuss project plans. A school super-intendent, or county supervisor, for instance, may be the odd person out in a conference room with other interested parties, public and private, who want to finalize a plan and argue that without cooperation from the school district, county, and so on, the whole project would fall apart. Political goodwill is thus one reason other units may participate at close to 100 percent despite other legal options.

Public-Sector Financial Involvement A last aspect of participation the survey considers is the financial involvement of the public sector. For a "public-private partnership" such as TIF to work, the predominant share of total investment typically comes from the private sector, while the public sector provides a smaller but critical share—critical because infrastructure improvement must occur for the private sector to find the area profitable for investment. The survey results show that Texas TIF districts fit this model, except for El Paso. In El Paso, a $40 million pro-ject was funded entirely by the public sector. If we consider only true "public-private" projects (i.e., exclude El Paso's), then for the fourteen TIF districts for which data is collected, the average planned project value is $137 million, and the average public-sector planned contribu-tion is $17.5 million, or approximately 13 percent of average total pro-ject value. The public sector on average, therefore, plans to provide less than one-eighth of the total investment in an average Texas TIF project.

Typical projects funded by TIF include street improvements, water and sewer improvements, lighting improvements, landscaping, side-walks and pedestrian overpasses, parking lots, and parks—with street, water, and sewer improvements being the most common. To help imple-ment improvement plans, TIF authorities have a variety of available techniques, including the purchase and sale of property, site clearance, and property condemnation. Thirty-eight percent of the districts have assisted in the purchase and sale of property. No other activity was reported by more than 30 percent of the responding districts.

To underwrite TIF expenditure, cities can choose a combination of at least three different financial arrangements. The first is to issue bonds and finance the project with debt, with the expectation that the sooner the public portion is completed, the sooner private investment begins to revitalize the area and meet the debt obligation with tax revenues from increased property values. A second option, "pay as you go," finances improvements with incremental tax revenue collected from property values that are rising due to market processes. This option, less risky than the first by avoiding such situations as heavy public debt combined with lack of business activity to generate revenues for debt retirement, allows for the customizing of infrastructure development to meet the needs of specific incoming businesses. The third option, allowing developers to pay up front for public improvements to be reimbursed as incremental tax revenues are collected, gives the developer an additional incentive to work for a successful project. Under this option, the developer is less likely to ignore the district after initial tenants have been found.

Twenty projects reported using one of the above options; three projects did not report financial arrangements. Of the twenty reporting projects, three are financing 100 percent of the public portion of the project with debt, and three others are financing parts of the public portion with debt in combination with other sources. Nine of the projects, nearly half of all Texas TIF projects, are fully funded on the pay-as-you-go option, and four are funded with a combination of pay-as-you-go and one of the other two financing arrangements. Three of the projects are fully funded by the developer, who will be repaid over time, and two projects are partially funded by the developer. Our analysis reveals no statistical relationship between the size of the project and the use of public debt but does show a trade-off between pay-as-you-go and developer-funded projects as project size increases. Larger projects are more likely to be funded by a developer who pays up front and is then reimbursed over time. This correlation between developer funding and size of project makes sense in two ways. City officials who use public funds may be risk averse and reluctant to publicly fund large projects. They may thus rely more heavily on developers as projects grow in value. Second, the larger projects are likely backed by developers who have "deep pockets" and who are willing to pay up front. Findings about project funding are summarized in table 10.4.

Expectations

To assess expectations about TIF, cities were asked a series of questions about the original condition of the land and their intent in pursuing TIF. Despite the absence of any minimum requirement for blight in the state legislation, most of Texas' TIF districts are in downtown or inner-city locations and have been formed with the intent of revitalizing dilapidated areas. Interest in central city revitalization appears unrelated to district initiation method: just over half the central city districts are city initiated and just under half are owner initiated. Of those that are city initiated, respondents report that their reason for using TIF as opposed to some other revitalization tool is that TIF is a relatively new tool and

TABLE 10.4
Financial Arrangements of Texas TIF Projects

Type of Funding	Percent of Districts (n = 20)						
	Overall	City Size		City Location		Initiation Method	
		Big	Small-Mid	Central	Sub/Edge	Owner	City
100% debt	15%	9%	22%	13%	25%	0%	27%
100% pay as collected	45%	45%	44%	44%	50%	44%	45%
100% developer	15%	27%	0%	19%	0%	33%	0%
Debt/pay as collected	10%	0%	22%	6%	25%	0%	18%
Pay as collected/ developer	10%	18%	0%	13%	0%	22%	0%
Debt/other	5%	0%	11%	6%	0%	0%	9%
Total	100%	100%	100%	100%	100%	100%	100%

helps to increase assessed value and tax revenue. Of those that are owner initiated, respondents report that using TIF is an opportunity to pursue a public-private partnership about which the private sector is highly organized and motivated.

Four of Texas' districts, however, are outside the central city. Two of these, both owner initiated, are in Houston. One is pursuing housing development, and the other is revitalizing Houston's Galleria area.[5] The other two, both city initiated, are in smaller "edge" cities—Grapevine in the Dallas-Fort Worth Metroplex region, and La Marque in Houston's Gulf Coast region—and were formed to develop factory outlet malls. Respondents in both cities justify using TIF for this purpose, claiming that but for TIF, these areas would never have developed. As an example of TIF used for this purpose, Grapevine's experience is elaborated at the end of this section.

Goals of Texas' TIF Districts   Respondents were asked to rate the importance of different goals on a three-point scale, with 3 being most important. We expected tax base growth to be among the most important goals since future tax revenue from the growth is needed to pay for public improvements. Not surprisingly, respondents indicate that increasing the tax base is the most important overall goal, with a mean score of 2.95. Business attraction is ranked second, as measured by mean score of 2.80. Close to 90 percent of all TIF districts rank business attraction and increasing the tax base as top priorities. Increasing residential housing is slightly less important than attracting business and increasing the tax base. To our surprise, we found that business retention and job creation are, on average, only somewhat important to cities using TIF. The relative lack of interest in these priorities may result from a dearth of pre-existing businesses in TIF districts coupled with the expectation that if businesses are attracted to an area, then job creation is expected to follow. There seems to be no difference in goal importance between older and newer TIF projects.

We did find differences in the importance of goals across central cities and suburbs, as well as across large and small cities. Officials of central city projects place a greater importance on residential housing development, business attraction and retention, job creation, and crime reduction than their counterparts in the suburbs or urban fringe. Suburban projects, however, place relatively greater importance on "increasing the tax base." These differences are not surprising since central cities typically contain the older housing stock and are more adversely affected by the general trend of business and population decentralization. Indeed, suburban and urban-fringe projects rank "increasing the tax base" far above any other goal, suggesting that some cities are turning to TIF as a revenue-raising tool to service the needs of an increasingly ex-urban population. Officials from larger cities, regardless of whether or not they are central cities, place relatively greater importance on housing development and crime reduction than the officials in relatively smaller cities. Smaller cities place greater emphasis on business attraction and retention than the larger cities. Goal importance across location of TIF district is summarized in table 10.5.

Results

Accomplishment of Goals   Close to half of the twenty-two TIF districts report success in attracting new business to their districts while four, or roughly one-fifth of the districts, all of which ranked business attraction as a top priority, report no new businesses specifically as a result of TIF (although three of these four nonetheless report a renewed downtown and satisfaction with their TIF experience). The other roughly one-third of the districts did not respond to this question about business attraction. Despite success in attracting business, most of the new businesses are in the low-paying consumer service sector, and many are chains (including, for example, retail outlets, food service establishments, and bank storefronts). Only one responding district, in downtown Dallas, has been successful in attracting a major employer to the area, the cor-

TABLE 10.5
Goals of Texas TIF Districts

| | | Mean Rank* (by type of TIF district) | | | |
| | | City Size | | District Location | |
Goal	Overall	Big	Small-Mid	Central	Suburb/Edge
Increased tax base	2.95	3.00	2.90	1.94	3.00
Business attraction	2.80	2.67	3.00	3.00	2.20
Residential housing	2.30	2.92	1.50	2.35	2.00
Business retention	2.17	2.00	2.40	2.32	1.50
Job creation	2.10	2.17	2.10	2.24	1.80
Crime reduction	1.80	2.38	1.40	2.00	1.00

*3 = very important; 2 = somewhat important; 1 = not at all important

porate headquarters of Blockbuster Video, which moved from outside the region.

One exception to the trend of using TIF to attract private investment that often, as it turns out, generates low-wage service-sector jobs, is in El Paso, which used TIF for civic improvement, including an arts festival plaza, an art museum, and a memorial. Ironically, El Paso's district has met some of the strongest opposition, including one of only two lawsuits filed against TIF use in the state. Opposition has since died down, however, as the city has refocused its spending efforts no longer on developing public goods but on fostering private investment.

Unintended Outcomes   In addition to inquiring about accomplishment of intended goals, we also were interested in what, if any, unintended outcomes are produced by TIF efforts. To learn about such possibilities, we asked cities a series of questions about the extent to which they focus attention specifically on traditionally marginal populations. One such population about which we were concerned was the *economically marginalized*, such as women, minorities, and low-income people, who traditionally do not have access to capital. We were interested in learning if TIF districts make any special effort to help these groups start or locate businesses within the district.

We found that none of the state's districts make any special effort to attract women- and minority-owned businesses into the area.[6] Given the underrepresentation of women and minorities on TIF boards of directors, it may not be surprising that districts also neglect the enabling of investment by this segment of the population. As mentioned above, many of the businesses opening in TIF districts are in the low-paying consumer service sector. It may be that by defining their goal as something simply called "business attraction," TIF planners are successful in attracting conventional business with ready access to capital but may miss opportunities to create specific conditions for less conventional types of investment, such as by women and minorities. TIF districts, in focusing on intended outcomes (e.g., courting conventional investment), may thus also produce unintended consequences, such as continued exclusion of investment opportunities by economically marginalized groups.

A second marginalized group that might need special attention is residents displaced by TIF redevelopment. As shown in table 10.2, most of the TIF districts are located in areas with economically disadvantaged populations. Given that state legislation empowers TIF boards to use a portion of incremental revenues to provide replacement housing, we expected that districts would make such a provision for poor and displaced residents. We found, however, that half of the state's districts make no special effort to help these residents find and purchase new housing. Of these, most are located in the inner city, yet they rank residential housing as no more than a moderately important goal. An additional one-fifth of the districts report having no such need since they displace no one in the (re)development process.

Only two of the districts, both in the inner city in Dallas and both ranking residential housing as a top priority, report assisting displaced residents in finding new housing. In both cases, these efforts are within the TIF district. Since Texas state law does not permit more than 10 percent of property within the zone to be used for residential purposes, these efforts are limited. The city of Dallas and other cities opting for this sort of assistance thus face a trade-off between helping displaced residents find housing outside the zone, with perhaps more residential opportunities but broader dislocation risks, or helping them find housing within the zone, with limited residential options but less displacement.

In addition, two thirds of the districts report using none of its revenue to provide or build low-income housing. Most of these are located in poor central city neighborhoods and rank residential housing as no more than a moderately important goal. A number of these districts report attracting new businesses to the TIF district, mainly in the low-paying consumer service sector. And yet they make no provision to build housing within the district that is affordable to workers in such jobs or to existing residents. Only a quarter of the districts, all in Dallas and Houston and all ranking residential development as a top priority, report using some of its revenue to provide or build low-income housing, in all cases within the TIF district.[7]

Cities' Assessments   Finally, we were interested in cities' own assessments of their TIF experiences. Respondents were asked to register their level of satisfaction on a four-point scale, with 4 representing very satisfied, 3 indicating somewhat satisfied, 2 indicating somewhat dissatisfied, and 1 indicating not satisfied. The mean score for the seventeen respondents is 3.59. The majority of zones are evaluated quite favorably by public officials, with officials of smaller cities and city-initiated and suburban zones indicating somewhat more satisfaction with TIF performance. Cities' own assessments of their TIF experiences across types of TIF districts is summarized in table 10.6.

Grapevine's Experience

An example of TIF use in Texas that has gained attention in the local press is in Grapevine, an edge city of roughly thirty thousand, predominantly white, residents in the Dallas-Fort Worth (DFW) metroplex. In recent years, Grapevine has increasingly attracted "yuppie" residents, who have moved to the urban fringe to build oversized homes within commuting distance of DFW. The city believed that a large-scale commercial development would augment the property tax base and provide needed revenues to service the needs of its growing population. Coincidentally, a developer was looking to locate an upscale factory outlet mall at the edge of the metroplex. Grapevine and another nearby city engaged in a "bidding war" for the mall development. The city could not afford to finance improvements on a 275-acre tract of vacant land on the city's edge out of sales tax revenues alone, so it opted to use TIF. According to the assistant city manager, the TIF package helped secure the deal for Grapevine.

TABLE 10.6
Cities' Own Assessment of Their TIF Experience

Satisfaction	Mean Score (by type of TIF district)						
		City Size		District Location		Initiation Method	
	Overall	Big	Small-Mid	Central	Sub/Edge	Owner	City
Level of satisfaction*	3.59	3.43	3.70	3.53	4.00	3.50	3.64

*4 = very satisfied; 3 = somewhat satisfied; 2 = somewhat dissatisfied; 1 = very dissatisfied

Grapevine passed the city-initiated TIF ordinance in February 1996. The project proposes to spend $28 million of public money on street, sewerage, lighting, and utilities improvements to leverage $200 million in private investment—the typical public-private ratio of 14 percent— for the upscale outlet mall. The city seems confident that the project will be successful as it funded its portion entirely by debt, to be paid off over twenty years—one of only three projects throughout the state to be funded entirely by debt. The board of directors is slightly smaller than the average city-initiated board of 10.4 members. Its nine-member board is one-third women and no minorities.

The district is one of the only districts in recent years to be initiated by a city. Most districts formed since 1989 are owner initiated, in central city areas, and faced little or no opposition. The few city-initiated districts since 1989, with the exception of Grapevine, are in downtown areas. These other districts experienced opposition to their TIF plan either by the public or the school district, or both, and enjoy less than 100 percent contribution rates by nonmunicipal taxing units.

Grapevine also experienced some opposition at the outset. Grapevine-Colleyville Independent School District (GCISD) initially opposed the use of TIF for a mall development, arguing that school revenue should not be locked up in such a project. Eventually, the school district, and other taxing units, agreed to participate at 100 percent. Having finally gotten into the spirit, the GCISD assistant superintendent is quoted as saying, "My personal belief is that it's incumbent on us to assist in economic development" (Jones 1996: 24). The school district's participation, however, also turns out to be a way to shelter its district tax revenues from Chapter 41 of the Texas Education Code, also known as the "Robin Hood plan," which redistributes property tax revenues from the wealthiest school districts to the poorer districts in the state (Olsson 1997; Jones 1996; Texas Senate Economic Development Committee 1996). Thus GCISD opted to participate in the TIF project to keep their revenue within the locale, even if tied up in a TIF fund, rather than allowing it to be redistributed to poorer school districts in other parts of the state.[8]

As mentioned earlier, there is frequent concern over the fairness and effectiveness of TIF. In this case, not only is there an opportunity cost for school budgets, both locally and (because of Texas' Robin Hood plan) statewide, when GCISD revenues are tied up in TIF, particularly for land that probably would have eventually developed without TIF. But, by engaging in competitive bidding with another city for the development, Grapevine also is using public money to support private investment that would have probably occurred anyway, although perhaps not within Grapevine city limits—a big windfall for the private development interests. Further, the city expects a total of five thousand new jobs at build-out as a result of the project. Yet these jobs will be in the low-wage consumer service sector and may very well not be filled by Grapevine residents. The city reports using none of its tax increment to provide or build low-income housing. While the new mall development may thus augment city coffers, it also will bring no net new jobs to the metroplex and indeed may externalize to adjacent cities the costs of housing and servicing the mall's low-income labor force. Grapevine's experience thus confirms the concerns raised above about the advantages of TIF, particularly, in a diverse and divided society, over who benefits and who pays the costs.

Despite such concerns as these, the city of Grapevine reports to be very satisfied to date with its use of TIF and with TIF's economic revitalization impact.

SUMMARY AND CONCLUSION

Our investigation and review of Texas' TIF experience confirms that TIF has some advantages and disadvantages as an economic development tool in Texas. A wide variety of Texas cities are using TIF and, on the whole, appear to be successful in their TIF endeavors. Cities generally have met with relatively little opposition to their plans and have managed to garner in most cases 100 percent contribution rates of nonmunicipal taxing units. They have been able to come up with feasible financing and project plans, with a typical public-private spending ratio of roughly 1:8. Close to three-quarters of all Texas TIF projects are being financed with the less risky nondebt options, either as revenue is collected or by the developer who is then reimbursed as revenue is collected. Most Texas districts, whether owner or city initiated, are using TIF to help redevelop dilapidated areas in poorer central city neighborhoods. On the whole, districts have also been fairly successful in attaining expressed goals, of which increasing the tax base and attracting new businesses rank top overall. Most Texas cities report that they are quite happy with their TIF experience.

Our analysis also shows, however, some problems with the use of TIF. Boards of directors typically do not represent Texas' population in terms of ethnic and gender mix, tending to underrepresent women and minorities. This underrepresentation may have implications more far-reaching than simply for board diversity. TIF districts in Texas make no special effort to attract investment by minority- and women-owned businesses. Such economic oversight may, in part, be linked with the political oversight of not fully including this segment of the population on TIF boards. It may also result from a focus on such popular but generic goals as "business attraction" that may bring new businesses but only from the traditional business community, to the continued exclusion of others. Many Texas TIF districts have been successful in attracting new businesses, mainly in the low-paying service sector. But only one-quarter of the districts use some of their incremental revenue to provide and build low-income housing affordable to workers in these new jobs. And only two Texas districts make any special effort to assist residents who are displaced by redevelopment to find and purchase new housing.

The state legislation provides for a great deal of flexibility in the TIF process. This flexibility, however, enables both TIF's successes and its problems. On the one hand, the law is poised to foster an experience successful from the city's and developer's viewpoints, encouraging either property owners or cities to initiate districts and discouraging occlusion by giving nonmunicipal taxing units the legal option not to contribute, or only partially contribute, to any project they perceive to be objectionable. It provides relatively few restrictions on the types of land that can be considered for inclusion in TIF districts, permitting TIF projects in areas that are not blighted as long as development is deemed not to occur but for TIF "in the reasonably foreseeable future." Overall, it grants little political red tape in the planning process. On the other hand, however, it contains very weak equity clauses, with no requirements about ethnic- and gender-balanced boards, replacement housing, or low-income housing (except for owner-initiated districts in Harris County) and contains no directive on the types of businesses that should benefit from the public funding of infrastructure improvements.

In an era of devolution, tax increment financing is becoming an increasingly accepted local development tool, and, with spreading use, its fairness is increasingly questioned. The Texas TIF experience, as currently practiced and legislated, displays both these characteristics. Texas state legislation is not only loose about the practice of TIF, but little track is kept, at the state level, of cities using TIF. Cities are required to submit an annual report with the State Attorney General's Office containing specific information about their projects. But neither the AGO nor any other state office maintains any formal registry or review process. The biggest issue facing the use of TIF in Texas could thus be accountability, particularly as concerns over the fairness of economic development initiatives become ever more apparent and pressing.

NOTES

1. This frequency of TIF use is about average for those twenty-nine states actively using it, except for California, Illinois, Michigan, and Minnesota, whose uses of TIF far exceed those of other states (Klemanski 1989).

2. Compare McCloskey (1985) for a remarkable investigation into the extent to which economics disciplines use metaphor and other rhetorical devices to persuade and shape the course of policy and social change.

3. Only one county in Texas has more than 2.1 million people: Harris County, the county seat of which is Houston, has a population of just under 3 million.

4. Houston also, in 1981, created one of the first TIF districts, and one of the nation's largest—a seven-mile-long zone along Buffalo Bayou. However, Houston's plan, created during the term of a lameduck mayor, was subsequently shelved by the new mayor and council who were highly critical of it. By 1990, when the city began creating several new and active districts, this early attempt had been all but forgotten.

5. Since the survey, we have learned that Houston has created at least ten new TIF zones, some of which are in poorer central city locations and some of which are in high-rent suburban/edge areas (cf. Derfner 1999).

6. The city of Dallas reports that it requires a "good faith" effort in hiring women and minorities for public contracts. But such an effort is admittedly quite different from any aimed at attracting women- and minority-owned businesses into the TIF area.

7. Those of Houston's districts created by property owner petition are required by state law to dedicate at least one-third of the surface area and one-third of the tax increment to building low-income housing.

8. As of 1 September 1999, the Texas State Legislature closed the "loophole" that allowed school districts to shelter tax revenue in TIF funds from the wealth sharing provision of Chapter 41. As a result, school district participation in TIF projects is anticipated to drop.

REFERENCES

Attorney General's Municipal Advisory Committee. 1996. Handbook on economic development laws for Texas cities: How to utilize existing statutory tools to promote local economic development. (April). Austin: Office of the Attorney General.

Beauregard, R. A. 1993. Constituting economic development: A theoretical perspective. In *Theories of local economic development: Perspectives from across the disciplines*, ed. R. D. Bingham and R. Mier. Newbury Park, CA: Sage.

Cole, R. L., D. A. Taebel, and R. V. Hissong. 1994. America's cities and the 1980s: The legacy of the Reagan years. In *Readings in state and local government: Problems and prospects*, ed. D. C. Saffell and H. Basehart. New York: McGraw-Hill.

Davis, M. A. 1982. Tax increment financing: Texas tries a new urban development tool. Austin, TX: House Study Group, Texas House of Representatives.

Derfner, J. 1999. A blight on the burbs. *American Prospect* (23 November): 23.

El Paso, City of. 1996. Tax increment finance district annual report, FY 1994–95. (March). El Paso: Department of Economic Development.

Goodman, R. 1979. *The last entrepreneurs: America's regional wars for jobs and dollars.* New York: Simon & Schuster.

Huddleston, J. R. 1986. Intrametropolitan financial flows under tax increment financing. *Policy Sciences* 19: 143–161.

Jones, K. 1996. Malled: Have wealthy metroplex school districts found a way around the state's school-finance law? *Texas Monthly*, October, 22–24.

Klemanski, J. S. 1989. Tax increment financing: Public funding for private economic development projects. *Policy Studies Journal* 17: 3 (Spring): 656–671.

Logan, J. R., and H. L. Molotch. 1987. *Urban fortunes: The political economy of place.* Berkeley: University of California Press.

McCloskey, D. N. 1985. *The Rhetoric of Economics.* Madison: University of Wisconsin Press.

Olsson, K. 1997. The chronicles of "Robin Hood"—Saving Texas schools. *The Texas Observer*, February 14, 21–23.

Paetsch, J. R. and R. K. Dahlstrom. 1990. Tax increment financing: What it is and how it works. In *Financing Economic Development: An Institutional Response*, ed. R. D. Bingham, E. W. Hill, and S. B. White. Newbury Park, CA: Sage.

Squires, G. D. 1996. Partnership and the pursuit of the private city. In *Readings in urban theory*, ed. S. Fainstein and S. Campbell. Cambridge, MA: Blackwell.

Texas Senate Economic Development Committee. 1996. Interim report on economic development incentives. July. Austin: Senate Economic Development Committee.

CHAPTER 11

Tax Increment Financing in Indiana

J. Drew Klacik

INTRODUCTION

In Indiana, as in many states, Tax Increment Financing (TIF) has become a commonly used local means of financing public infrastructure improvements intended to stimulate private-sector investment and job creation. By conducting surveys of practitioners in local governments in Indiana, this chapter reviews and investigates Indiana's TIF experience and the extent of variations in the uses and structures of TIF. It presents results from two surveys (1993 and 1996) of all Indiana jurisdictions sponsoring TIF districts and accumulating incremental assessed value (AV) between 1989 and 1995. It aims to provide insights into the legislative and administrative decisions that have led to the current variety of TIF structures found in Indiana. Indiana's experience in the use of TIF demonstrates that TIF programs within a state can vary widely in terms of types of activities financed, financing methods chosen, the size and type of areas selected as a TIF district, and the length of time required to complete the project. These findings may remind us that because of wide variations in the uses and structures of TIF, we should not base our judgement of TIF on our assessment of merely one good example or a bad one.

TIF IN INDIANA

The General Assembly passed TIF-enabling legislation in 1975; however, the first TIF districts in the state were created by South Bend in 1979. A constitutional challenge by the South Bend Public Transportation Corporation versus the city of South Bend delayed the collection of the first incremental revenue until 1985, when the Supreme Court upheld the constitutionality of TIF. Mishawaka and Indianapolis soon created TIF districts. By 1989, ten Indiana cities and four Indiana counties had created TIF districts, and the total incremental assessed value (AV) was approximately $69 million. By 1992, the number of cities creating at least one TIF district had increased to thirty-one, and the number of counties creating a TIF district increased to six. In 1992, the total incremental AV in Indiana's TIF districts amounted to over $367 million. By 1995, fifty-three cities and twelve counties had created at least one TIF district and total AV exceeded $494 million.

This analysis presents data from two surveys (1993 and 1996) of all Indiana jurisdictions sponsoring TIF districts and accumulating incremental AV between 1989 and 1995. Eighty-five districts were identified and surveyed. For the purposes of this analysis, a TIF district is a designated geographic area created for a specific purpose. In Indiana, a TIF district may be created by either a municipal or a countywide redevelopment commission. The city, town, or county whose redevelopment commission created the TIF district is considered the sponsoring organization. Thus one organization may sponsor a number of TIF districts. The survey findings provide insight into the wide variety of local adaptations of TIF. TIF districts are grouped and presented according to the following: the purpose of the TIF; the principal use of TIF funds; whether the TIF district was declared as an economic development area or as a redevelopment area; whether the TIF district has incurred debt, is spending as incremental revenue is collected, or using a combination of both methods to finance public investment; and whether the TIF district includes real property only or both real and personal property. These categorizations recognize that TIF districts are created in different forms to achieve a variety of policy goals and will serve as the basis for future subjective and quantitative evaluations of TIF.

Number of TIF Districts

Figure 11.1 illustrates that the number of TIF districts in the state of Indiana has more than quadrupled since 1989. The use of TIF continues unabated. The creation of twenty-one new TIF districts between 1994 and 1995 was the greatest annual increase in the number of TIF districts in the state. Furthermore, additional districts created but not yet collecting incremental AV include the new Toyota factory in Gibson County, the Qualitech Steel facility in Hendricks County, and the AK Steel Facility in Spencer County.

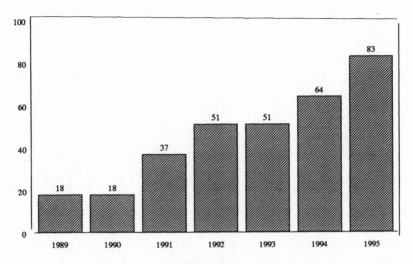

FIGURE 11.1
Number of TIF Districts with Incremental AV 1989–1995

Incremental AV

Incremental AV is the amount of assessed value within the TIF district above the base AV within the district when it was established. The growth in incremental AV has been even more dramatic than the fourfold increase in the number of TIF districts. As figure 11.2 indicates, total assessed value in TIF districts has increased from $69 million in 1989 to $494 million in 1995, an increase of over 600 percent. Over the same period, gross taxable AV in the state increased by 59.7 percent. The decline in personal property AV has likely occurred as a result of depreciation rather than disinvestment.

TIF Sponsorship

Sponsorship describes the unit of government that creates and activates the TIF district. As figure 11.3 indicates, in 1989, only ten cities and towns and five counties were sponsoring TIFs and collecting incremental revenue. The fifteen sponsors had established a total of eighteen TIF districts. These pioneer TIF districts were principally in Indiana's larger, more industrialized cities and towns. The county-sponsored TIFs were created to address the needs of three of the largest economic development projects in the state: GM Truck and Bus Facility, in Allen County; I/NTEK and I/NKOTE steel facility in St. Joseph County; and the Subaru/Isuzu joint venture in Tippecanoe County. By 1992, thirty-one cities and towns and seven counties were

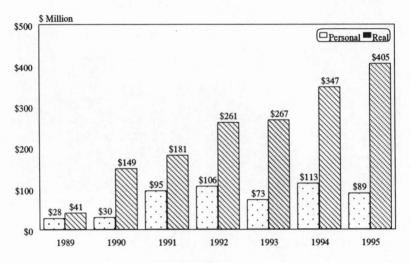

FIGURE 11.2
Total Incremental AV 1989–1995

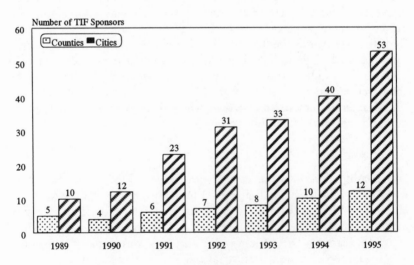

FIGURE 11.3
Cities and Counties Sponsoring TIF

sponsoring a total of fifty-one TIF districts. At the end of the study period, fifty-three cities and twelve counties were sponsoring a total of eighty-five TIF districts.

Reasons for TIF Designation

This category separates TIFs according to the sponsor jurisdiction's motivation in creating the TIF district. There were a variety of motivations. However, they can be grouped into three categories. The first group includes all TIF districts created in response to a specific project with committed private-sector investment. The second category includes all TIF districts that were created in a proactive effort to capture unknown yet anticipated private investment in an area believed, by the TIF sponsor, to have development potential. The third purpose was neighborhood revitalization. Figure 11.4 describes the number of districts in each category.

Specific project TIF districts occurred most commonly. These specific project TIF districts were created in response to a committed private-sector investment or a series of committed private-sector investments. The uses of TIF funds are usually a part of the public private negotiation, and the use of TIF is contingent upon the private-sector firm committing to the project. Examples of specific project TIFs include many of the largest economic development projects occurring in the state. The United Airlines Maintenance Center is located in a TIF dis-

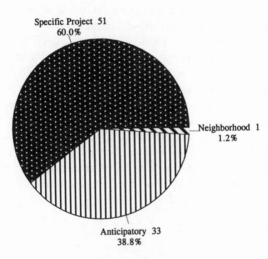

FIGURE 11.4
All TIFs: Reason for TIF

trict, as is Circle Centre Mall in downtown Indianapolis, the General Motors Truck and Bus Facility in Allen County, and the Subaru/Isuzu joint venture in Tippecanoe County.

Many other specific projects have been the catalysts for the designation of TIF districts. Retail shopping expansion/improvement projects have occurred in a number of cities and towns, including Muncie, Roschester, Fort Wayne, and Rensselaer. Other specific project TIFs include the construction of downtown parking garages and convention center improvements. Fort Wayne, Elkhart, and Terre Haute created TIF districts to assist in financing the construction of parking garages. A number of cities, including Kendallville, Lafayette, LaPorte, Mishawaka, Muncie, and South Bend, have designated a portion of their downtowns as TIF districts. These downtown revitalization TIFs are linked to private investment usually in the form of hotel, office, or retail development. As rural counties begin to use TIF with greater frequency, specific project TIFs for distribution centers located at undeveloped expressway interchanges have become common. North Vernon and Rensellear have capitalized on I-65 interchanges to develop distribution centers, and Allen County has similarly taken advantage of its proximity to I-69.

A proactive TIF involves the creation of a TIF district based on anticipation of private investment. A proactive TIF differs from the specific project TIF in that the private investor(s) and the schedule of private investment is not known at the time of the TIF district's designation. Another way of viewing proactive TIFs is to view the sponsor government as playing the role of speculative real estate developer, usually without incurring the risk of buying property. The sponsor jurisdiction identifies the land that it views as having excellent private-sector development potential, designates the land as ready for development, and proactively sets up a TIF district to finance the necessary infrastructure improvements. As might be expected, many of the proactive TIF districts are created to capture the assessed value accruing from new private investment made in potential industrial or office/commercial parks. The new investment is then used to fund additional infrastructure.[1] Additionally, the initial AV growth rates in proactive TIFs tend to be slower than in specific project TIFs.

One TIF district is attempting to spur neighborhood revitalization. South Bend has designated one of its oldest residential neighborhoods as a TIF district and has used TIF revenue in conjunction with other source revenue in its revitalization efforts.

Use of Funds

Infrastructure construction and repair is the singularly dominant use of TIF revenue. In 1996, of the eighty-five reporting TIF districts, seventy-five were created principally for financing infrastructure improvements. Infrastructure investment includes sewer expansion/repair, storm drainage, street construction/expansion, water supply, park improvements, bridge construction/repair, curb and sidewalk improvements, traffic control, and street lighting. In three cases, land acquisition was a subcomponent of infrastructure investment. In other cases, building demolition and other site improvements were funded through TIF. Five TIF districts were created principally for land or building purchases, with the debt being retired as the result of a taxable lease or private purchase. Five TIF districts dedicated their revenue for public parking structures or other downtown revitalization efforts, such as landscaping and street lighting.

Type of Incremental Assessed Value Collected

There are three possible options for the collection of incremental assessed value: real property, personal property, or both real and personal property. In Indiana, sixty-seven TIF districts depend solely on real property assessed value to generate incremental revenue, eighteen TIF districts collect revenue from both personal and real property, and no districts are based solely on personal property.

Method of Finance

There are also three options available to finance public investment through TIF: (1) incur debt, (2) spend as revenue is collected, or (3) use both debt and the spending of additional revenue. According to a survey conducted in 1996, the vast majority of Indiana TIFs use debt financing (52 TIF districts, about 61 percent). While only eight of the TIF districts based their funding strategy on using both debt and spending as additional revenue is collected, many others have used any additional TIF increment for further infrastructure investment in the TIF district. There is no evidence of any TIF district returning any unexpected excess incremental revenue to the general taxing units. A limited number of TIF districts entered into preproject agreements that assure the general taxing units of receiving a share of the potential incremental revenue. Twenty-four TIF districts do not intend to incur debt and will only spend TIF revenue as it is collected.

Types of Areas Designated as TIF

In Indiana, TIF districts may be designated as either an economic development area (EDA) or as a redevelopment area (RDA). While redevelopment areas require the finding of blight, economic development areas require a finding of significant economic development benefit. The use of EDA designation began in 1989. Since 1993, EDA designations have outnumbered RDAs by nearly three to one and there are now more EDAs than RDAs in Indiana. By 1996, forty-nine TIF districts had been designated as EDAs, but there had been only thirty-six RDA TIF districts.

The permitting of economic development area TIFs represents a dramatic change in how and where TIF is used. With a blight finding (RDA), a TIF district is most likely to be used in a deteriorating portion of the sponsor community.[2] The infrastructure in the RDA is likely insufficient for re-use, and disinvestment has probably occurred. When used in this manner, TIF is an urban revitalization tool, likely used to redirect property taxes to finance infrastructure repair or replacement, one of the few local public mechanisms available to offset the advantages of suburban development. In practice, the finding of blight is a local matter, and in some instances blight standards may be lenient enough to enable the use of TIF for projects that do not involve revitalization. In intent and in most instances, a redevelopment TIF represents a public effort to intervene in the private disinvestment process and stimulate growth in areas where private investment is not otherwise likely to occur. This is generally true in Indiana, as most redevelopment TIFs are located in urban areas, and their principal purpose is downtown revitalization or the reuse of urban manufacturing facilities.

When an economic development area TIF is created based on a finding of significant economic impact, a TIF district might be located at any site where "significant" economic growth might occur. The new property taxes resulting from the economic growth is captured and used to pay for the infrastructure the new growth required. Thus in Indiana, since EDA designation has been permitted, the state has experienced a phenomenal increase in the number of greenfield TIFs. Whether in a former cornfield or at a key undeveloped interchange, these TIFs are likely to support the development of suburban retail facilities, office complexes, distribution centers, or industrial parks. When used in this manner, an EDA TIF represents a public effort to capitalize on private investment by capturing the property tax generated by the new growth. While it cannot be denied that without infrastructure, these projects of *significant* local economic impact would not occur, it is clear that TIF in Indiana is no longer solely a revitalization tool but is used in conjunction with suburban and urban growth. This change in policy makes TIF a tool available for use by redevelopment and economic development officials, increases the potential uses of TIF, and creates additional flexibility for local officials to address a wider range of local objectives. It does, however, deny the older, blighted urban areas of a region the competitive advantage of TIF use.

The fact that the Indiana legislature has permitted the use of EDA TIFs is confirmation of the increased reliance of TIF as an infrastructure funding mechanism, regardless of where the growth occurs. The expanded use of TIF has the potential to create a conflict between those who advocate local TIF decisions and those who advocate the statewide oversight of TIF. The determination of the proper use of TIF is not simple and in fact might best be analyzed relative to the goals of the community. Local practitioners in Indiana have long recognized this dilemma. In an effort to ensure a balance between local control and statewide oversight, redevelopment officials have established the Redevelopment Association of Indiana. The association membership consists of professional staff and appointed redevelopment commission members from the vast majority of cities, towns, and counties using TIF. In addition to self-monitoring the use of TIF, the Redevelopment Association members provide training and education forums for its members (as well as communities considering TIF) and work cooperatively to develop suggested improvements to existing TIF law.

INDIANA EXPERIENCE AND INNOVATIONS

The practitioner interview portion of the survey provided insight into the evolution of TIF policy within Indiana. Three key issues emerged: (1) the relationship between TIF and infrastructure; (2) TIF and public input; and, (3) TIF financing innovations.

TIF and Infrastructure

The most common idea stressed by redevelopment officials was that TIF is the only mechanism available for the financing of infrastructure construction and repair. Most TIF literature describes TIF as an economic development tool, an incentive to be considered and analyzed in the same way as tax abatements. From this perspective, the key question is whether or not any incentive, TIF included, can affect a business's location decision. Based on survey discussions, many practitioners argue for a different set of questions: Could the public infrastructure necessary for economic growth be built without the use of TIF? and Would the private investment occur without the public infrastructure investment?

Few would argue that projects such as the Subaru/Isuzu factory in Tippecanoe County or the GM Truck and Bus Facility in Allen County would have selected their current sites without interstate access, sewers, water, electricity, and access roads, the infrastructure provided through the use of TIF. The need for public infrastructure investment to engender economic growth is generally accepted by the redevelopment directors and other economic development practitioners. What is often controversial, to practitioners and taxpayers alike, is who is going to provide the infrastructure, and how the public portion of the infrastructure bill will be paid. In Indiana, with its existing antitax climate, TIF may be the only politically acceptable tool for financing infrastructure. Furthermore, in an ideal situation, TIF may function as an infrastructure user fee.

The use of public infrastructure investment to attract a Wal-Mart, Meijers, or other suburban retail establishments to a specific site is more controversial. Many argue that public incentives are ineffective in influencing the location decisions of market-based retail establishments. There is some concern about the expanding use of TIF for projects that do not appear to meet the "but for" infrastructure test. However, the imposition of use standards would undermine TIFs flexibility. The general argument is that the use of TIF is a local policy decision, and the imposition of certain standards or the exclusion of specific projects might undermine the validity of a local decision. However, the concern remains that the overuse of TIF may lead to the imposition of additional restrictions by the state legislature.

The practitioners are trapped between the public's desire for more and better jobs and the public's desire to not pay more taxes. In the public's eye, public officials are damned if they raise taxes but are also damned if it is perceived that the city is not growing or at least maintaining its current standard of living. In effect, the public wants more but doesn't want to pay for it. If the public is presented with a referendum for a general obligation bond, it is voted down, and the mayor is branded as protaxes. If the public is asked if the city should pursue economic growth, the answer is "Yes, but don't raise my taxes." TIF provides a tool complex enough (and often misunderstood even by public officials) to provide the public perception that the city is building infrastructure, attracting economic growth, and not raising taxes (whether true or not).

In the final analysis, the fundamental question concerning TIF and infrastructure should be: Are cities, towns, and counties that use TIF purchasing additional infrastructure, or is the use of TIF merely enabling communities to direct traditional property tax revenue to other uses?

TIF and Public Input

One of the principal criticisms of TIF is that it is a means for local officials to avoid the referendum-style voter approval campaigns that are typical of the general obligation bond process (Klemanski 1990). In

Indiana, the public debate concerning TIF projects generally falls into one of two categories. The first category of public debate is focused on the merits of the project rather than on the use of TIF as a financing mechanism. The second category of public debate does focus on the use of TIF as a financing mechanism rather than the validity of the project.

Project Merit In most cases, when the local practitioners report public opposition to the creation of a TIF district, the opposition is focused on the project rather than on the use of TIF. In suburban Indianapolis, Hendricks County residents were concerned about the environmental impact of a steel processing plant. Plant opponents quickly realized that the declaration of a TIF district was critical to financing the improvements necessary to make the plant operational, and that if they could undermine the TIF district they could stop the plant. The public hearing for the TIF district provided a convenient focal point for opponents to voice their complaints. The public complaints were focused on issues of noise, air, traffic, and other environmental factors. Few remonstrators directly addressed the use of TIF. In a similar situation in Indianapolis, the city attempted to create a TIF district for developing a section of its canal district, and residents of the area flooded the TIF hearing with remonstrance, most of which was focused not on the use of TIF but on the fear that the declaration of a redevelopment area permitted the use of eminent domain and the residents feared a loss of their property. Of course antitax and anticorporate welfare rhetoric was used by opponents of the project. However, it seemed to be a means to sway public sentiment rather than the principal concern of the most-concerned opponents. Proponents of the projects responded that TIF would not raise property taxes. Neither side provided any analytical support for its argument, and in both of these cases, the public remonstrance halted the projects.

The Use of TIF and Public Schools In Indiana, local school boards have been the principal opponent to the use of TIF rather than the project for which TIF is used. The local school districts fear that the use of TIF will result in increased financial obligations without an increase in property tax revenue. In at least two instances, a TIF district was established in order to provide the water and sewer infrastructure necessary for new residential development. The local school board contended that while the residents of the new homes would certainly include school age children, all the property taxes from the homes would accrue to the TIF districts. The school board was concerned that the increase in students without the commensurate gain in assessed value would place undue burden on the property tax payers of their school district. During the debate concerning the use of TIF to retire a portion of the city of Indianapolis's commitment for the United Airlines Maintenance Center, the local school boards were concerned that the anticipated residential growth would place undue burden on the school district, again without the property tax benefits of the new private investment.

Local school concerns have led to a series of legislative actions, as well as an increase in the practice of negotiated agreements between local school boards and redevelopment commissions. The state legislature has passed a law requiring that all affected taxing units be notified, through written notice, of the creation of a new TIF district. The notification must include the redevelopment commission's estimated economic impact of the development, as well as estimates of the impact on the taxing unit. In practice, many of the sponsoring jurisdictions had, in response to earlier controversy, begun to provide notification, though usually not a formal estimate of impact.

The adoption of the notification law has had seemingly little impact on the creation of TIF districts as the growth has continued unabated. However, it may be partially responsible for the initiation of the negotiated TIF. In this form, the sponsoring redevelopment commission reaches a formal or informal estimate concerning the use of TIF funds and/or the maximum amount of incremental AV to be captured by the TIF district. In one Indiana community, the redevelopment commission and the school board negotiated the annual revenue stream the schools would receive from new property within the TIF district. The revenue stream for the schools takes precedence over the revenue for the redevelopment commission's financing commitments.

Financing Options

Indiana's practitioners have become more sophisticated in the use of TIF as an infrastructure-financing mechanism. Originally, the use of TIF financing was made more expensive through higher interest rates and the need for capitalized interest. The higher interest rate arose as a result of increased risk arising from the uncertainty of future private investment and the lack of any public-sector guarantee. The capitalized interest, often for two or three years, occurred as a result of the public investment in infrastructure usually being made in advance of the private investment.

Decreasing the high cost associated with the early use of TIF has been the impetus for two Indiana innovations. The first innovation involves the use of developer agreements, and the second, the use or support of other types of public revenue. There are two principal forms of developer agreements. In the first, the developer guarantees a revenue amount. In this form of agreement, the developer either guarantees the total amount of private investment or a minimum annual revenue amount. The effect of either guarantee is to assure that either through its property tax payments or the provision of additional revenue, the redevelopment commission, and thus the buyers of the TIF bonds, have a guarantee that the necessary revenue to retire debt will be available. The second form of a developer guarantee is a more recent development. In this form the private developer of the property benefiting from the TIF buys the TIF bonds, generally with an extremely low interest rate, and then uses the property taxes it pays to retire the bonds. If the private firm does not generate enough property taxes, the difference is its responsibility. In the first case, the private guarantee reduces risk and results in the buyer requiring a lower interest rate. In the second case, the interest rate has generally been either nominal or zero.

The use of a second form of public revenue, usually local option income taxes, has served to reduce investor risk, as well as the need to capitalize interest. In some instances, the local option income tax is actually the principal form of revenue, accompanied by a relatively small amount of TIF revenue. Then, as the amount of incremental property tax revenue increases, the use of the local option income tax is reduced. In other instances, debt is incurred based upon nonincremental revenue, and the future TIF revenue is used to pay back the revenue originally used. In some instances a jurisdiction has used cash reserves and then rebuilt the reserve using TIF. In most of these cases the availability of another form of revenue reduced investor risk and thus interest rates. Other TIF sponsors have merely used additional public revenues to provide a guarantee to investors that should TIF revenue be insufficient to cover the debt requirement in any year other public revenue will make up the difference. In these cases, while the interest rate may be diminished, the additional cost of capitalized interest is often incurred.

CONCLUSION

The Indiana TIF experience indicates, as in other states, that Indiana communities are becoming increasingly reliant on TIF to finance the infrastructure costs necessary to engender new private investment. While there are other alternatives, TIF will continue to be the most politically acceptable choice for local officials trapped between a no new tax mandate and the need to appease the progrowth members of the community.

In summary, while TIF may not be a perfect tool, after careful consideration of the issues above and alternative financing options, it may be the best tool available to achieve goals of public interest that likely would not have occurred without the use of TIF.

NOTES

1. To date, the amount of incremental revenue generated has been too limited to have dramatic impact.

2. It is likely that the few nonurban pre-EDA TIFs used a rather lenient definition of blight.

REFERENCE

Klemanski, John S. 1990. Using tax increment financing for urban redevelopment projects. *Economic Development Quarterly* 4 (February): 23–28.

CHAPTER 12

Using TIF to
Provide Affordable Housing:
A Fiscal Impact Analysis of the
King Park TIF District
in Urbana, Illinois

Andrea Elson, Garrit Knaap,
and Clifford Singer

Tax increment financing (TIF) has become an increasingly popular method of financing investments in urban infrastructure, facilitating commercial and industrial redevelopment, and fostering private investment in declining residential areas. The popularity of TIF stems in large part from its political advantages: it does not require the assessment of new taxes; it does not require increases in property taxes; and it does not require the issuance of general obligation bonds (Royse 1992). Instead, TIF enables local authorities to finance redevelopment projects with the property tax proceeds that accrue from property value appreciation. What is more, in this era of diminished state and federal financial support, TIF remains one of a few remaining economic development tools available to local governments.

For tax increment financing to succeed, however, a number of conditions must hold. First, public investments in the TIF district must cause property values in the district to rise. Second, property value increments in the district must generate sufficient tax revenues to cover the costs of the public investment. Third, TIF must not impose excessive burdens on overlapping tax districts—such as school districts. The extent to which these conditions hold can never be known a priori. Insights about whether these conditions are likely to hold, however, can be gained using a TIF fiscal impact model. We present one such model here.

In this chapter we present a fiscal impact model we developed to analyze a TIF redevelopment project in Urbana, Illinois. We then use the model to address the following questions: How will a TIF redevelopment project affect property values in the district? Will public investments in the TIF district generate sufficient revenues to cover expenditures? How will the TIF redevelopment project affect the local school district? What parameters of the redevelopment project most significantly affect the financial performance of the district? And, how will the TIF district perform under alternative redevelopment scenarios? In addressing these particular questions, we seek to accomplish two general objectives: (1) to illustrate how to analyze the fiscal impacts of redevelopment projects in a TIF district; and (2) to assess the feasibility of using tax increment financing for residential redevelopment.

THE TIF-3 DISTRICT IN URBANA, ILLINOIS

The city of Urbana, Illinois, created its third tax increment financing district in 1989 (see Proposed Tax Increment District Number 3 map). The area, commonly referred to as the "TIF-3 district" or the "King Park Neighborhood" includes land currently in residential, industrial, commercial, mobile home, public park, or other use. The city's plan for redevelopment in the King Park Neighborhood is described in the North Campus and King Park Neighborhood Redevelopment Plan:

> Public incentives will be used to transform the Redevelopment Project Area into a stable business environment that will attract private investment through the provision of infrastructure, land write downs, land acquisition and assembly, and public facilities and incentives. The stage can then be set for the conservation and redevelopment of the entire Redevelopment Project Area with private capital made possible through public investment. . . . Because of the magnitude of required public investment, tax increment financing must assume the lead role in catalyzing private redevelopment by eliminating the conditions of deferred maintenance, blight, obsolescence of public facilities, land speculation and assembly, and other conditions which have precluded intensive private investment. Through the Redevelopment Plan and Projects, and utilizing real estate tax increments, the City can serve as the central force for marshaling the assets and energies of the private sector for a unified public/private redevelopment effort. (City of Urbana 1990)

Urbana's plan for the TIF district has three major objectives: redevelopment of an existing residential neighborhood, redevelopment of a commercial area along a street bordering the University of Illinois, and

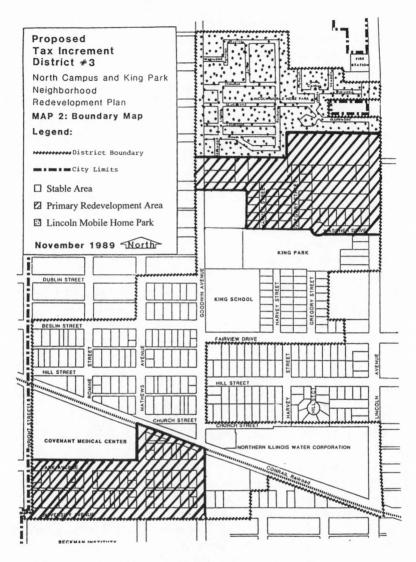

Proposed Tax Increment District #3

North Campus and King Park Neighborhood Redevelopment Plan

MAP 2: Boundary Map

Legend:

〰〰〰〰 District Boundary

▬ ▪ ▬ ▪ ▬ City Limits

☐ Stable Area

▨ Primary Redevelopment Area

⊡ Lincoln Mobile Home Park

November 1989

redevelopment of the Lincoln Mobile Home Park. Some of the redevelopment activities in the residential neighborhood were completed before this analysis was conducted. In accordance with the plan, the city acquired approximately thirtyfive dilapidated or vacant residential parcels, demolished them, re-subdivided the land, and managed the construction and sale of approximately thirty new homes to low- and middle-income residents. These actions were unusual in that the redevelopment activities were initiated by the city and financed through tax increment financing. Based in part on the success of these redevelopment projects, the city plans to redevelop additional single-family homes in this neighborhood.

Urbana's plans for redevelopment in the commercial area of the TIF district involve land assembly and financial incentives but less direct municipal participation. The southern edge of the district borders a major thoroughfare, and recent developments on the campus of the University of Illinois have increased the value and development potential of property in this area. Plans for the area include the private construction of a national suite hotel, coupled with a restaurant and office complex.[1]

Once the commercial redevelopment is complete, the city plans to redevelop the Lincoln Mobile Home Park. Redevelopment of the nineteen-acre Lincoln Mobile Home Park, which comprises most of the northern boundary of the TIF district, has been a long-term city objective. The city describes the park as "an aging, poorly designed, densely developed facility with marginal living conditions" and believes the future of the park may play a significant role in the long-term health of the King Park Neighborhood (City of Urbana 1990). Because there has been little interest by the private sector in redeveloping the park, the city plans to participate extensively in the redevelopment project.[2]

THE TIF FISCAL IMPACT MODEL

The TIF Fiscal Impact Model was designed to analyze the fiscal impacts of alternative redevelopment strategies in Urbana's TIF-3 district.[3] The model is based on the presumption that investments in the TIF district will be recaptured through increases in property taxes over the life of the district. Figure 12.1 illustrates the growth in property value expected of a representative parcel in the TIF district.

In the figure, the preredevelopment assessed value (market value equivalent) for a vacant, residential lot starts at approximately twenty thousand dollars and increases slowly over time. As a result of redevelopment (i.e., the construction of a new dwelling on the lot), the assessed value of the property rises to approximately forty-six thousand dollars. After redevelopment, property values increase at a higher rate, where the rate depends on the extent of redevelopment in the vicinity of the redeveloped parcel.[4]

As illustrated in figure 12.2, the model captures the contribution of each parcel to the TIF fund at three stages of the redevelopment process: preredevelopment, redevelopment, and postredevelopment, each of which may differ in length for each parcel. The preredevelopment stage

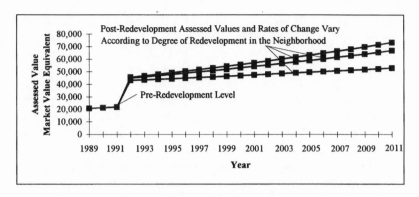

FIGURE 12.1
Assessed Value by Year

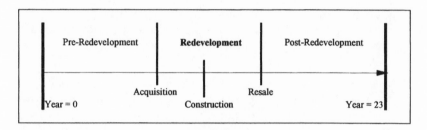

FIGURE 12.2
Stages of Redevelopment

includes the period between the establishment date of the TIF district and the date at which the parcel is acquired from the city and removed from the tax rolls. Factors that influence the fiscal contribution during this stage include the assessed value of the parcel at the beginning of the stage, the property tax rate, the rate of property value appreciation, the date at which the parcel is purchased for redevelopment, and the discount rate. The redevelopment stage includes the period after the parcel is acquired by the city and before it is returned to private ownership. Because the parcel is assumed to be exempt from taxation during this stage, the tax rate does not affect the contribution of the parcel during this stage. Factors that influence the fiscal contribution during this stage include the purchase price and date, the cost of residence relocation, the cost of redevelopment, the sales price and date, and the discount rate. The postredevelopment phase includes the period after the parcel has been redeveloped and returned to private ownership to the terminal date of the TIF district. Factors that influence the fiscal contribution at this stage include the date at which the parcel returns to the tax roles, the assessed value after redevelopment, the rate of appreciation, the terminal date of the TIF district, and the discount rate.

The model allows parameter values for each parcel to differ at each stage of the redevelopment process. Preredevelopment property values may change at one rate, for example, while postredevelopment values may change at a different rate. Parcels at some locations may sell at a higher price or take longer to sell than others. By allowing policymakers to vary assumptions regarding property values, dates of purchase and sale, property tax rates, and rates of property value appreciation, the model facilitates analyses of alternative development decisions. Key factors that determine property values include the following:

1. *Appreciation*—Appreciation rates are used to project the growth of property values (land plus improvements) construction costs, and sales values over time. These rates are based on historical trends and are constant throughout the district and over the stages of development.

2. *Depreciation*—Depreciation rates, which vary by neighborhood and by redevelopment stage, are used to project the improvement component of property values and the demolition and relocation components of redevelopment costs. Variation in the depreciation rate of improvement values allows net appreciation rates to vary throughout the district and over time. The demolition depreciation rate allows demolition expenses to decrease with the age of the structure. Finally, relocation depreciation rates allow relocation costs to decrease as residents anticipate redevelopment and move. The depreciation of demolition and relocation costs plays a critical role in the analysis of redevelopment in the Lincoln Mobile Home Park.[5]

3. *Neighborhood Effects*—The model also allows the incorporation of neighborhood or "spillover" effects. If, for example, ten lots in a neighborhood are redeveloped, and one lot remains dilapidated, the assessed value of the nonredeveloped lot might benefit from the improved neighborhood. Similarly the assessed values of the ten redeveloped lots might suffer from the continued presence of a dilapidated structure. Further, sales prices in completely redeveloped areas may prove slightly higher than in areas where the degree of redevelopment remains less certain. These effects can be captured in the model by allowing deprecation rates to vary with the share of parcels in the neighborhood that have been redeveloped.[6]

The TIF Fiscal Impact Model aggregates the fiscal impacts of every parcel in the TIF district and presents the results in present value terms. The manner in which the parameters are used to determine the fiscal impacts of each parcel are presented in appendix A. A description of the variables in the model is presented in table 12.1.

THE BENCHMARK SCENARIO

The ability of the TIF Fiscal Impact Model to analyze alternative development scenarios depends on the use of appropriate parameter values. For expositional purposes, the parcels were grouped into three areas—a "stable" area (where the city is no longer or not involved in specific redevelopment activity), the "primary redevelopment" area, and the area of the Lincoln Mobile Home Park. Although most parameter values vary by area, certain procedures and parameter values are used for all three areas. All beginning land and improvement values, for example, are based on 1989 assessed values and expressed in 1989 dollars. Based on historical trends, a general inflation rate for property values of 2.5 percent, a discount rate of 6 percent, and a terminal horizon of twenty-three years are used for the entire district. Parameter values for the rest of the variables vary according to specific characteristics of the area and planned redevelopment activities.

The "Stable" Area

The stable area consists of parcels that the city has already redeveloped or has no plans to redevelop. These parcels are primarily residential but also include isolated industrial uses and parcels redeveloped by entities other than the city. Table 12.2 describes each variable and summarizes the source and logic from which the parameter values were derived for this area. The variables marked "N/A" for "not applicable" are not relevant because the city has no plans to invest funds in the stable area. Improvement depreciation rates were set so that the difference between the inflation rate and the depreciation rate equals the nominal rate of depreciation observed in the area between 1983 and 1993.

The "Primary Redevelopment" Area.

The primary redevelopment area comprises approximately forty single-family residential lots in the middle of the TIF district and various commercial lots along the southern boundary of the TIF district. The benchmark scenario for the primary redevelopment area assumes that redevelopment has occurred (and will continue to occur) according to the redevelopment plan. Residential redevelopment is assumed to occur between 1994 and 1996, and the commercial redevelopment (the suite hotel and the office park) is

TABLE 12.1
Variable Names and Descriptions

Description	Variable Name
Beginning Value of Land	BEGLAND
Beginning Value of Improvements	BEGIMP
Postredevelopment Value of Land	ENDLAND
Postredevelopment Value of Improvements	ENDIMP
Initial Cost of Acquiring Fixed Real Value Assets	FIXDCOST
Initial Cost of Acquiring Depreciating Assets	IMPSCOST
Initial Cost of Evacuating Assets	RELOCOST
Real Cost of Construction	CONSCOST
Real Sale Value with Degree of Redevelopment Uncertain	SALEVAL?
Real Sale Value with Degree of Redevelopment Certain	SALEVAL!
Total (Net) Tax Revenue Rate	TAXRATE
Tax Rate Refunded to Taxing Districts	REVRATE
Assessed TIF Base	TIFBASE
Redevelopment Fraction	REDEV
Inflation Rate for Land and Improvements	LANDINFL
Initial (real) Depreciation rate	REALDEPR
Depreciation Rate of Acquisition Costs	DEMODEPR
Depreciation Rate of Evacuation Costs	RELODEPR
Inflation Rate for Construction Costs	COSTINFL
Loan/Interest Rate	DISCRATE
Time from Acquisition to Construction	CONSWAIT
Time from Acquisition to Sale	SALEWAIT
Final Depreciation of First Unimproved Parcel	SMALLM1
Final Depreciation of Last Unimproved Parcel	SMALLM2
Final Depreciation of First Improved Parcel	SMALLM3
Final Depreciation of Last Improved Parcel	SMALLM4
Time of Acquisition/Demolition	DEMOTIME
Construction Time	CONSTIME
Time of Sale/Reenter Tax Rolls	SALETIME
Lifetime of the Study	TAU

assumed to occur in 1995 and 1996, respectively. Table 12.3 describes each variable and summarizes the logic and source from which the data were taken for the primary redevelopment area.

The Lincoln Mobile Home Park.

Many of the parameter values for the Lincoln Mobile Home Park are the same regardless of redevelopment scenario. These include the beginning

TABLE 12.2
Parameter Values and Sources for the Stable Area

Variable Name	Values	Source/Logic
BEGLAND	1,318,570	1989 EAV * 3
BEGIMP	2,694,380	1989 EAV * 3
ENDLAND		N/A
ENDIMP		N/A
FIXDCOST		N/A
IMPSCOST		N/A
RELOCOST		N/A
CONSCOST		N/A
SALEVAL?		N/A
SALEVAL!		N/A
TAXRATE	0.0296	Aggregate FY 94–95 Tax Rate / 3
REVRATE	0.0296	Aggregate FY 94–95 Tax Rate / 3
TIFBASE	3,466,110	Official TIF Base Values * 3
REDEV	0 or 1	Determined on an Individual Basis
LANDINFL	0.025	2.5% per City's Fiscal Plan
REALDEPR	0.00	Assumed negligible
DEMODEPR		N/A
RELODEPR		N/A
COSTINFL		N/A
DISCRATE	0.06	6% per City's Suggestion
CONSWAIT		N/A
SALEWAIT		N/A
SMALLM1	0.00	Assumed negligible
SMALLM2	0.00	Assumed negligible
SMALLM3	0.00	Assumed negligible
SMALLM4	0.00	Assumed negligible
DEMOTIME	Varies by Parcel	Actual Time, Unless Noted
CONSTIME	Varies by Parcel	Actual Time, Unless Noted
SALETIME	Varies by Parcel	Actual Time, Unless Noted
TAU		23 Years (Duration of TIF-3 District)

land and improvement values, tax rate, base assessed value, and discount rate. Depreciation rates are determined as in the primary redevelopment area. The parameter values for the remaining variables depend on the redevelopment scenario. The benchmark scenario for the park represents one redevelopment program and follows the residential redevelopment program observed in the primary redevelopment area. Specifically, the benchmark scenario for the Lincoln Mobile Home Park assumes acquisi-

TABLE 12.3

Parameter Values and Sources for the Primary Redevelopment Area

Variable Name	Values	Source/Logic
BEGLAND	2,409,147	1989 EAV * 3
BEGIMP	2,938,050	1989 EAV * 3
ENDLAND	5,041,645	Actual Postredevelopment EAV * 3
ENDIMP	10,224,737	Actual Postredevelopment EAV * 3
FIXDCOST	331,659	Acquisition + Infrastructure Costs (1989$), Actual or Budgeted
IMPSCOST	39,388	Demolition Costs (1989$), Actual or Budgeted
RELOCOST	58,905	Relocation Costs (1989$), Actual or Budgeted
CONSCOST	1,950,855	Construction Costs (1989$), Actual or Budgeted
SALEVAL?	1,940,434	Adjusted According to Location (1989$)
SALEVAL!	1,962,373	Adjusted According to Location (1989$)
TAXRATE	0.0296	Aggregate FY 94–95 Tax Rate / 3
REVRATE	0.0296	Aggregate FY 94–95 Tax Rate / 3
TIFBASE	5,100,246	Official TIF Base Values * 3
REDEV	0 or 1	Determined on an Individual Basis
LANDINFL	0.025	2.5% per City's Fiscal Plan
REALDEPR	0.00	Assumed negligible
DEMODEPR	0 to 0.025	Generally 2.5%
RELODEPR	0 to 0.025	Generally 2.5%
COSTINFL	0.0416	4.16% per Appraisal Cost Manual
DISCRATE	0.06	6% per City's Suggestion
CONSWAIT	0 to 3	Actual or Predicted Value
SALEWAIT	0 to 3	Actual or Predicted Value
SMALLM1	0.00	Assumed negligible
SMALLM2	0.00	Assumed negligible
SMALLM3	0.00	Assumed negligible
SMALLM4	0.00	Assumed negligible
DEMOTIME	0 to 6	Actual Time, Unless Noted
CONSTIME	0 to 6	Actual Time, Unless Noted
SALETIME	0 to 6	Actual Time, Unless Noted
TAU	23	23 Years (Duration of TIF-3 District)

tion of the entire park in 1994 for $1,000,000, the construction of ninety-six residences in 1995, the sale back to private homeowners in 1995, and a final assessed value of approximately $5,664,000. Table 12.4 describes each variable and summarizes the sources and logic from which the parameter values were chosen for the Lincoln Park benchmark scenario.

THE BENCHMARK RESULTS

A primary purpose of the TIF Fiscal Impact Model is to estimate the fiscal impacts of alternative redevelopment scenarios. We do so by changing parameter values—such as the times of purchase, the dates of construction, and the postredevelopment property values—and comparing the results to the benchmark scenario. We begin by presenting the results of the benchmark scenario in three parts: impacts on property values, impacts on tax revenues and cash flows, and total fiscal impacts.

Property Values with Redevelopment

As described earlier, the effects of TIF on property values are projected by extrapolating the existing rate of growth (or decline) without redevelopment, capturing the effects of redevelopment, and projecting the growth in property values after redevelopment. The results for each of the three input areas are illustrated in figure 12.3.

As shown in figure 12.3, property values in the stable area are projected to increase at approximately .89 percent per year over the life of the district. Property values in the primary redevelopment area are projected to increase at an uneven rate before redevelopment (based on observed changes in property values before 1993), exhibit a large one-time increase as a result of redevelopment, and increase at approximately 2.4 percent per year after redevelopment. Property values in the Lincoln Mobile Home Park are projected to remain constant before redevelopment, fall as homes are removed, rise after new houses are constructed, and rise at approximately 1.5 percent per year after redevelopment.

Property Values without Redevelopment.

Just as the model can be used to project property values with TIF redevelopment, the model can project the path of property values without TIF redevelopment, although the extent to which redevelopment would occur without the TIF is somewhat ambiguous. Property values for the stable and Lincoln Mobile Home Park areas are fairly simple to project without TIF redevelopment as no redevelopment would likely occur. Property values in the primary redevelopment area, however, are more

TABLE 12.4
Parameter Values and Sources for the Lincoln Mobile Home Park

Variable Name	Values	Explanation
BEGLAND	276,900	1989 EAV * 3
BEGIMP	79,800	1989 EAV * 3
ENDLAND	460,800	96 Lots * $4800 (Same Range as Eads' 2nd Lots)
ENDIMP	5,203,200	96 Lots * (Avg Sale Price - Exemption) - Value of Land
FIXDCOST	442,453	C + D + E > Amount Budgeted for Acquisition in 1992, 1989$
IMPSCOST	132,736	C + D + E > Amount Budgeted for Acquisition in 1992, 1989$
RELOCOST	176,981	C + D + E > Amount Budgeted for Acquisition in 1992, 1989$
CONSCOST	7,287,679	Amount Budgeted for Site Preparation in 1992, 1989$ + Construction Costs of $69,000 per Unit (1989$)
SALEVAL?	6,624,000	Assuming $69,000 (Similar to Eads' 2nd)
SALEVAL!	6,720,000	Assuming $70,000 (Similar to Eads' 2nd)
TAXRATE	.0296	Aggregate FY 94–95 Tax Rate / 3
REVRATE	0.0296	Aggregate FY 94–95 Tax Rate / 3
TIFBASE	338,070	Official TIF Base Values * 3
f	1	Complete Redevelopment Assumed
landinfl	.0250	2.5% per City's Fiscal Plan
realdepr	0.00	Assumed negligible
delta	.1000	10% Assumed
epsilon	.1000	10% Assumed
costinfl	.0416	4.16% per Appraisal Cost Manual
discrate	.06	6% per City's Suggestion
conswait	1	1 Year between Acquisition and Construction
salewait	2	2 Years between Acquisition and Sale
smallm1	0	Assumed negligible
smallm2	0	Assumed negligible
smallm3	0	Assumed negligible
smallm4	0	Assumed negligible
demotime	5	1994 Acquisition
doittime	6	1995 Construction
saletime	7	1996 Sale
tau	23	23 Years to Represent Duration of TIF-3 District

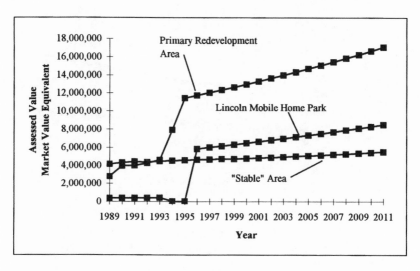

FIGURE 12.3
Assessed Value by Year for Each Redevelopment Area

difficult to project because some redevelopment (namely Eads' First Subdivision) occurred without the use of TIF funds. Therefore, the benchmark projection presumes that the Eads' first redevelopment would occur without the TIF district, but no other residential or commercial redevelopment would occur.

An illustration of the path of property values with and without the use of TIF redevelopment is presented in figure 12.4 for the entire district. Figure 12.5 indicates that redevelopment through tax increment financing increases the level of property tax assessments in the TIF district. In addition, the postredevelopment assessed values increase at a faster rate with than without TIF redevelopment—a result of the assumptions in the model regarding the inflation, depreciation, and neighborhood-effect variables.

Tax Revenues

Once the assessed values have been projected for the life of the TIF district, the base value can be subtracted from projected assessed values and multiplied by the tax rate to yield an estimate of revenues to the TIF fund. Figure 12.6 illustrates the path of tax revenues over the life of the TIF district. Because the tax rate is assumed to remain constant over the entire life of the TIF district, the path of revenues in figure 12.6 is quite similar to the path of assessed values in figure 12.4.

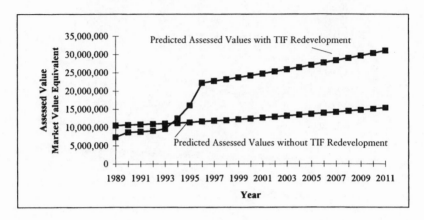

FIGURE 12.4
Predicted Assessed Values with and without TIF Redevelopment

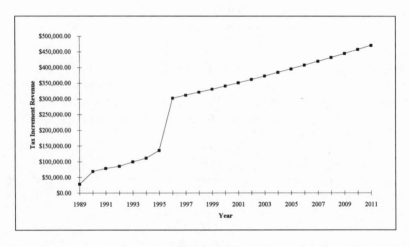

FIGURE 12.5
Tax Increment Revenue by Year

Cash Flow

Cash flows to the fund throughout the life of the TIF district can be found by combining the flow of tax revenues with the flows of investment expenditures and sales receipts. The results are presented in figure 12.6 with one major adjustment: the redevelopment and resale of properties in the Lincoln Mobile Home Park are both assumed to occur in 1997, instead of 1996 and 1997, respectively. This modification was

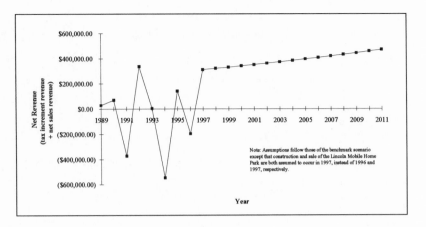

FIGURE 12.6
Net TIF Revenue by Year

made in order to eliminate the distortion in scale necessary to display a net loss of approximately $7 million in 1996, followed by a net gain of approximately $6.5 million in 1997. Although eliminated for expositional purposes in figure 12.6, the cash-flow implications of the Lincoln Mobile Home Park redevelopment are extremely significant. The longer it takes to sell redeveloped homes in the Lincoln Mobile Home Park, the longer the city will have cash tied up in the redevelopment project.

Even after removing the $7 million disruption in cash flow due to the purchase and resale of the Lincoln Mobile Home Park, figure 12.6 indicates that the cash flows to the TIF fund are quite volatile during the period of redevelopment. Not until all major redevelopment projects (such as the hotel, the planned office park, and the Lincoln Mobile Home Park) reenter the tax rolls does the TIF fund maintain a steady and positive cash flow. Cash flow, therefore, represents a major issue in such redevelopment projects.

Total Fiscal Impacts

The total fiscal impact of the benchmark scenario can be found by calculating the net present value of the path of cash flows to the TIF fund for each of the redevelopment stages. Table 12.5 presents the total fiscal impacts of the benchmark scenario for each area disaggregated into four components: the preredevelopment contribution, the postredevelopment contribution, the amount rebated to other taxing bodies, and the net sales revenue from the city's involvement in redevelopment. The table indicates that the benchmark redevelopment plan results in a contribution of approximately $1,577,774, the largest portion of which arises from the stable area.

TABLE 12.5
Fiscal Impact by Stage and Area

Revenue Service	Stable Area	Primary Redevelopment Area	Lincoln Mobile Home Park	Total
Preredevelopment Contribution	62,655	177,742	48,182	288,578
Postredevelopment Contribution	1,840,547	1,703,237	1,607,646	5,151,430
Amount Rebated to Others	-1,240,282	-929,183	-110,851	-2,280,316
Redevelopment Proceeds	0	-388,958	-1,192,960	-1,581,918
Total	$662,919	$562,838	$352,017	$1,577,774

Table 12.5 illustrates the fiscal impacts of various elements of the redevelopment process. In the Lincoln Mobile Home Park, for example, the contribution of the net sales proceeds (sales revenue less construction costs) equals approximately -$1,192,960. Because of the dramatic difference between pre- and postredevelopment property values, however, the loss on the cityfunded construction portion of redevelopment is more than offset by the increase in tax increment revenues, resulting in a positive overall contribution.

It is interesting to note that the postredevelopment contribution to the TIF fund from the stable area exceeds that of the primary redevelopment area and the Lincoln Mobile Home Park. This occurs because the model was structured so that the postredevelopment contribution includes the entire contribution of a given parcel when a parcel is not subject to redevelopment activity. The fact that most of the parcels in the stable area are not subject to redevelopment results in a large post-development contribution and a corresponding zero predevelopment contribution. Because some of the parcels in the stable area have been redeveloped (albeit by entities other than the city of Urbana), however, the aggregate preredevelopment contribution is greater than zero.

Impacts on the School District

Because the model generates forecasts of future property values, it can also be used to predict fiscal impacts on other taxing bodies, such as a school district. Figure 12.7 presents property tax revenues forecast for

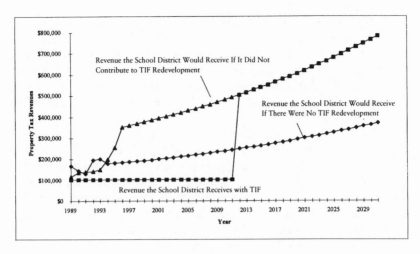

FIGURE 12.7
School District Revenues by Year with or without TIF Redevelopment

Community School District Number 116 under three different conditions. School district revenues under the benchmark redevelopment scenario are represented by the lowest line in the graph in figure 12.7. In the benchmark case, the school district receives property tax revenues in an amount equal to its tax rate times the base value of all the parcels in the TIF district—assumed to be constant over the life of the TIF district. The revenue the school district would receive, if it were allowed to collect on the current (and projected) total assessed values instead of the base value, is shown by the highest line in figure 12.7. As redevelopment nears completion, the difference between the two streams of revenue becomes quite substantial.[7] The middle line in figure 12.7 represents the amount of revenue the school district would receive without redevelopment.

The property tax revenue projections for the school district can also be used to analyze the fiscal impacts of TIF-funded redevelopment on the school district over the long run. As shown in figure 12.7, the revenue the school district will receive (based on the TIF base value) remains constant over the life of the district, while the revenues the district would have received (if there were no TIF redevelopment) rises slowly over time. The present value of the difference between these two revenue streams until the terminal year (2011) represents the cost to the school district of participation in the redevelopment project. After the terminal date, however, the base value is no longer frozen, and the school district receives revenues as depicted by the highest line in figure

12.7. The present value of the difference between this revenue stream and the revenue stream if there were no TIF redevelopment, after the year 2011, represents the benefit to the school district of participation in the redevelopment project. Because the revenue stream with TIF redevelopment rises faster than the revenue stream without redevelopment, the benefits of TIF redevelopment to the school district may eventually offset costs.

Figure 12.8 presents the net discounted present value of the revenue stream predicted for the school district with and without TIF redevelopment for more than one hundred years after the creation of the district. The figure reveals that if the discount rate is 6 percent, the benefits from the increased tax base outweigh the loss of revenue to the TIF fund sometime between the years 2029 and 2039, eighteen to twenty-eight years after the end of the TIF district. With a discount rate of 9 percent, however, the lost revenue is not recovered during the period depicted in the graph. These results suggest that TIF redevelopment must be viewed as a long-term investment for those taxing bodies that forego current increases in tax revenues and that the fiscal impacts of TIF to such taxing bodies depend critically on the discount rate.

Sensitivity Analysis

Although the results of the model seem plausible, they merely reflect computations based on the benchmark parameter values. If the assumed parameter values are incorrect, the projections will be incorrect.[8] To identify those variables that have the greatest influence on projected fis-

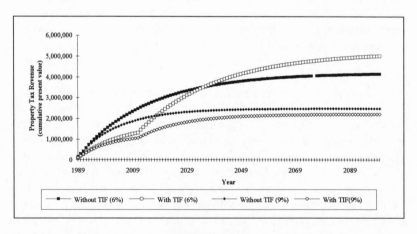

FIGURE 12.8
Present Value of School District Revenues with Alternative Discount Rates

cal impacts, we conduced a sensitivity analysis of the parameter values for each area of the TIF district.

To perform the sensitivity analyses, the value of each parameter was increased by a factor of one-tenth (i.e., multiplied by 1.10). The resulting changes in the net fiscal impact (for each area) were then compared to the results in the benchmark scenario. The results are presented in table 12.6. If a 10 percent change in the parameter value caused the projected total contribution to change by more than 10 percent, we call the results sensitive to that parameter value.

In the stable area, the results are sensitive to only four variables. Two of the variables (the beginning improved values and the assessed TIF base value) are based on official county records and thus can be assumed to be constant and known with reasonable certainty. The values of other variables (such as the property tax rate and the refund rate) might change over time, but the property tax rate and the tax refund rate will always equal each other. If both variables increase by 10 percent, the overall contribution will increase by 10 percent.

In the primary redevelopment area, the results are sensitive to nine variables (the end improvement value, construction costs, sales prices, property tax rates, refund rates, the TIF base, the redevelopment fraction, the discount rate, and the lifetime of the TIF district). As in the stable area,

TABLE 12.6
Results of Sensitivity Analysis

Spreadsheet Notation	Stable Area	Primary Redevelopment Area	Lincoln Mobile Home Park
BEGIMP	13.91%	2.45%	0.30%
ENDIMP	3.45%	21.77%	41.95%
FIXDCOST	0.00%	−5.31%	−11.46%
CONSCOST	0.00%	−31.40%	−185.39%
SALEVAL!	0.00%	31.26%	167.83%
TAXRATE	28.71%	33.42%	47.04%
REVRATE	−18.71%	−16.51%	−3.15%
TIFBASE	−18.71%	−16.51%	−3.15%
REDEV	3.59%	17.33%	11.46%
LANDINFL	7.10%	8.96%	16.69%
DISCRATE	−6.52%	−11.10%	−34.44%
CONSTIME	0.00%	3.08%	20.35%
SALETIME	−0.04%	−8.46%	−45.97%
TAU	7.99%	18.12%	45.52%

some variables, such as the TIF base value, the property tax and refund rate, the lifetime of the TIF district, and the discount rate, are parameter values known with reasonable certainty. Other variables, such as the end improvement value, construction costs, and sales values, are variables over which the city has little influence but could significantly affect the fiscal impact of the scenario. Only the redevelopment fraction is a sensitive variable that the city can influence through its development policies.

The sensitivity analysis for the Lincoln Mobile Home Park benchmark scenario indicates that the results are *in*sensitive only to the beginning improvement value, the refund rate, and the TIF base. Thus, the end improvement value, acquisition costs, sales prices, and land appreciation rates are variables over which the city has little influence but could significantly affect the fiscal impacts of the scenario. Finally, the redevelopment fraction, the construction time, and the sale time are variables to which the results are sensitive but which the city can influence through its development policies.

For all three areas, however, the sensitivity results may reflect the influence of one or two particular parcels. The predicted postredevelopment value of the suite hotel, for example, greatly exceeds the value of the typical single-family residence, although both influence the results in the primary redevelopment area. This means that in the primary redevelopment area, the results may be sensitive to the end improvement value simply because of the impact of the hotel's postredevelopment value. If the same test of sensitivity were performed on the primary redevelopment area without the exceptionally high-valued hotel, the variables to which the results are sensitive might differ substantially. Thus certain parcels may require special consideration when evaluating the influence of particular parameter values.

Of all the variables in table 12.6, only the property tax rate is disproportionally influential in all three areas. The lack of consistency with which the other variables influence the results reflects the diversity of property in the three areas and their redevelopment projections in the baseline scenario. The results generally seem plausible after considering the nature of the parcels contained in the three areas. For example, because beginning improvement values capture the largest portion of assessed values in parcels that will not be redeveloped (i.e. the stable area), it seems reasonable that a 10 percent increase in beginning improvement values may have a disproportionate influence on the overall contribution to the TIF fund. Similarly, in the primary redevelopment area, end improvement values represent the largest portion of assessed values for parcels that will be subject to redevelopment, and it therefore seems reasonable that the end improvement value might have a disproportionate influence in this area. The same reasoning applies to the Lincoln Mobile Home Park.

ALTERNATIVE DEVELOPMENT SCENARIOS

Although the sensitivity analysis demonstrates that the fiscal impacts of the redevelopment project are sensitive to a number of variables, many of the variables are ones over which the city has little control. A variable that the city can control, and the variable with which the city was most concerned, is the date (or dates) at which the redevelopment of the Lincoln Mobile Home Park should begin. Seven of the ten scenarios that follow, therefore, differ only in the dates at which redevelopment in the park would begin. Table 12.7 presents the fiscal impacts of these scenarios.

Table 12.7 indicates that the present discounted value of the contribution of the Lincoln Mobile Home Park to the fund over the life of the TIF district would equal approximately $352,017 if the parcel were redeveloped according to the provisions of the benchmark, Scenario (1). Scenarios (2), (3), (4), and (5) depict the results from acquiring and constructing homes and reselling the properties two years prior to, one year prior to, one year after, and two years after the dates in the benchmark scenario, respectively. The results imply that the total, net contribution of the Lincoln Mobile Home Park to the fund increases the earlier redevelopment occurs. A closer examination of the components of the total indicates that, although net sales proceeds from the construction process increase as construction is postponed (due to the combination of increased sales prices and decreased acquisition, demolition, or relocation costs), the corresponding decrease in postredevelopment property tax revenues causes the net overall contribution to decrease. Scenarios (2) and (3), in spite of their relatively large values for the total contribution, are illustrative only as they assume redevelopment already occurred.

Scenario (6) presents the results if acquisition and construction occur in three equal, yearly installments that start at the same year as in the benchmark scenario; scenario (7), meanwhile, indicates the results when complete acquisition occurs in the same year as in the benchmark scenario, but construction and sale fall into three equal, yearly installments starting the year after acquisition. Scenario (8), the highest contributor of the eight scenarios, presents the results if the city incurs the same acquisition, demolition, relocation, and infrastructure costs as in the benchmark scenario but does not pay for the construction of the homes nor realize any revenue from their sale. In spite of the absence of costs directly attributable to construction, the results from scenario (8) prove only slightly higher than those of the benchmark scenario, implying that perhaps the costs of acquisition, demolition, relocation, and infrastructure prove more significant than the costs incurred in the actual construction of homes.

TABLE 12.7
Fiscal Impacts of Alternative Redevelopment Scenario

Scenario	(1)	(2)	(3)	(4)	(5)
Revenue Source	Benchmark Scenario	Redevelop Two Years Earlier	Redevelop One Year Earlier	Wait One Additional Year	Wait Two Additional Years
Preredevelopment Contribution	48,182	29,974	39,247	56,792	65,088
Postredevelopment Contribution	1,607,646	1,879,497	1,741,193	1,478,692	1,354,173
Amount Rebated to Others	−110,851	−109,070	−109,987	−111,665	−112,431
Net Sales Proceeds	−1,192,960	−1,277,036	−1,233,468	−1,155,202	−1,119,920
Total	$352,017	$523,366	$436,985	$268,617	$186,910

Scenario	(6)	(7)	(8)	(9)	(10)
Revenue Source	Buy in 3, Sell in 3 Phases	Buy in 1, Sell in 3 Phases	TIF Funds Not Used for Construction	Scenario (8) Plus 85% Rebate	No Redevelopment
Preredevelopment Contribution	56,687	56,687	48,182	7,227	65,088
Postredevelopment Contribution	1,480,170	1,480,170	1,607,646	241,147	101,028
Amount Rebated to Others	−111,649	−111,649	−110,851	−110,851	−124,823
Net Sales Proceeds	−1,156,027	−1,300,016	−1,169,214	−1,169,214	0
Total	$269,181	$125,192	$375,762	($1,031,691)	$41,293

Scenario (9) is the same as the previous scenario but includes a rebate of 85 percent of the predicted tax increment revenue to the developer. The inclusion of the rebate significantly changes the character of the scenario and essentially decreases the revenue from the preredevelopment and postredevelopment fiscal impacts to 15 percent of that of scenario (8). Finally, scenario (10) provides the results for the Lincoln Mobile Home Park if no redevelopment activities occur and the park continues its historical trend in assessed values. The total contribution to the TIF fund is smaller than the other scenarios, although eliminating redevelopment as an option also results in a positive value over the life of the TIF district.

Although assumptions and inputs could also be varied for the stable and primary redevelopment areas, the variables presented in the benchmark scenarios for both of the areas prove unlikely to change dramatically, and sample scenarios would provide little additional important information.

AN ASSESSMENT OF THE FISCAL IMPACT MODEL

The analyses presented above demonstrate that the TIF Fiscal Impact Model can serve as a tool for policy analysis and decision making. By determining the net fiscal impact of alternative development scenarios, the model identifies the financial consequences of alternative public policies. In addition, the process of choosing parameter values forces policy analysts to consider the factors that shape property values and redevelopment potential in a given area. Such consideration may prove to be an extremely useful exercise in itself. The model not only sets the stage for examining the implications of various redevelopment policy choices but also establishes equations that can themselves be used for other, related purposes. The ability to predict future levels of assessed property values and the subsequent impact on other taxing bodies affected by redevelopment decisions, for example, could prove critical in obtaining and maintaining support for various redevelopment programs. Fortunately, it is in such capacities that the model excels.[9]

Despite its ability to incorporate depreciation, inflation, and neighborhood effects in the prediction of future property values, the accuracy of the TIF Fiscal Impact Model, like all models, depends on the accuracy of the parameter values. Sensitivity analyses demonstrated that the projected fiscal impacts are quite sensitive to several parameter values—especially for some areas of the TIF district. What is more, many of these parameter values, such as the sales price of redeveloped homes and dates at which such homes could be sold, remain highly uncertain. For policy decision making, therefore, the model should be exercised using the range of parameter values over which the parameters might reasonably vary.

Finally, although the model provides insights into the fiscal impacts of redevelopment policies, it cannot provide unambiguous policy guidance. Redevelopment activities may result in externalities that may not be capitalized into property values and thus are not considered by the model. Therefore, the benefits to the city in other dimensions, such as sales taxes, public safety, and urban aesthetics must also be considered. As with most municipal policy issues, the fiscal impacts of residential revitalization comprise but one of many important dimensions of the issue.

USING TIF TO PROVIDE AFFORDABLE HOUSING

Despite its limitations as a policy development tool, the TIF Fiscal Impact Model demonstrates that tax increment financing can serve as a feasible method of financing residential redevelopment. As with more common industrial and commercial TIF projects, the financial viability of TIF residential redevelopment depends on the cost of redevelopment, the tax rate, and the increase in property values in the TIF district. To the extent that the parameter values used to analyze the King Park redevelopment plan are reasonably accurate and representative, however, the fiscal impact exercises suggest that using TIF to finance residential redevelopment is fiscally viable. In residential redevelopment projects like those in Urbana, the cost of redevelopment equals the gap between the cost of redeveloping substandard housing units and the price at which redeveloped units are sold to low-income families. That gap, therefore, cannot be excessively large. How large that gap can be, although not addressed here, can be examined using the model. Further, the fiscal impacts of redevelopment, based on the Urbana case study, are better the earlier the redevelopment occurs within the life of the TIF district.

The fiscal impacts of residential redevelopment using TIF on the school district, however, present more complex policy issues. Depending on the rate of discount, it may take several years after the termination of the TIF district before the gain in property tax revenues compensate for the loss of revenues during the life of the district. What is more, residential redevelopment is likely to add to school district cost during the life of the district. Thus TIF districts may create intergenerational redistributions of wealth for the constituents of overlapping taxing bodies. The Urbana experience suggests, however, that TIF residential redevelopment can produce a net fiscal surplus even to overlapping taxing bodies, provided the time horizon is not too short and the discount rate is not too high. With these caveats, therefore, our analysis of the TIF-3 district in Urbana suggests that residential redevelopment represents a viable method of using TIF for the purposes for which it was originally designed—to eliminate urban blight and to revitalize low-income neighborhoods.

NOTES

1. The hotel and restaurant have since been built.

2. Since this chapter was written, the Lincoln Mobile Home Park has been razed and is being redeveloped. To address concerns about displacement (such as those described by Reingold in this volume), the city went to great lengths to help residents relocate. For example, the city spent over $250,000 on relocation benefits. Residents were given comparable homes, if their homes weren't removable or reparable, or the value of a comparable home. Of the eighty-one families relocated, 42 or 51 percent received mobile home cash equivalencies ranging from $2,107 to $11,198 and averaging $6,402. The city also established the Benefit Review Committee to which residents could appeal if they felt their benefits were inadequate. Finally, city staff worked with each household to find alternative housing, assist with budgeting and credit reports, and help them stay within the Urbana school district if they so desired. Of the twenty-eight residents who responded to a postrelocation survey, twenty-four indicated that they were better off than when they lived in the Lincoln Mobile Home Park.

3. For general information on fiscal impact analysis, see Burchell and Listokin (1980).

4. Throughout this chapter, we assume assessed values closely reflect market values. As shown by Ritter and Oldfield (1990), however, this assumption may not hold in a TIF district.

5. By city ordinance, new mobile homes are not permitted in the park, thus the rate at which demolition and relocation costs depreciate in the Lincoln Mobile Home Park relative to the rate at which construction costs appreciate plays a critical role in determining when redevelopment in the park should take place.

6. These types of effects were not included in the examples that follow.

7. Some of this difference, however, would actually be made up through increases in state aid.

8. A comparison of predicted property values and tax revenues to actual values and revenues from 1989 to 1994 suggests that the parameter values yield reasonably accurate forecasts during this time period.

9. A comparison of actual and predicted assessed values and tax increment revenues in the early years of the TIF project demonstrates that the structure of the model is sound, although the true test of the model depends not on its ability to replicate past trends but on its ability to predict future values.

REFERENCES

Burchell, Robert W., and David Listokin. 1980. *A practitioner's guide to fiscal impact analysis.* New Brunswick, NJ: Center for Urban Policy Research.

Kelly, Andrea. 1991. Toward the application of optimal control principles to tax increment financing: A financial analysis of the city of Urbana's TIF-3 redevelopment project. Master's Thesis, University of Illinois at Urbana-Champaign.

Ritter, Kevin, and Kenneth Oldfield. 1990. Testing the effects of tax increment financing in Springfield, Illinois: The assessor's role in determining policy outcomes. *Property Tax Journal* (June): 141–47.

Royse, Mark. 1992. Advantages and disadvantages of tax increment financing. *Economic Development Review* (Spring): 84–86.

Urbana, City of. 1990. *North campus and King Park neighborhood redevelopment plan.* Urbana: City of Urbana.

APPENDIX A

This appendix gives a mathematical description of the TIF Fiscal Impact Model used in the main text. The estimate market value of a property before it is affected by redevelopment (i.e., for time $\tau < s$ where s is the "starting" time for redevelopment) is taken to be

$$V = (B_1 + I_1 e^{-p\tau})e^{g\tau}$$

where g is a general dollar value inflation rate, and p is an inflation-adjusted ("real") depreciation rate on the initial value of improvements, I_1, over the initial property lot value, B_1. If a fraction f of the property in a set of parcels is lost to the tax base by public purchase or tax rebate subsidies during a time $s < \tau < u$, then the value of the remainder during that time period is

$$V = (B_1 + I_1 e^{-p\tau})(1 - f)e^{g\tau}$$

Between the time u when the property is returned to the tax base and the time τ at which we are interested in its value, we assume that said value is

$$V = [(B_1 + I_1 e^{-pu}M_1)(1 - f) + (B_2 + I_2 e^{-pu}M_2)f]e^{g\tau}$$

where for $j = 1,2$

$$M_j = (1 - f)e^{-m_j(\tau - u)} + fe^{-m_{j+2}(\tau - u)}$$

The inclusion of the factors M_j allows for a linear interpolation between depreciation rates in the total absence and complete accomplishment of redevelopment for unimproved and improved parcels (as specified by the constants M_j for $j = 1$ through 4).

Let the net revenue rate S for demolition at time s, construction at time $t = s + w$, and sale at time $u = s + x$ be defined by

$$Se^{-ht} = -[C + De^{-\delta\tau} + Ee^{-\varepsilon\tau}]\Delta(\tau-s) - F\Delta(\tau-t) + [G(1-f) + Hf]\Delta(\tau-u)$$

where the relevant property here of the function Δ is that

$$\int_0^\tau X(\tau)\Delta(\tau - c)d\tau = X(c)$$

for positive $\tau > c$, for any constant, c.

A simple and useful approximation for the rate of discount is to use a common loan and interest rate, l. Now let T be the net tax rate on TIF parcel increments of estimated market value V (after accounting for any reductions for development incentive subsidy). For generality we allow in this formulation a different tax rate R on the TIF base to account for subsidy possibilities. With this preparation, we can now write down the evolution of the contribution of a property to the TIF fund balance as

$$\frac{dK}{d\tau} = lK + TV - RL + S$$

Here $L = A$ for $\tau = s$ or $u < \tau$ and $L = (l\text{-}f)A$ for $s < \tau < u$, where A is the market value corresponding to the TIF base used for computing tax financing increment revenues for each parcel group.

Defining the net present value of the contribution of each set of parcels to the TIF fund balance as

$$Q = e^{-l\tau}K$$

it can be verified by substitution that the above equation integrates to

$$Q = \int_0^\tau \varepsilon^{-l\tau}(TV - RL + S)d\tau$$

To evaluate this result for $\tau > u$, we break the integral up as

$$Q = Q_u + Q_\tau + Q_R + Q_S$$

where

$$Q_u = T\int_0^u e^{-\sigma\tau}(B_1 + I_1 e^{-p\tau})d\tau - Tf\int_s^u e^{-\sigma\tau}(B_1 + I_1 e^{-p\tau})d\tau$$

$$Q_z = (1-f)Q_1 + fQ_2$$

$$Q_R = -RA\int_0^t e^{-l\tau}d\tau + RAf\int_s^u e^{-l\tau}d\tau$$

$$Q_S = -e^{-\eta s}(C + De^{-\delta s} + E^{-\varepsilon s}) - e^{-\eta t}F + e^{-\eta u}[(1-f)G + fH]$$

where $\sigma = l\text{-}g$ and $\eta = l\text{-}h$. Here, for $j = 1,2$

$$Q_j = T\int_u^t e^{-\sigma\tau}(B_j + I_j e^{-p\tau}M_j)d\tau$$

Now let $\mu_j = \sigma + m_j$ for $j = 1$ to 4 and $\rho = \sigma + p$. also let

$$s_k = e^{-\sigma t_k}$$
$$r_k = e^{-\rho t_k}$$
$$l_k = e^{-l t_k}$$

and

$$m_{jk} = e^{-(p-m_j)u}e^{-\mu_j t_k}$$

for $t_1 = s$, $t_2 = u$, and $t_3 = \tau$. Then the above integrals can be expressed as

$$Q_u = T[B_1(1 - s_2)/\sigma - fB_1(s_1 - s_2)/\sigma + I_1(1 - r_2)/\rho - fI_1(r_1 - r_2)/\rho]$$
$$Q_R = -RA(1 - l_3)/l + fRA(l_1 - l_2)/l$$
$$Q_j = T\{B_j(s_2 - s_3)/\sigma + I_j[(1 - f)(m_{j2} - m_{j3})/\mu_j + f(m_{j+2,2} - m_{j+2,3})/\mu_{j+2}]\}$$

The correspondence between the mathematical symbols used here for compactness and the spreadsheet parameter names used in the main text is as follows:

A TIFBASE
B_1 BEGLAND
B_2 ENDLAND
C FIXDCOST
D DEMOCOST
E RELOCOST
F CONSCOST

G	SALEVAL?
H	SALEVAL!
I_1	BEGIMP
I_2	ENDIMP
R	REVRATE
T	TAXRATE
f	REDEV
g	LANDINFL
h	CONSINFL
l	DISCRATE
m_1	SMALLM1
m_2	SMALLM2
m_3	SMALLM3
m_4	SMALLM4
p	RELDEPR
t	CONSTIME
t_1	DEMOTIME
t_2	SALETIME
t_3	TAU
w	CONSWAIT
x	SALEWAIT
δ	DEMODEPR
ε	RELODEPR

CHAPTER 13

Are TIFs Being Misused to Alter Patterns of Residential Segregation? The Case of Addison and Chicago, Illinois

David A. Reingold

In 1977, Illinois adopted tax increment finance (TIF) legislation, granting local municipalities (cities, villages, and incorporated towns) the authority and flexibility to use projected increases in property tax revenues for (re)developing areas that would not be attractive to the private sector except for the TIF funds.[1] Legislation like the Illinois Tax Increment Allocation Act is thought to be a reaction by local government to the gradual erosion of federal support for urban revitalization projects of the 1950s and 1960s (Paetsch and Dahlstrom 1990).

One of the perceived differences between early urban renewal programs and their more contemporary counterparts is the problem of misuse. Early urban renewal used federal funds to clear slum and blighted areas, razing whole blocks and entire neighborhoods, displacing large numbers of residents and businesses, and reinforcing patterns of residential segregation. In many cases, these programs had devastating consequences for the residents and communities that made up the mostly poor nonwhite areas of inner cities (Halpern 1995; Hirsch 1983). In contrast, the prevailing concern over contemporary urban renewal programs, such as tax increment finance, is that local officials have been able to subsidize the development of desirable property in growing areas with few or no signs of slum or blight. Since the viability of a TIF district depends on anticipated increases in property tax revenue, and systemic urban blight and decay frequently suppress property values, some observers fear that TIF is not a viable option in many of these communities and will be used primarily only in more affluent areas. However, as Elson and her colleagues demonstrate in the previous chapter, TIF has been used to successfully build affordable housing, changing the trajectory of property values in a low- and moderate-income residential area.

These shifting concerns over the misuse of urban renewal efforts likely reflect changes in federal law, most notably the passage of civil rights legislation in the 1960s. Local authorities are now held accountable by the U.S. Department of Justice under federal law for the use of urban renewal funds (federal or local) that discriminate on the basis of race, ethnicity, creed, gender, or other criteria. However, the passage of federal laws effectively forbidding the use of urban renewal efforts for regulating patterns of residential segregation has not eliminated this practice.

In 1997, the Village of Addison, Illinois, located twenty miles west of Chicago's downtown, tentatively agreed to an out-of-court settlement (without admitting guilt) estimated at $20 to $25 million for undertaking a TIF project that, allegedly, violated the Fair Housing Act of 1968 and, as a consequence, the civil rights of approximately forty-five Hispanic households. The lawsuit was initiated by several housing advocacy groups and asserts that Addison's Board of Trustees created TIF districts under the "guise of redevelopment" in the village's two largest Hispanic residential communities with the intent of reducing the Hispanic population and discouraging future Hispanic settlement.

Whether or not the law recognizes wrongdoing in the Addison case, it raises a number of important questions: Are TIFs being misused by local authorities to solidify patterns of residential segregation much like urban renewal funds were misused forty years ago? Is there a relationship between the racial and ethnic composition of a community and its likelihood of TIF designation? Are TIFs initiated by municipal governments more likely to target mostly poor, nonwhite communities compared to TIFs initiated by private developers? Answers to these questions have important implications for understanding the actual purpose of TIFs and the potential for their misuse.

To address these issues, this chapter will begin with a more detailed look at the Addison case. This will be followed by a description of the spatial distribution of TIFs in Illinois, an analysis of Chicago's neighborhoods with TIF districts, and an assessment of whether a TIF's initiation status (either developer or city initiated) effects the type of community targeted for (re)development with TIF funds.

THE ADDISON CASE[2]

The Village of Addison was incorporated in 1884 but remained a detached rural area until after World War II. In the 1950s, developers began building to meet the growing consumer demand. By 1960 the population had risen to sixty-seven hundred, up from 916 in 1930. During the next ten years, rapid growth pushed its population over twenty-four thousand in 1970. With the completion of a major expressway in the 1970s, connecting Addison to Chicago's central city, Addison's population grew to almost thirty thousand, and increased only slightly in the 1980s and 1990s.

For the most part, Addison remains a residential area. Most of the housing was built during its latter period of explosive population growth. Almost two-thirds of Addison's homes are in single-family units, and, in 1989, the median home value was almost $125,000 (with a significant amount of variation).

Even though Addison is predominantly a residential area, the Village is largely dependent on an industrial base. Forty-two percent of Addison's total assessed valuation is from industrial or commercial property. Addison has one of the largest industrial parks in the state and has over one thousand businesses, which employ more than eleven thousand workers; major employers include an Ace Hardware distribution center, a regional United Parcel Service center, Krach Corporation, and KDA Kitchen Manufacturers. Some of Addison's economic activity is the result of its locational advantage: it is both situated close to O'Hare International Airport and has access to the interstate. These advantages, however, have not spilled over into its retail sector. There are only about six shopping centers in the community, and Addison lacks a civic square or a central downtown area to promote retail activity.

In general, Addison can be considered a stable middle- and upper-middle-class area. In 1989, almost 60 percent of Addison residents worked in white-collar occupations, and 44 percent of families in the village earned more than fifty thousand dollars per year. Less than 4 percent of its families lived below the federal poverty line, and fewer than 5 percent of the labor force was unemployed.

Despite its middle-class status, Addison has experienced moderate change in ethnic composition during the past several decades. While Addison's population remains almost 90 percent white, the Hispanic and Asian-Pacific populations increased during the 1980s from 6 percent to 13 percent and from 3 percent to 6 percent, respectively. This change is reflected in an increase of foreign-born residents from 13 percent to 19 percent, as well as an increase in the proportion of Addison households headed by single women (from 8 percent to 13 percent). These shifts, however, have not been accompanied by higher levels of residential instability. In 1979, approximately 49 percent of households had lived in a different house in 1975; by 1989, this figure had decreased to 39 percent. Perhaps many of Addison's residents lack either the will or the means to relocate.

The adoption of two TIF districts by the village's board of trusties in Addison's Green Oaks and Michael Lane neighborhoods in 1993–94 dovetails with several of the changes taking place in Addison. Most notable is the in-migration of mostly Hispanic and Asian-Pacific households into these two areas. For some village officials and residents, these changing patterns of residential location were perceived to be lowering the value of surrounding homes, creating unsafe conditions because of overcrowding, causing higher incidences of vandalism such as gang graffiti, and putting the town's future at stake (Girona 1997).

Another factor was the town's retail sector, which had lagged behind its industrial base. The adoption of TIF districts near two existing shopping centers located in Green Oaks and Michael Lane was likely seen as a needed catalyst to spur the development process, which would have been anchored by these existing retail establishments. Whether the land assembly process was going to result in residential development and/or commercial development is unclear, since the village board had not formalized contractual agreements with private developers at the time the suit had been brought; nevertheless, TIF districts used effectively in these areas may have boosted both retail and residential development.

Even though Green Oaks and Michael Lane include several commercial areas, the two communities are largely residential. Much of the existing housing stock in these two areas, totaling approximately forty acres, had been built in the 1960s and 1970s and was constructed as part of a coordinated development plan. Before the proposed TIFs were adopted, there were approximately eight hundred residential units in the two communities, and roughly two-thirds of the residents in these areas were Hispanic.

The TIF adoption process appeared routine.[3] The Addison Board of Directors hired a private consulting firm to study the feasibility of TIF adoption in and around Green Oaks and Michael Lane. The firm found that these areas were "considered blighted due to aged condition of property, depreciation of physical maintenance, deleterious land use, inadequate utilities, obsolescence, code violations [such as overcrowding and inadequate off-street parking], excessive vacancies, and an absence of effective community planning for the area" (United States District Court 1997).

These assessments were later denied in the plaintiffs' class action suit against the village. According to the plaintiffs, the problem of overcrowding simply reflected cultural and socioeconomic differences between longtime Addison residents who are mostly native-born whites and the newly arrived mostly foreign-born Hispanics. Some of the other code infractions that made these areas eligible for TIF designation were interpreted as only minor code violations, such as repairing a hole in a screen, painting rust spots on an awning, removing dust on window sills, replacing toilet paper roll holders, repairing cracks in linoleum floors, and removing stains from porcelain bathroom fixtures. As for the parking problems, Addison's zoning ordinance requires at least two off-street parking spaces per dwelling unit. The plaintiffs claimed that the village intentionally created the shortage of parking in the Green Oaks and Michael Lane neighborhoods in 1989–90 when it enacted and/or began enforcing a municipal ordinance that prohibits curbside parking in certain areas between 2 and 5 A.M. The claims of obsolescence and alleged depreciation of physical maintenance were denied by the plaintiffs since most of the housing in the TIF areas, as well as most other areas of Addison, was constructed within the past several decades and was not in substantial disrepair. Similarly, the plaintiffs argued that the village's finding that the TIF areas had excessive vacancies, deleterious land use, inadequate utilities, and absence of effective community planning was unsubstantiated and, in some cases, fabricated.

Despite these inconsistencies, public hearings for both proposed TIF districts were held in March and September 1994. Soon after each hearing, the board successfully passed both plans. The land assembly process began with a series of condemnation lawsuits filed by the village in order to acquire property for redevelopment. As a result, at least eight buildings with thirty-two units were raised, including four apartment structures.

The assertion that TIF designation was being used to limit Hispanic residential settlement largely depended on a claim that the TIF boundaries were intentionally gerrymandered so as to exclude equivalent housing stock located in predominantly white areas that were contiguous with Green Oaks and Michael Lane. Specifically, two housing complexes, adjacent to the Green Oaks TIF and largely occupied by whites, were excluded from this development plan. Perhaps even more damaging is the assertion that Addison took no condemnation or demolition action against several predominantly white housing complexes within the Green Oaks TIF, even though they were reported to be in similar condition as the demolished property.

The out-of-court settlement plan, worked out between the village and the U.S. Justice Department, is estimated to cost the village between $20 and $25 million for fines, damages, and redevelopment measures. Part of the agreement requires the village to pay about $1.8 million to nearly 170 displaced families, as well as another $2.5 million in attorneys' fees. The village also agreed to build affordable housing to replace what it demolished, construct a recreational park and a parking lot in Green Oaks, and convert an existing building into a neighborhood resource center.[4]

The apparent misuse of TIF districts in Addison to displace Hispanic residents and influence residential segregation has many similarities to the type of misuse that occurred during the urban renewal efforts of the 1950s. But it is far removed from concerns that TIFs may provide subsidies to affluent areas that would have developed without public funds. Clearly, TIF misuse can occur in a variety of ways.

Even though the Addison case appears to be an isolated incident, it is possible that TIF is being abused to alter patterns of residential segregation but has escaped public attention and legal scrutiny. One way to indirectly test whether the Addison case is, indeed, an isolated incident is to look at the characteristics of communities with TIF districts.

WHAT TYPES OF COMMUNITIES ADOPT TIF?

Figure 13.1 presents the spatial distribution of TIF districts in Illinois. As of 1994, the state had 325 TIF districts: 158 in downstate counties, 98 in suburban Cook County (the county that includes the city of Chicago), 42 in collar counties (DuPage, Lake, McHenry, Will), and 27 in Chicago.[5] Much of the recent TIF growth has occurred since 1987 (more than 50 percent) and is concentrated in Chicago. These trends reflect an increased attention to TIF due to the state's brief promotion of sales tax TIFs in the mid-1980s and the elimination and/or curtail-

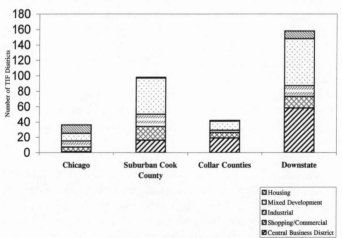

FIGURE 13.1
Illinois TIF Districts by Region & Type, 1977–1994

Source: Taxpayers' Federation of Illinois, May 1995
Notes: Collar counties include Du Page, Kane, McHendry and Will.

ment of other alternative financing options in the late 1980s, such as the Urban Development Action Grant Program and Industrial Revenue Bonds Act, both of which were frequently used by urban municipalities. Overall, roughly 40 percent of TIF districts were created for mixed development; 30 percent for central business district projects; 14 percent for industrial projects; 12 percent for commercial projects, such as shopping malls; and 5 percent for residential development projects.

Dye's (1997) analysis of municipalities in northeastern Illinois that adopted TIF compared to those that did not found that TIF-adopting municipalities were more likely to be larger (in terms of population) and poorer (in terms of per capita income). Non-TIF-adopting municipalities experienced faster growth in population and faster growth in per capita income. While no differences were found in per capita property tax base, TIF-adopting municipalities have substantially higher tax rates. Nevertheless, the best predictor of a municipality's decision to adopt TIF is size of population. Larger municipalities are significantly more likely to adopt TIF.

Overall, these findings seem to suggest that in northeastern Illinois, TIF adoption is not taking place in municipalities that are either desperately poor or extremely affluent. Rather, TIF-adopting municipalities appear to be somewhere in between these two extremes where the process of decay may be in its early stages, threatening more serious long-term decline and necessitating redevelopment.

Unfortunately, the use of municipalities as the unit of analysis limits our understanding of the characteristics of communities that are targeted for TIF. TIF districts frequently designate small geographic areas within municipalities, not entire cities, towns, villages, or incorporated areas. If the geographic area in and around the TIF varies from the overall characteristics of the municipality, studies that rely on municipal-level data may not accurately describe the actual characteristics of areas with TIFs. Therefore, analyzing differences between municipalities may fail to capture much of the variation within municipalities.

Overcoming this problem is difficult since limited information exists on the socioeconomic characteristics of TIF districts. While TIF redevelopment plans frequently contain substantial descriptive information on the targeted area, most of these reports focus on findings of slum and blight, as specified in state TIF legislation and do not provide basic community-level characteristics.

The tendency to use municipalities as the unit of analysis is, in part, a by-product of how the U.S. decennial census and other administrative records from public agencies are aggregated. For a variety of reasons, information from these sources is reported at the municipal level but is not reported for geographic areas that constitute the ecological boundaries of actual communities. One notable exception is the city of Chicago, where each community in the city contains a mutually exclusive set of enclosed census tracts,[6] which allows for a more detailed investigation of the type of communities with TIF.

The community characteristics presented in this analysis are from the 1990 U.S. decennial census (except for several measures that also use data from the 1980 U.S. decennial census in order to estimate change over time). Even though these data have many advantages, one shortcoming is that they do not provide information at the time of TIF adoption. Community-level characteristics for a TIF adopted prior to 1990 may be affected by the activities related to the TIF. We would likely expect this type of measurement error to underestimate the area's overall level of distress since the TIF funded project may already have begun revitalizing the area. Conversely, community characteristics for a TIF adopted after 1990 may fail to account for some of the community's most recent changes so may underestimate the community's well-being. Fortunately, these measurement issues are likely minimized since Chicago did not enact its first TIF district until the mid-1980s and since many of the city's TIF districts were created within a few years of the 1990 census figures.

Table 13.1 presents the average socioeconomic characteristics of community areas with and without TIF districts in Chicago, as well as the overall city averages for these measures.[7] It is interesting to note that virtually all of Chicago's forty-four TIFs are contained within the boundaries of these community areas. The summary statistics for Chicago community areas with and without TIF are calculated by tabulating the appropriate community area means and averaging them to produce a summary statistic for each community characteristic. In contrast, the citywide figures are the average characteristics of the entire city and not the average of all seventy-seven community area means in the city. The averages of community area means with and without TIF, in other words, are not weighted by the size of the community area.

The decision to use unweighted data stems from several considerations. The relative size of a TIF district, including its physical boarders and its population, does not appear to be closely related to the relative physical size of a community area. Moreover, the area contained within any given TIF district is considerably smaller than its surrounding community area. As a result, weighting summary community-level TIF statistics on the size of the surrounding neighborhood may mask substantial variation at the community level.

In general, Chicago communities with TIF tend to have similar socioeconomic characteristics as communities without TIF, and both are relatively consistent with citywide averages. While communities with

TABLE 13.1
Average Community Characteristics of TIFs in the City of Chicago
(Standard Deviations in Parentheses)

	Community Areas with TIF	Community Areas without TIF	City of Chicago Averages
Percentage Poor,	23.3	18.5	18.0
1990	(17.6)	(17.8)	
Percentage Change Poor,	17.2	12.0	8.0
1980–1990	(30.2)	(42.2)	
Percentage Black,	40.4	44.5	39.0
1990	(35.9)	(45.2)	
Percentage Change Black,	77.6	35.3	–2.0
1980–1990	(161.8)	(86.4)	
Percentage Hispanic,	15.3	12.9	13.0
1990	(17.4)	(20.2)	
Percentage Change Hispanic,	43.1	41.7	36.0
1980–1990	(97.4)	(110.0)	
Percentage Change Population,	–3.9	–9.5*	-7.0
1980–1990	(16.7)	(12.6)	
Percentage Change Different	11.3	6.9	7.0
House in 1975 and 1985	(12.8)	(13.2)	
Percentage of Female-Headed	24.4	21.6	20.7
Households, 1990	(17.4)	(17.0)	
Median Family Income ($),	33,763.69	32,583.42	30,707.00
1990	(18,651.8)	(13,938.57)	
Percentage High School	64.5	65.7	66.0
Graduates, 1990	(15.4)	(13.4)	
Percentage of Units Owner	18.6	33.5**	22.0
Occupied, 1990	(20.5)	(27.3)	
Median Home Value ($),	145,001.50	93,713.96**	77,600.00
1990	(131,217.1)	(57,732.64)	
Median Gross Rent ($),	450.67	442.1	445.00
1990	(129.7)	(99.0)	
N	44	44	

Source: Adapted from the Chicago Department of Planning and Development
(1997).
Note: Two-tailed t-tests; * = $p < .10$; ** = $p < .05$. The figures for median family income, median home value, and median gross rent in this table and all subsequent tables are not adjusted for inflation. Figures for Chicago community areas with and without TIF are the averages of community area(s) means.

TIF tend to have slightly higher poverty rates, more Hispanic residents, and more female-headed households, the magnitude of these differences is relatively small and statistically insignificant. The most dramatic difference between TIF and non-TIF communities is the percentage of homeowners (or owner-occupied units) and median home value. Specifically, the homeownership rate for an average community with TIF is 18.6 percent. In contrast, the homeownership rate for an average community without TIF is 33.5 percent. This means that communities with higher rates of owner-occupied units are less likely to be associated with TIF. This makes sense since homeownership is frequently associated with stable communities that are not in need of public funds for revitalization. However, communities with TIF have a median home value of $145,001, while communities without TIF have a median home value of only $93,713. This suggests that TIF is actually being utilized to subsidize the redevelopment of middle- and upper-class communities.

Aggregate estimates of community change between 1979 and 1989 also reveal some differences between communities with and without TIF. During the 1980s, communities with TIF experienced rising poverty rates, as well as growing black and Hispanic residential settlement. The dramatic increase in black settlement in TIF communities is heavily influenced by a few Chicago neighborhoods that had almost no black residents in 1979 but had fifty or seventy-five black residents in 1989. These patterns, however, are not revealed in the citywide averages since increases of this size are marginal, given the magnitude of the city's total population.

To investigate the characteristics of TIF-adopting communities over time, table 13.2 compares the average socioeconomic characteristics of community areas in Chicago with TIF by its initiation date. The first time period (before 1989) reflects TIF activity in the Harold Washington administration, including Eugene Sawyer's two-year term as acting mayor after Washington's unexpected death. The second time period (1989–95) captures the first two administrations of Richard J. Daley. The third time period (1996–97) includes the first two years of Daley's third term in office. As reflected in the number of TIFs adopted in each time period, most TIF activity in Chicago has occurred since Daley became mayor, escalating considerably in his third term, hence the phrase "the city that TIFs" (Hinz 1997).

In general, there are only modest differences in the average community characteristics of Chicago TIFs over these three time periods. The racial and ethnic composition of these communities is relatively consistent, as are the overall poverty rate and the percentage of female-headed households. A notable exception is the slight tendency under the Washington and Sawyer administrations to target communities with large and

TABLE 13.2

Average Community Characteristics of Chicago TIFs by Initiation Date
(Standard Deviations in Parentheses)

	Initiated Before 1989	Initiated Between 1989 and 1995	Initiated Between 1996 and 1997
Percentage Poor	22.7	21.1	26.2
	(11.6)	(18.4)	(19.2)
Percentage Change Poor,	31.4	17.6	10.7
1980–1990	(19.6)	(31.2)	(32.4)
Percentage Black	44.5	39.4	39.9
	(38.9)	(37.7)	(34.6)
Percentage Change Black,	109.1	85.0	55.3
1980–1990	(153.6)	(186.7)	(141.2)
Percentage Hispanic	14.5	15.4	15.5
	(14.0)	(18.7)	(18.2)
Percentage Change Hispanic,	13.8	59.2	36.1
1980–1990	(51.9)	(119.2)	(82.8)
Percentage Change Population,	−4.3	−5.3	−2.2
1980–1990	(9.7)	(8.4)	(25.2)
Percentage Change Different House	7.0	10.1	14.3
in 1975 and 1985	(9.3)	(13.5)	(12.9)
Percentage of Female-Headed	23.3	23.0	26.8
Households	(11.5)	(18.5)	(18.5)
Median Family Income ($)	25,906.13	34,550.28	36,073.76
	(6,309.6)	(18,037.4)	(22,365.7)
Percentage High School Graduates	62.9	65.3	66.1
	(14.6)	(15.6)	(16.1)
Percentage of Units Owner	11.9	27.5**	10.8
Occupied	(8.8)	(24.6)	(13.7)
Median Home Value ($)	90,291.57	134,363.30	180,044.50
	(41,482.0)	(131,947.8)	(148,988.4)
Median Gross Rent ($)	410.43	443.80	475.29
	(70.1)	(111.2)	(165.2)
N	7	20	17

Sources: Adapted from the Chicago Department of Planning and Development
(1997).

Note: Two-tailed t-tests; * = $p < .10$; ** = $p < .05$; asterisks to the left show contrast with TIFs initiated between 1989 and 1995; asterisks to the right show contrast with TIFs initiated between 1996 and 1997.

growing numbers of black residents, probably because the political base of both mayors was in the black community. In contrast, the Daley administration's early use of TIF tended to target communities with larger increases in their Hispanic populations, likely reflecting the importance of the Hispanic vote in Daley's first election. A consequence of this shift away from black communities is that TIF is no longer being used to combat the deleterious consequences of extreme poverty concentration. While the newest TIFs are not targeting the most depressed communities, they are targeting areas with greater levels of economic distress, compared to the citywide averages. However, these areas also have relatively high median home values.

This pattern appears to reflect the recent use of TIF in and around several very affluent communities that include pockets of poverty. Those opposed to the use of TIF under these circumstances usually argue that TIF is intended to be used only as a development tool of last resort in places that are slum and blighted and would not develop but for the TIF funds. The overall value of residential property in these newly adopted TIF districts is thought to be an indication that these distressed areas would eventually be revitalized as a result of the community's overall economic viability. In contrast, those who support the use of TIF in these types of communities usually argue that these pockets of poverty are not benefiting from the economic strength of the community and that development of these distressed areas will not take place in a timely, planned, and coordinated manner without TIF. Unfortunately, it remains unclear whether or not TIF in these types of neighborhoods is appropriate and good public policy.

The most revealing aspects of this comparison, however, are not the average community characteristics, but the level of variation (as measured in the standard deviations) of these community characteristics over time. For example, while TIFs adopted under the Daley administration have targeted communities with a slightly higher average poverty rate, this administration has used TIFs on a much broader range of communities compared to previous administrations. The use of TIF in neighborhoods with higher and lower levels of poverty is reflected in the substantially larger standard deviations for TIFs initiated since 1989 (11.6 for TIFs initiated before 1989, 18.4 for TIFs initiated 1989–95, 19.2 for TIFs initiated in 1996–97). Clearly, TIF is being used in Chicago to address areas threatened by early stages of urban decay, as well as more severally distressed areas characterized by prolonged and persistent disinvestment.

These figures also suggest that the use of TIF during the early years of the Daley administration is associated with the gentrification of Chicago's neighborhoods. This is revealed in the tendency of newer TIF districts to have lower levels of residential stability (as measured by the percentage change of residents living in a different house in 1975 as compared to 1985), higher median family incomes, higher median home values, and more owner-occupied units. These patterns suggest that TIF has been associated with neighborhood change, specifically gentrification, since residential turnover appears to be attracting slightly more affluent residents who can afford more expensive homes. Unfortunately, these descriptive figures cannot distinguish between TIF as a cause of neighborhood change or TIF as used to further bolster already gentrified areas.

DOES TIF INITIATION STATUS MATTER?

One of the interesting questions raised by the Addison case is whether municipal governments are targeting communities based on their ethnic and racial composition. One way to investigate this issue is to compare the characteristics of communities with private developer-initiated TIFs to the characteristics of communities with city-initiated TIFs. In Chicago, the TIF process can be initiated by either a private developer(s) seeking capital investment for a particular project or by the city's Department of Planning and Development, which then seeks private developers to pursue the (re)development objectives of a particular project. The city's targeting of communities with particular characteristics might suggest possible misuse.

The figures presented in table 13.3 illustrate that roughly two-thirds of all TIFs in Chicago are developer initiated. The city's reliance on private developers to spur the TIF process has steadily declined since the election of Mayor Daley. Before 1989, none of the city's seven TIFs were city driven, whereas almost half of all TIFs adopted since 1995 have been city-initiated.

It should not be much of a surprise that developer-initiated TIFs tend to be located in slightly more affluent communities since there is usually less risk involved in these projects. The only substantial difference between developer- and city-initiated TIFs is the percentage of Hispanic residents in the community. Specifically, developer-initiated TIFs are in communities with an average Hispanic population of 11.6 percent, whereas city-initiated TIFs are in communities with an average Hispanic population of 23.2 percent. The central question, then, is obvious: What accounts for this disparity?

One explanation is that the city is targeting Hispanic communities in order to regulate patterns of Hispanic residential settlement, much like the village of Addison targeted Green Oaks and Michael Lane. This

TABLE 13.3
Average Community Characteristics of Chicago TIFs by Initiation Status
(Standard Deviations in Parentheses)

	Developer Initiated	City Initiated
Percentage Poor	22.0	26.0
	(16.9)	(19.5)
Percentage Change Poor, 1980–1990	16.7	18.0
	(31.9)	(27.9)
Percentage Black	41.0	39.0
	(37.2)	(34.0)
Percentage Change Black, 1980–1990	83.1	66.8
	(172.9)	(143.9)
Percentage Hispanic	11.6**	23.2
	(12.1)	(24.2)
Percentage Change Hispanic, 1980–1990	61.2*	4.2
	(110.7)	(40.8)
Percentage Change Population, 1980–1990	–6.4	1.2
	(10.4)	(25.5)
Percentage Change Different House in	11.7	10.2
1975 and 1985	(10.8)	(16.5)
Percentage of Single Female-Headed	23.5	26.7
Households	(16.6)	(19.4)
Median Family Income ($)	34,466.40	32,257.89
	(18,227.8)	(20,148.3)
Percentage High School Graduates	67.2	60.8
	(14.2)	(17.3)
Percentage of Units Owner Occupied	19.4	16.6
	(20.4)	(21.0)
Median Home Value ($)	146,698.40	141,365.10
	(135,923.3)	(125,367.4)
Median Gross Rent ($)	455.93	439.36
	(114.8)	(161.3)
N	30	14

Sources: Adapted from the Chicago Department of Planning and Development (1997).
Note: Two-tailed t-tests; * = p < .10; ** = p < .05.

conclusion seems highly unlikely since the rate of Hispanic change between 1979 and 1989 in communities with city-initiated TIFs is much lower than that of communities with developer-initiated TIFs. This suggests that city-initiated TIFs are targeting stable Hispanic communities, rather than communities undergoing racial and/or ethnic change. The same cannot be said for developer-initiated TIFs, which are more likely to be in communities with relatively small yet rapidly growing Hispanic communities.

It is possible that because of the Addison case, private developers may be avoiding the use of TIFs in projects located in and around established Hispanic communities. It is important to remember that all (re)development projects, including those that use TIF, involve some level of risk for borrowers and lenders. Risk is usually a function of a given geographic area's economic potential. However, there are other components of risk, including the threat of litigation. Even the perception that the use of TIFs in Hispanic communities increases the threat of legal action could have the consequence of stifling (re)development activity in these areas. But why would local municipalities such as the city of Chicago be immune to the perceived increased risk associated with TIF in Hispanic communities? After all, the city's Department of Planning and Development continues to pursue TIF projects in these areas in spite of what happened in Addison. One major difference between a large municipal government such as the city of Chicago and private developers is the amount of liability each can accept. A $25 million settlement against a large municipal government may have no effect or only a marginal effect on its fiscal health, while a settlement of this size against a private corporation may directly or indirectly threaten its existence.

THE QUESTION OF TIF MISUSE TO ALTER PATTERNS OF RESIDENTIAL SEGREGATION

Overall, the Addison case clearly illustrates how TIFs might be used to adjust patterns of residential segregation, but the analysis of Chicago's community areas with TIF districts did not reveal any patterns that conclusively demonstrate a pattern of abuse. The tendency for TIFs to be used in communities with a wide range of socioeconomic characteristics demonstrates the breadth of this development tool and its potential to address various degrees of urban decay. The tendency for city-initiated TIFs to target communities with stable Hispanic populations is likely an indication that the city views these areas as important sources of economic growth rather than places that threaten the overall viability of the city.

The examples of Addison and Chicago, and their implications for

TIF misuse elsewhere, deserve further comment. The Illinois Tax Increment Allocation Act sets forth relatively stringent criteria for the TIF adoption process compared to those of other states. The alleged TIF misuse in Addison, therefore, is not likely a result of a weak but for clause or a permissive factors test, and suggests that states with more flexible adoption criteria may be at even greater risk for the type of TIF misuse that occurred in Addison. Similarly, one might expect that Chicago's notorious reputation as one of the nation's most segregated cities would make it more likely to engage in the use of TIF to reinforce patterns of residential segregation. The preliminary finding that TIF in Chicago is being used appropriately implies that residentially integrated municipalities are probably not engaging in this type of TIF misuse.

The potential misuse of TIF, whether real or perceived, has resulted in several policy changes at the city and state levels. Under a new city policy, "any expenditure of tax increment financing funds [by the city of Chicago] will require the advanced approval of the city's Office of Budget and Management" (Hinz 1997). Previously, the planning commissioner and comptroller made these decisions on their own. While this new level of oversight is a response to the city's increasing use of TIF for (re)development projects, it also reflects an awareness of potential TIF abuse highlighted by the Addison case.[8]

Even though the state has not directly responded to the Addison case by adopting new TIF regulations, the legislature is considering a bill that would reform the Illinois Tax Increment Allocation Redevelopment Act. Some of the changes proposed in House Bill 525 include these:

1. The adoption of formal definitions for the factors required to designate an area as blighted;

2. The formulation of a housing impact study and guaranteed relocation assistance equal to that required by the Federal Relocation Assistance Act for proposed TIF districts that call for the removal and/or demolition of ten or more inhabited residential units and/or contain seventy-five or more inhabited residential units;

3. The disclosure of a municipality's plans for TIF-adoption via mail notices to residential units if 10 or more units are to be removed;

4. The appointment of at least one member of the Joint Review Board (an oversight panel required by state law to review the spending of tax money on development projects) to be an affordable housing advocate if ten or more units are to be removed;

5. The holding of a pre-designation public hearing if more than fifty residential units are in the proposed TIF district. (Metropolitan Planning Council 1997)

Unfortunately, it remains unclear whether these new regulations, if adopted, would prevent the future misuse of TIF for the purpose of altering patterns of residential segregation.

In conclusion, the Addison case clearly illustrates the potential costs associated of misusing TIF. Municipal officials need to make sure that residents of a targeted area do not perceive their actions as hostile or unfriendly. This may even require proactive campaigning to generate community support for proposed TIF projects. Neighborhoods undergoing gentrification, like those frequently targeted by the city of Chicago, have the potential to generate significant community opposition to TIF, given the heightened fears of displacement. Neighborhood-based organizations in a wide range of communities, including areas threatened by early stages of urban decline and more severely distressed areas, may be able to play an important role in managing this fear; however, these organizations need well-trained staff so that they can effectively work with and informally monitor developers and municipal officials who are implementing very complex TIF projects. Similarly, neighborhood-based organizations that advocate for the interests of the disadvantaged need to educate residents in a responsible manner so that they can work with developers and municipal employees to adopt TIFs that do not adversely impact certain groups.

ACKNOWLEDGMENTS

I would like to thank Peter Skosey and Kathy Dehm for their assistance on this project.

NOTES

1. Illinois TIF legislation has undergone several revisions since its initial inception. By 1984, 147 TIF districts had been adopted, but only 26 districts in the state produced any growth in the equalized assessed value of the land within the targeted (re)development area. In 1985, a state initiative gave municipalities the authority and funding to create TIF districts based on the amount of growth in sales tax revenue to all districts created before 1 January 1987. As a result, the number of new TIF districts grew to 137 at the time this sunset provision went into effect. Concern that the state had an unacceptable liability for these newly created sales tax districts resulted in further revisions to existing TIF legislation. Specifically, "the changes both limited and phased out over time the amount of sales tax growth a TIF district could use to make a claim for state aid. It also restricted the percentage of a municipality's total EAV [equalized assessed value] and total area that could be included in a district and mandated that the DOR [Department of Revenue] conduct a review of all TIF districts that had been certified to receive state aid" (Taxpayers' Federation of Illinois 1995).

2. Background information on the Village of Addison is from U.S. Census figures found in *The Local Community Fact Book, 1990* (Chicago Fact Book Consortium 1990).

3. One of the first steps in designating an area as a TIF district in Illinois is determining whether the property meets certain conditions, also known as a "factors test." An improved area (in contrast to a vacant area) can be declared blighted and become a TIF district if at least five of the following factors are present: age; dilapidation; obsolescence; deterioration; illegal use of individual structures; presence of structures below minimum code standards; excessive vacancies; overcrowding of structures and community facilities; lack of ventilation, light, or sanitary facilities; inadequate utilities; excessive land coverage; deleterious land use or layout; depreciation or lack of physical maintenance; or lack of community planning.

4. Again, it is important to note that no finding of guilt or innocence was established in the Addison case, and the out-of-court settlement sealed all relevant documents. As a result, it is unclear whether the village engaged in a conspiracy or was simply oblivious to the nature of its actions.

5. The geographic distribution of TIF in Illinois is somewhat atypical of national trends. For example, Klemanski (1990) reports that 28 percent of central city jurisdictions use TIF, compared to 11 percent of suburban jurisdictions and 9 percent of independent jurisdictions.

6. The aggregation of census data by communities in Chicago dates back to the early part of this century when Ernest Burgess was laying the foundation of what would become the Chicago School of Sociology. After conducting extensive research on Chicago, Burgess and his colleagues concluded that the city was made up of interdependent, "natural" community areas; as a result of his efforts, he was able to ensure that census tracts did not overlap the boundaries of local communities, allowing for a wealth of information on each community. These categories remain relevant today even though several modest changes in the boundaries of actual communities have occurred since the original delineation of these community areas (Venkatesh 1997).

7. This analysis provides only descriptive socio-economic characteristics of communities with TIF, and does not estimate the determinants of the TIF-adoption process or the causal impact of TIF on neighborhood change. These limitations result from the relatively small number of observations, i.e., TIF districts in Chicago.

8. It is important to note that the Addison case alone did not precipitate this administrative change. Mayor Daley has come under some public pressure for using TIF to provide financial benefits to his supporters, including private real estate developers and law firms with close ties to city hall and the mayor's family. The city has also been criticized for spending TIF funds on luxury furniture for the planning commissioner's office.

REFERENCES

Chicago Department of Planning and Development. 1997. *Existing tax increment financing districts*. Chicago: City of Chicago.

Chicago Fact Book Consortium. 1990. *Local community fact book: Chicago metropolitan area, 1990.* Chicago: University of Illinois Press.

Dye, Richard F. 1997. A comparative analysis of tax increment financing in northeastern Illinois. In *Assessing the impact of tax increment financing in northeastern Illinois: An empirical analysis and case studies,* ed. R. Calia. Chicago: The Civic Federation.

Girona, Jose P. 1997. Addison's TIF plan challenge as being racist. *The Chicago Tribune* (May 11): Section 4, 1.

Halpern, Robert. 1995. *Rebuilding the inner city.* New York: Columbia University Press.

Hinz, Greg. 1997. The city that TIFs. *Crain's Chicago Business* (July 7): 1a.

———. 1997. Tighter controls over TIF spending. *Crain's Chicago Business* (August 4): 4b.

Hirsch, Arnold R. 1983. *The making of the second ghetto: Race and housing in Chicago, 1940–1960.* Cambridge: Cambridge University Press.

Illinois Department of Revenue. 1992. *1992 Illinois property tax statistics.* Springfield: State of Illinois.

Klemanski, John S. 1990. Using tax increment financing for urban redevelopment projects. *Economic Development Quarterly* 14 (February): 1.

Metropolitan Planning Council. 1997. *Recommendations for House Bill 525, reform of the Illinois Tax Increment Allocation Redevelopment Act* (August 19).

Paetsch, James R., and Roger K. Dahlstrom. 1990. Tax increment financing: What it is and how it works. In *Financing economic development: An institutional response,* ed. R. D. Bingham, E. W. Hill, and S. B. White. New York: Sage Publications.

United States District Court for the Northern District of Illinois Eastern Division. 1997. In *Plantiffs v. Village of Addison, Illinois.*

Venkatesh, Sudhir A. 1997. A city of community areas: How sociologists built Chicago. Unpublished manuscript. Harvard University Society of Fellows.

CHAPTER 14

The Use of Tax Increment Financing in Redeveloping Brownfields in Minnesota

Jeff Zachman
and
Susan D. Steinwell

Although the problem of underutilized, contaminated property had been recognized earlier, the term *Brownfields* emerged nationally in the 1990s as a moniker for those properties with a real or perceived stigma of pollution that complicated, or even inhibited, their purchase, sale, financing, refinancing, redevelopment, and ultimate reuse. TIF and several of Minnesota's environmental laws, including the Minnesota Environmental Response and Liability Act (MERLA), have allowed for the successful redevelopment of many Brownfields in the state (Minnesota State Legislature 115B.01–241, 1996).[1]

We have selected for analysis two case studies employing TIF within the context of Minnesota's Brownfields regulatory climate. Both case studies involve redevelopment of properties in two neighboring suburbs in the same county within the Twin Cities metropolitan area; both further involve contaminated (or formerly contaminated) properties. The first case concerns the redevelopment of a federal and state superfund site in the city of New Brighton. Although many elements of the first case make it a complex story, not the least of which is the site's superfund status, the use of TIF is fairly straightforward. The second case study regards the redevelopment of industrial property in the city of Roseville, Minnesota. This case shows how elements of TIF law may be used to address the redevelopment of contaminated property, and particularly property where contamination problems were unknown at the time redevelopment began. Together, these two case studies show how TIF and MERLA have been used to redevelop properties with significant environmental problems.

BROWNFIELDS REGULATORY
ENVIRONMENT IN MINNESOTA

A review of the Brownfields regulatory environment is necessary to understand how tax increment financing has been used in Minnesota within the context of Brownfields redevelopment. The nationwide emergence of Brownfields as a community issue is partially the result of environmental cleanup laws, such as "Superfund," as well as the attendant potential liability associated with merely owning contaminated property. Historically, MERLA, which is Minnesota's counterpart to CERCLA, exacted a negative impact on property values and redevelopment potential. Moreover, the effects of superfund liability on real estate activity typically had their strongest impact on urban centers (Schwehr 1991).

The legacy of the Twin Cities of Minneapolis and St. Paul, as well as their surrounding suburbs, is that of a moderately sized industrial base around which the cities expanded. Residential development and a general shift from heavy to light industry often placed modern community needs at odds with older industrial sites that were built at a time when environmental laws and compliance requirements were few or nonexistent. The fear of environmental liability has, in fact, been one of the forces responsible for "urban sprawl" both in the Twin Cities metropolitan area and in other areas throughout the Midwest (Larson and Harley 1995). Liability fears and the potentially high costs associated with cleaning up and redeveloping older industrial sites prompted many private and public developers to direct their attention away from Brownfields and toward "Greenfields," agricultural or undeveloped areas surrounding the urban core.

Against this backdrop, city planners and private developers searched for ways to capitalize on the presence of acres of underutilized land in the urban core. Many metropolitan areas face pressures to extend their service area boundaries at a tremendous cost to both infrastructure budgets and the environment. Given this, and given the reality that urban core areas continue to suffer from a lack of new development, which can maintain living-wage jobs, middle-class households, and property tax revenue, it was time to take action. The idea of coupling environmental liability relief with public financing incentives evolved as a viable solution to the Brownfields dilemma.

The first legislative attempt to resolve Brownfield redevelopment issues was a three-paragraph amendment to MERLA enacted in 1988. With this, parties interested in property transfer and redevelopment obtained the statutory tools and administrative cooperation to investigate and remediate contaminated sites. In exchange for reimbursing the Minnesota Pollution Control Agency (MPCA) for its staff review time, these parties could receive limited liability protection and the benefit of technical oversight and approval from an expanded MPCA staff specifically dedicated to providing such assistance to the public. The Minnesota State Legislature and MPCA eventually expanded the initial effort into an award-winning comprehensive program of liability assurances, technical guidance, and environmental protection known as the "Land Recycling Act of 1992."[2]

The Land Recycling Act has subsequently undergone several amendments and is administered by the MPCA as the Voluntary Investigation and Cleanup (VIC) Program.[3] VIC's hallmark is both successes in responding to the needs of the private sector in a timely way and a "menu" of liability and administrative assurances that are often tailor made to individual site investigation, cleanup, and development efforts. Both responsible and voluntary parties may receive a variety of written assurances that acknowledge their investigation and cleanup actions and provide liability protection, depending on the scope of those actions. Parties may select from the VIC's menu the form of assurance best suited to the site and particular transaction dynamics. The most comprehensive protection is afforded by the "Certificate of Completion of Response Actions," which acknowledges a thorough investigation of soils and groundwater at a site; sets the standards for cleanup; severely limits the state's ability to reopen its cleanup decisions; and protects innocent purchasers from future liability in the event the cleanup fails or new information regarding site pollution becomes known. The least comprehensive form of protection is a "no action" letter. This, in essence, states that the MPCA, while reserving its right to reopen the matter, is satisfied with the cleanup and will request no further action of the voluntary party.

While VIC program liability assurances have greatly helped in returning polluted urban land to productive use, there are those who, due to ignorance of the VIC program, claim a fear of complexity, lack of sufficient financial incentives such as TIF, or other reasons in their argument to maintain a preference for Greenfields development. Moreover, the VIC program is a state-run program that is grounded in state law. For those fearful of the federal government's superfund enforcement program, VIC initially offered little assurance that the United

States Environmental Protection Agency (EPA) would not become involved in a property's cleanup. Federal dollars dedicated to the support of state superfund programs and the cleanup of heavily polluted sites on the federal National Priorities List (the NPL or Superfund List) are managed through the regional offices of the EPA. CERCLA and other federal statutes give the federal government jurisdiction to intervene, supervise, or assume control of the cleanup of contaminated properties. The MPCA addressed this issue by entering into a Memorandum of Agreement with the EPA's Region 5 office in Chicago.[4] The Memorandum of Agreement states that when a site in Minnesota (other than federal NPL sites) has been investigated or remediated in accordance with the practices and procedures of the VIC program, and after the MPCA has issued one of several available assurances, the EPA "will not plan or anticipate any federal action under superfund law unless, in exceptional circumstances, the site poses an imminent and substantial endangerment or emergency situation" (Notice of Availability 1997). Such language is intended to provide VIC recipients with assurances that the EPA will not question or reopen state decisions regarding cleanups.[5] The Memorandum of Agreement provides good faith assurances from the federal government regarding its future interest in a property and, together with other federal actions, such as prospective purchaser and lender liability guidance, has further stimulated confidence in private redevelopment of Brownfields in Minnesota.

TAX INCREMENT FINANCING IN MINNESOTA

In Minnesota, tax increment financing is a method of financing public and other qualifying improvements from the increased property taxes generated from new development that would not occur "but for" the assistance of the public authority (Minnesota State Legislature 115B.175, 1996). TIF powers are primarily exercised directly by cities or governmental units that are controlled by cities. Like municipalities, housing and redevelopment, port, economic, and rural development finance authorities all may exercise TIF powers under Minnesota law. Special laws also have granted TIF powers to other local units of government. In general, TIF may be used to finance six basic types of activities: redevelopment or renewal of blighted areas, provision of low- and moderate-income housing, economic development, development of sites where soil conditions must be corrected, hazardous substance cleanup sites, and development and redevelopment of mined underground spaces (Minnesota State Legislature, 469.176, 1996).

A soil condition district is defined as a type of tax increment financing district where the presence of hazardous substances, pollution, or contaminants requires removal or remedial action and the estimated costs of such an environmental cleanup exceed the current fair market value of the land (Minnesota State Legislature, 469.174, 1996). There are some exceptions to the requirement that the proposed removal and remedial action exceed the property's fair market value. Prior to 1995, soils-condition TIF districts were available only as a vehicle to correct geotechnical conditions necessary to permit new construction. The statute was amended in 1995 to allow public bodies with TIF powers to create a soils-condition TIF district to finance the costs of an environmental cleanup through TIF.

In addition to a soils-condition district, a hazardous-substance TIF subdistrict may be created to use the tax increment to finance the costs of cleaning up sites contaminated by hazardous substances. An authority may use TIF to pay for an environmental cleanup under a plan approved by the MPCA, or to finance the costs of an environmental cleanup when the private parties responsible for the pollution cannot be identified and superfund money is not available (Minnesota State Legislature, 469.175, 1995). A hazardous-substance subdistrict is essentially a TIF district within a TIF district. To collect the extra funds that are needed to finance a hazardous waste cleanup, Minnesota law allows the original net tax capacity in hazardous-substance subdistricts to be reduced substantially. The original net tax capacity is essentially the base from which the tax increment generated by the redevelopment is measured; that is, it is the amount of property taxes generated by a particular district at the time when the TIF district is created. Reducing the original tax capacity increases the amount of the tax increment available to the TIF authority. A hazardous-substance subdistrict can likewise include land that is adjacent to the contaminated areas. Minnesota law also allows the period of time for collecting the tax increment generated from the hazardous-substance subdistrict to be extended beyond the normal statutory limits (Minnesota State Legislature, 469.176, 1995). After the TIF authority certifies that the costs of the cleanup, as set forth in the MPCA-approved cleanup plan, have been paid or reimbursed, the original net tax capacity is restored to the subdistrict.

The additional tax increment generated in a hazardous-substance subdistrict must be used only to pay for or reimburse specific associated costs; these include the expense of the hazardous substance, pollutant, contaminant, and petroleum clean-ups and testing, demolition, and soil corrections. Other related administrative and legal charges, including MPCA's cost of reviewing the developments' environmental cleanup plans or litigation expenses of the Minnesota attorney general to bring a cost recovery action against a responsible party under MERLA or

CERCLA, are covered as well. If litigation succeeds in recovering the environmental cleanup costs, such funds will be treated as excess increment to be distributed by the county auditor as directed under Minnesota Statute 469.176 subd. 2.

CASE STUDY 1: THE MACGILLIS AND GIBBS
SUPERFUND SITE—NEW BRIGHTON, MINNESOTA

The MacGillis and Gibbs Company and the Bell Lumber and Pole Company operated separate wood treatment facilities on adjacent parts of a sixty-eight acre NPL site in the city of New Brighton. Wood treatment began at the site in the 1920s. The adjacent sites are treated as a single NPL site by the EPA due to their proximity and similarity in wood treatment processes. The MPCA treats the properties as two separate sites. Little else ties these two sites together, as each had different regulatory and remedial trajectories. The Bell Lumber and Pole Company, acting as a "responsible party" under state and federal superfund program oversight, implemented an approved remedy for contaminated soils, groundwater, and debris at its property. Facility operations that in the past caused site pollution and community criticism (principally odors), have been moved into enclosed buildings with process and air-emission treatment controls.

By contrast, Bell Pole's neighbor, the MacGillis and Gibbs Company, lacked the resources to finance the cleanup of its property and became the focus of local, state, and federal attention from at least 1984 until August 1997, when the property was conveyed to the city of New Brighton. The MacGillis and Gibbs site was significantly contaminated. Estimates of the total 1997 environmental cleanup bill range from between $20 million and $25 million. Both the EPA and the MPCA had placed environmental liens against the property. Dilapidated buildings, stockpiled debris, and abandoned equipment could be seen throughout the twenty-four-acre site. The company's failure to pay real estate taxes on portions of its property since at least 1982 created a lien of back real estate taxes totaling at least $600,000 by 1997.

New Brighton, which has long taken an active role in environmental issues, had targeted the MacGillis and Gibbs property as an impediment to realizing the full potential of the city's Brighton Corporate Park redevelopment area. The city grew impatient with the perceived slow pace of the publicly financed environmental cleanup and began actively encouraging the EPA and the MPCA to initiate the federal and state-financed clean-up of the property as soon as possible. In the end, the city commenced condemnation proceedings against MacGillis and Gibbs to hasten the company's wind-down of operations, commencement of the environmental cleanup, and redevelopment of the site. When the city authorized use of tax increment financing at the area encompassing the MacGillis and Gibbs property, council members agreed that the TIF law's mandated but for test was easily met: unlikely private investment meant that any environmental cleanup and the return of the property to the tax rolls would not occur but for the active participation of the city.

The availability of federal and state superfund money relieved the city from the burden of directly financing the environmental cleanup of the MacGillis and Gibbs property. The fact that the site required cleaning with public funds, however, presented a redevelopment issue. The city was concerned that even after the property was clean, redevelopment by private parties would be stymied by the fear of "after-acquired" environmental liability. The MacGillis and Gibbs property was subject to environmental liens in favor of the EPA or the MPCA. In addition to those liens, both agencies could seek to recover the cleanup funds that the federal government and the state had spent directly from future owners of the property. The city knew that no one would be interested in buying property that was subject to a $25 million lien or that could be the subject of litigation brought by the federal and state governments to recover their cleanup costs. Liability assurances from the MPCA's VIC program alone would be inadequate in the MacGillis and Gibbs case because the site was a federal superfund site and because federal funds were being used to finance the cleanup. VIC assurances, thus, were and remain best suited to sites where the federal government has not been involved.

To increase the chances that redevelopment would succeed, New Brighton negotiated a covenant not to sue with the EPA, the United States Department of Justice, the State of Minnesota, and the MPCA. This covenant, which is also known as a "prospective purchaser agreement," states that neither the federal nor the state government will seek to recover its cleanup costs from the city or the city's buyers. In exchange for that promise, the city offered to provide the EPA and the MPCA with certain benefits, including easement rights across the property, restrictive covenants governing the way the property may be developed and used, and a share of the city's net gains upon resale of the MacGillis and Gibbs property. The covenant not to sue provides that the city will retain only 20 percent of its net gains upon resale, but will first be able to deduct its out-of-pocket costs of acquiring the property and reselling parcels to third parties, as well as the cost of acquiring a large off-site parcel for storm water retention.

Other city development costs are to be recovered through the tax increment. The twenty-four-acre MacGillis and Gibbs site is within a

TIF district known as "Brighton Corporate Park III." Funds generated by the tax increment will be used to finance the costs of constructing infrastructure, including a road, storm sewers and utilities, clearing the site, and relocating nearby property owners. Projections made by the city of New Brighton in late 1996 showed that the Brighton Corporate Park III would ultimately be economically viable only if the city were able to resell a substantial portion of the park to a potential taxpayer by late 1997 or early 1998. For that reason, the city was negotiating to sell a portion of the MacGillis and Gibbs site to a local manufacturer interested in expanding its operations within the city concurrent with the city's work on the covenant not to sue.

The city considered creating a hazardous-substance TIF subdistrict within the Brighton Corporate Park III district to help recapture at least a portion of the costs related to the property's contamination. Even though the city's development costs were great, the city elected to not create the hazardous substance subdistrict, partly because it would spend a relatively small sum in direct environmental cleanup costs and partly because such subdistricts can be unpopular among other taxing jurisdictions, such as school districts. Hazardous-substance subdistricts are unpopular because they essentially eliminate the ability of other local units of government to collect any taxes from a particular property for many years. More significantly, however, the city determined that the financial payoff from creating the hazardous-substance subdistrict would have been minimal. By 1997, the twenty-four-acre MacGillis and Gibbs property had an original tax capacity of only $25,861, a relatively small amount given the property's size and location. The county assessor's office had reduced the property's assessed valuation in recognition of its contamination. Even if the original tax capacity of the MacGillis and Gibbs property had been written down to zero, the maximum amount the city would have recognized in additional TIF revenue would have been $25,861 per year from the property.

The MacGillis and Gibbs case illustrates one of the shortcomings in Minnesota's hazardous-substance subdistrict TIF mechanism. "The more severe the problem, the less likely a hazardous substance subdistrict is going to help because the county will have the property's value on the books for much less than a property should be worth," explains Kevin Locke, New Brighton's director of community development. If the environmental contamination has been a recognized condition, chances are that the value of the property for real estate tax purposes has been substantially reduced. Therefore, when the price of environmental remediation totals millions of dollars, it may make little economic sense for a public body with TIF powers to finance an environmental cleanup of any magnitude using the additional funds generated by a hazardous-substance subdistrict alone. The additional tax increment from the hazardous-substance subdistrict "write-down" may not be sufficient to finance the environmental cleanup. In the case of MacGillis and Gibbs, for example, the estimated cost of the environmental cleanup of the property totaled $25 million; but the funds generated by a hazardous-waste subdistrict alone would have annually generated only one-tenth of a percent of the cleanup's estimated total costs.

CASE STUDY 2: THE TWIN LAKES DEVELOPMENT DISTRICT—ROSEVILLE, MINNESOTA

A few miles to the south of the MacGillis and Gibbs site in New Brighton is the Twin Lakes Development. The city of Roseville authorized the use of tax increment financing to foster the economic redevelopment of Twin Lakes. The city and a development and construction company, Ryan Twin Lakes Limited Partnership (Ryan), entered into a development agreement, which specified that Ryan would acquire the land, raze and clean off the existing structures, and construct new structures for industrial and commercial uses. Ryan's prepurchase environmental investigations showed few reasons to be concerned. In fact, prior to Ryan's acquisition and construction, petroleum releases from off-site trucking terminals were thought to be Twin Lakes' only environmental problem, a problem viewed as manageable.

After acquiring the land, demolishing the buildings, and preparing the land for construction, Ryan discovered that portions of the property were seriously contaminated. The company found that low-lying areas of the property had been filled with demolition debris, telephone poles, and other materials. Elsewhere, Ryan discovered broken and undocumented sewer lines that had leaked effluent contaminated by solvents. In the end, it was determined that the site was contaminated by creosote, solvents, and petroleum, with cleanup estimated at $2.7 million. With the economic viability of the area in jeopardy, Roseville ultimately amended its redevelopment plan and tax increment financing plan to create a hazardous-substance subdistrict at Twin Lakes. The original net capacity of portions of the Twin Lakes development was written down to $0, which generated an adjusted additional tax increment of $1,546,045. Even though the pre-TIF values of the Twin Lakes development district were relatively high, the hazardous-substance subdistrict would not generate enough extra increment to cover the estimated total cleanup costs. The remainder of the estimated $2.7 million needed to finance the additional development costs came from adjusting the financial components of the development agreement between Ryan and the city. For example, the development's density and the minimum market values of the improvements to be constructed were increased to generate a greater tax increment.

With the financing, Ryan was able to clean up the land and build the improvements that the city had envisioned at Twin Lakes. The ultimate success of the project, however, also depended on removing the "environmental contamination" stigma from the site. When the cleanup was complete, the MPCA's VIC program ultimately issued Ryan one of the first Certificates of Completion under the Land Recycling Act. The certificate acknowledges that the Twin Lakes cleanup was completed to the satisfaction of the state and, more importantly, assures Ryan, all future owners, occupants, mortgage lenders, and others who may become associated with the property, that the MPCA will not order them to clean up and pay the costs of cleaning up historic contamination.

CONCLUSION

As the two case examples illustrate, both TIF and the Land Recycling Act can provide real estate developers and lenders with the financing and liability protection needed to address redevelopment needs. Even so, additional protection and financing are sometimes needed. Because the typical environmental cleanup is a multimillion-dollar undertaking, creating a hazardous-substance subdistrict under Minnesota law will generally produce insufficient funds alone to pay for or to finance an environmental cleanup. Property that is known to be contaminated frequently has a reduced valuation for real estate tax purposes. Even when the contamination is unknown, the value of property targeted for redevelopment may be depressed. Under either scenario, the additional tax increment generated by creating a hazardous-substance subdistrict may not produce sufficient funds to pay for or finance a multimillion-dollar environmental cleanup.

Minnesota law does allow a soils condition district (as opposed to a hazardous-substance subdistrict) to be created to pay for the costs of an environmental cleanup through TIF. A city or other public authority, however, may be reluctant to direct all of the tax increment from a district toward environmental cleanup alone. Other development costs, including land acquisition and infrastructure reconstruction, need to be financed as well. Finally, as helpful as the Land Recycling Act and VIC program have been in encouraging redevelopment of Brownfields, additional assurances, and even covenants not to sue from the federal government, may be needed in some cases.

Laws passed after the Land Recycling Act was enacted established two competitive environmental cleanup grant programs that are administered separately by the state Department of Trade and Economic Development and the Metropolitan Council, a regional governmental body in the seven-county Twin City metropolitan area.[6] Under these grant programs, a municipality must match at least 25 percent of a cleanup project's costs. The local match may be paid with tax increment, regional, state, or federal funds available for the redevelopment of Brownfields or with other funds available to a municipality. Under 1997 legislation, for example, if a city establishes a TIF district or hazardous-substance subdistrict to pay for part of the local match requirement under the grant programs, the district or subdistrict will not be subject to state aid reductions under Minnesota's Statute 273.1399. Both grant programs, at least implicitly, recognize that TIF alone may generate insufficient funds to finance what may be a multimillion-dollar environmental cleanup. Additional funds, whether from private parties (those responsible for the pollution or volunteers) or through other public programs, will likely be needed to help finance the significant costs of an environmental cleanup.

NOTES

1. Other Minnesota environmental statutes have been successfully used to promote economic redevelopment and environmental remediation. Notably, the Minnesota Petroleum Tank Cleanup Act provides responsible parties and volunteers with up to 90 percent of the costs of cleaning up properties contaminated by leaking petroleum tanks. A similar fund for properties contaminated by dry cleaning chemicals also exists. See Minnesota State Legislature 115B.47–51 (1996).

2. The Land Recycling Act consisted of a set of amendments to MERLA. See Minnesota State Legislature, 115B.175–179 (1996).

3. The Minnesota VIC Program received one of the Ford Foundation's 1994 Innovations in State and Local Government Awards recognizing exemplary new programs and policies that address important social and economic issues. The award carried a one hundred thousand dollar grant. Nominees were evaluated against a number of criteria, including their creativity and the transferability of programs to other jurisdictions. Several states have since modeled their voluntary cleanup programs on the Minnesota VIC Program.

4. The Memorandum of Agreement addressing Minnesota VIC Program assurances is, in actuality, an addendum to the Superfund Memorandum of Agreement (which addresses all state and federal superfund activity) between the EPA and the Minnesota Pollution Control Agency. It is documented in a 3 May 1995 letter from Valdus V. Adamkus, EPA regional administrator in Chicago, to Mr. Charles W. Williams, commissioner of the Minnesota Pollution Control Agency.

254 JEFF ZACHMAN AND SUSAN D. STEINWELL

5. At the writing of this chapter, the U.S. EPA has issued a Notice of Availability of Final Draft Guidance for Developing Superfund Memoranda of Agreement (MOA) Language Concerning State Voluntary Cleanup Programs. See *Federal Register* (9 September 1997). This notice accepting public comment outlines guidance for developing MOA that would preclude highly contaminated sites, as determined by a scoring program, from being eligible to participate in Minnesota's VIC program and, therefore, from receiving certain state-issued liability protection. Many Brownfields sites (including highly contaminated sites) that have already received liability protection under Minnesota's existing MOA with the EPA were investigated and remediated quickly in the VIC Program, in part due to the existence of the MOA. The new guidance, if finalized as currently drafted, threatens to reduce private and public investment activity in Brownfields and slow redevelopment by involving the EPA.

6. There are several programs or funding sources that provide financing necessary for the cleanup of Brownfields in Minnesota, all of which have some administrative role played by the Minnesota Pollution Control Agency or the Minnesota Department of Agriculture: the state Department of Trade and Economic Development administers the Contaminated Land Cleanup Grant Program (used for response action implementation costs); the Metropolitan Council administers the Metropolitan Livable Communities Act Grant Program (also used for response action implementation costs); the state Department of Revenue administers the Petro Fund (used for tank-related petroleum cleanups); the Agricultural Chemical Compensation and Reimbursement Account (used for agricultural chemical cleanup); and the Dry Cleaner Fund (used for dry cleaning chemical cleanup). During the 1997 legislative session, funding for some of these programs was expanded or further secured, and eligibility requirements were broadened. New funds and programs were also created: the state Department of Trade and Economic Development now provides grants for preliminary investigation costs and the cost of development of response action plans (including the costs of site acquisition, related demolition, and site preparation). See Minnesota State Legislature, Chapter 246 (1997). The Department of Trade and Economic Development can now provide grants for cleanup of sites impacted by petroleum contamination where no tank-related release can be established and at larger, tank farm sites (both types of sites are excluded from Petro Fund as a source of cleanup funds). See Minnesota State Legislature, Chapter 200, Article 2 (1997). New provisions of the Tax Bill give the two Twin Cities' metropolitan counties the authority to collect a fee on mortgage registrations and deed filings for use in Brownfields redevelopment. See Minnesota State Legislature, Chapter 231 (16:13–16) (1997).

REFERENCES

Larson, M., and M. Harley. 1995. *The urban environment and economic development: Brownfield strategies for midwestern cities.* St. Paul: Minnesota Environmental Initiative.

Minnesota State Legislature. 1995. Petroleum Tank Cleanup Act. In *Statutes*, 115C.

———. 1996. The Land Recycling Act. In *Statutes*, 115B.175–179.
———. 1996. In *Statutes*, 115B.47–51, 1–241
———. 1996. In *Statutes*, 469.174–179.
———. 1997. *Laws*, Chapter 200 (2), 231 (16:13–16), and 246.
Notice of Availability. 9 September 1997. *Federal Register* (62): 174.
Office of Technology Assessment. 1995. *State of the states on Brownfields: Programs for cleanup and reuse of contaminated sites.* Washington, D.C.: Office of Technology Assessment.
Schwehr, M. 1991. *A report on the effects of environmental contamination on real property.* Prepared for the Site Assessment Unit, Program Development Section, Ground Water and Solid Waste Division. St. Paul: Minnesota Pollution Control Agency.

CHAPTER 15

Conclusion

Craig L. Johnson

Tax increment financing (TIF) has become a useful, effective tool for local governments to finance capital projects in support of economic (re)development. TIF was originally justified as a local method of self-financing the redevelopment of blighted urban areas. Clearly, TIF projects have been successful at spurring the redevelopment of blighted areas in numerous instances in many states. Along with successful commercial and industrial projects, TIF has also been successful at redeveloping residential property, building affordable housing, and assisting in the revitalization of low- and moderate-income neighborhoods. In addition, TIF has been effective at tackling modern, technical redevelopment problems, like redeveloping contaminated sites such as Brownfields.

TIF is also a fiscal tool used to overcome problems associated with local fiscal stress. TIF has been adopted by cities facing various forms of fiscal stress, including tax and expenditure limitations, infrastructure demands from population growth, and declines in intergovernmental aid. TIF has been used in communities with a wide range of socioeconomic characteristics, demonstrating its breadth as a modern development tool and its potential to address various degrees of urban decay. Moreover, there is empirical evidence that TIF programs in Michigan accelerated property value growth, and TIF programs in Indiana raised property values and employment levels. Yet the verdict from the empirical research is still out. More research is needed on the net benefits of different types of TIF programs in jurisdictions with different socioeconomic characteristics across multiple states.

TIF laws are on the books in forty-eight states, but the application of generic TIF concepts varies widely from state to state; for example, tax increment financing is fundamentally different in California, Texas, Illinois, and Minnesota. As the use of TIF spreads and our understanding evolves of TIF's strengths and weaknesses, successes and failures, state laws governing TIF are starting to exhibit a common framework for addressing the basic issues.

This book has provided a detailed analysis of the fundamental concerns in using TIF. One basic issue deals with the impact of TIF on overlapping taxing entities, such as school districts. Once a TID is established, overlapping taxing entities do begin to lose revenue. This can be viewed as their financial contribution to the redevelopment, which might not occur without their assistance. Indeed, overlapping taxing entities should not be allowed to free ride, it is argued that they should pay for development that will ultimately benefit them in the long run. However, as research in this volume indicates, any net benefits to school districts, for example, will likely only occur over a long time horizon, even for cash flows discounted at a low discount rate.

Recognizing the inherent unfairness of imposing a TID on the tax base of an overlapping jurisdiction, many states have adopted legislation to protect the fiscal integrity of affected taxing entities. For example, "pass-through" arrangements may automatically rebate a portion of lost revenue back to affected jurisdictions. In addition, some states give affected jurisdictions the right *not* to participate in a TIF project or give them the right to choose their level of participation (10 percent, 30 percent, 50 percent, etc.). Such provisions ameliorate the problem in a way that maintains the fiscal integrity of overlapping jurisdictions and broadens the base of support for a development project, which may ultimately result in more TIF-supported (re)development, not less.

The chapters in this book have also illustrated how TIF is applied across the nation, in broad stroke, as well as in detail. While some states have experimented with nonproperty tax increment financing, especially sales tax increment financing (STIFs), such taxes are less suited for use in tax increment finance programs than are property taxes. The most attractive areas for generating nonproperty tax increment flows are not blighted urban areas, but rather undeveloped tracts or areas with the potential for manufacturing or wholesaling development that will add to the regional export base. STIFs are attractive for malls or similar commercial developments. But because retail sales tax flows fluctuate with the general economy and as retail establishments in the development area open and close, their revenue base is volatile, not as stable as the property tax base.

Finally, TIF is a process for allocating public resources, not just a redevelopment finance technique. TIF projects must be carefully planned, continually monitored, diligently implemented, critically evaluated, and ultimately terminated. The laws of a state that govern the TIF process must be structured to channel the political process and financial subsidies in ways that further the public interest. A finding of blight in a TID creates the link between the activities of private developers and the public purpose necessary for government to exercise the powers of eminent domain and support a project using tax dollars. In addition, if the development would have occurred without the expenditure of public TIF funds (i.e., the "but for" test was not passed), then a larger public purpose has not been served, and development should be left to the private sector. But while theoretically elegant, the but for test is difficult to implement in practice. Yet, the idea behind the but for test is one of the factors that make TIF financing such an appealing—and effective—tool for financing seemingly intractable problems, such as downtown blight and Brownfields redevelopment. Therefore, even though a blighted finding and but for test may not always be strictly enforced, or used at all, they are fundamentally sound "first" principles and do provide the underpinning justification for TIF and should not be eliminated. Indeed, as the use of TIF spreads in the nation, we need to develop more objective, practical ways of implementing the basic principles, not discard them.

ABOUT THE AUTHORS

Enid Arvidson: Enid Arvidson is assistant professor in the School of Urban and Public Affairs at the University of Texas at Arlington. She holds a master's degree in regional planning and a doctorate in economics from the University of Massachusetts, Amherst. Her published work and research is on urban and economic restructuring. Her teaching interests include urban and regional economics, urban political economy, community development, gender issues, and qualitative methods (School of Urban & Public Affairs, POB 19588, University of Texas, Arlington, TX 76019, Tel: 817-272-3349, Fax: 817-272-5008, E-mail: *enid@uta.edu*).

Jeffrey I. Chapman: A professor at the School of Public Affairs, Arizona State University, Jeffrey Chapman has written extensively in the area of state and local public finance. He authored *Proposition 13 and land use,* edited *Long term financial planning: Creative strategies for local government,* and served as co-editor of *California Policy Choices.* Currently the director of the College of Public Programs, Chapman also teaches courses in the areas of public finance, public policy, microeconomics, and intergovernmental management. He has a bachelor's from Occidental College and a master's and a doctorate from the University of California, Berkeley (Arizona State University, P.O. Box 870603, Tempe, AZ 85287-0603, Tel: 480-965-1046, Fax: 480-965-9248).

Richard Cole: Dean of the School of Urban and Public Affairs and professor of Political Science and Urban Affairs at the University of Texas at Arlington, Richard Cole received his master's in political science from the University of Texas and his doctorate in political science from Purdue University. He is the author of many books and articles in the fields of political science, urban affairs, and public policy analysis. His teaching interests fall primarily in the areas of American government and politics, urban and state politics, intergovernmental relations, research design and analysis, and public policy analysis (School of Urban and Public Affairs, POB 19588, University of Texas, Arlington, TX 76019. Tel: 817-272-3071, Fax: 817-272-5008).

Andrea Elson: Andrea Elson works for a Chicago-based urban planning and development consulting firm where she specializes in tax increment financing and real estate finance. She has experience in all aspects of the tax increment financing process, including the implementation and financing of tax increment financing redevelopment projects in more than twenty cities throughout Illinois and the Midwest. Elson has a master's degree in urban and regional planning from the University of Illinois at Urbana-Champaign and an undergraduate degree in business administration from the University of Notre Dame (Trkla, Pettigrew, Allen and Payne, Inc., 222 S. Riverside Plaza, Suite 1616, Chicago, IL 60606, Tel: 312-382-2108, Fax: 312-382-2128, e-mail: *ak4945@aol.com*).

Rod Hissong: Associate professor of urban affairs in the School of Urban and Public Affairs at the University of Texas at Arlington, Rod Hissong earned a master's degree in economics from Iowa State University and a doctorate in economics from Rice University. His research is in urban public finance and economic development. He teaches in the areas of urban economics, urban public finance and management, and social science research methods (School of Urban and Public Affairs, POB 19588, University of Texas, Arlington, TX 76019).

Carlyn Johnson: Professor of law and public affairs in the School of Public and Environmental Affairs at Indiana University, Carlyn Johnson has published extensively on school finance issues in Indiana and is the coauthor of *Financing Indiana's public schools* (School of Public and Environmental Affairs, BS 4061, 801 W. Michigan Street, Indiana University, Indianapolis, Indiana 46202, Tel: 317-274-2895, E-mail: cjohnson@iupui.edu).

Craig L. Johnson: Craig Johnson teaches public finance courses at Indiana University's School of Public and Environmental Affairs, where he is associate professor of public finance and policy analysis. He has published and presented widely on municipal securities market and tax increment financing (School of Public and Environmental Affairs, Room 229, Indiana University, Bloomington, IN 47405. Tel: 812-855-0732. Fax: 812-855-7802. E-mail: *crljohns@indiana.edu.*).

J. Drew Klacik: Policy analyst for the Center for Urban Policy and the Environment, Indiana University, Drew Klacik's principal areas of research have been economic development policy and the integration of economic development and community development policies. Prior to joining the Center, Mr. Klacik was a principal planner for the city of Indianapolis's Division of Economic Development. His primary responsibilities included tax increment financing projections and fiscal and economic impact analysis (Center for Urban Policy and the Environment, EE 3rd Floor, 342 North Senate Avenue, Indiana University, Indianapolis, IN 46202. Tel: 317-261-3016, Fax: 317-261-3050, E-mail: *dklacik@iupui.edu*).

Gerrit Knaap: Professor of urban and regional planning at the University of Illinois at Urbana-Champaign, Gerrit Knaap's publications include *The regulated landscape: Lessons on state land use planning from Oregon*, which he coauthored, and *Environmental program evaluation: A primer*, which he coedited (Department of Urban and Regional Planning, University of Illinois at Urbana-Champaign, 111 Temple Buell Hall, 611 Lorado Taft Drive, Champaign, IL 61820. Tel: 217-333-9595, Fax: 217-244-1717, E-mail: *g-knaap@uiuc.edu*).

Kenneth A. Kriz: Kenneth Kriz is an assistant professor at the University of Minnesota's Humphrey Institute of Public Affairs. He received his doctorate in public finance from Indiana University's School of Public and Environmental Affairs. (150 Humphrey Center, 301 19ᵗʰ Avenue South, Minneapolis, MN 55455, Tel: 612-626-2011, Fax: 612-625-3513, E-mail: *kkriz@indiana.edu*).

Robert G. Lehnen: Professor at the School of Public and Environmental Affairs, Indiana University, Robert Lehnen has authored numerous texts concerning Indiana school finance issues, including *Financing Indiana's public schools*. This current study, which, in conjunction with Carlyn Johnson, detailed issues of inequity in Indiana school finance, initiated a statewide debate that resulted in the reform of the Indiana school finance formula in the 1993 session of the Indiana General Assembly. (School of Public and Environmental Affairs, BS 4069, 801 W. Michigan Street, Indiana University, Indianapolis, IN 46202. Tel: 317-274-3466. Email: *rlehnen@iupui.edu*).

Joyce Y. Man: Joyce Man is an associate professor of economics and public affairs at Indiana University's School of Public and Environmental Affairs. She received her doctorate in economics from Johns Hopkins University. Her teaching and research interests include state and local taxes, intergovernmental relations, infrastructure financing, and urban and regional economic development policies. She has published articles on the effects of the property tax and the local sales tax, the relationship between infrastructure investment and economic development, and the uses and impacts of state and local economic development policies (School of Public and Environmental Affairs, 801 W. Michigan Street, Indiana University, Indianapolis, IN 46202. Tel: 317-274-1078, Fax: 317-274-7860, E-mail: *yman@iupui.edu*).

John L. Mikesell: Professor of public and environmental affairs at Indiana University and specializing in government finance and budgeting, John Mikesell has worked on fiscal studies for several states, including New York, Minnesota, Indiana, and Hawaii. In addition, he has served on the Revenue Forecast Technical Committee of the Indiana State Budget Committee for two decades. He is editor-in-chief of *Public Budgeting and Finance* and author of *Fiscal Administration.* He is co-author with John Due of *Sales Taxation, State and Local Structure and Administration.* Professor Mikesell earned his doctorate in economics from University of Illinois. (School of Public and Environmental Affairs, SPEA 230, Indiana University, Bloomington, IN 47405. Tel: 812-855-0732, Fax: 812-855-7802, E-mail: *mikesell@indiana.edu*).

Samuel Nunn: Samuel Nunn is a professor at Indiana University's School of Public and Environmental Affairs. He is also an associate director of the Center for Urban Policy and the Environment. His research focuses on capital infrastructure systems within cities and local economic development policy. He also has more than eight years of municipal administrative experience in economic development planning. He received his doctorate from the University of Delaware. (Center for Urban Policy and the Environment, 342 North Senate Avenue, Indiana University, Indianapolis, IN 46202. Tel: 317-261-3043, Fax: 317-261-3050, E-mail: *snunn@iupui.edu*).

David A. Reingold: Dr. Reingold is an assistant professor at Indiana University's School of Public and Environmental Affairs. He received his doctorate in sociology from the University of Chicago and has published articles on community participation and work disincentives in public housing and on the ability of local housing authorities to conduct economic development initiatives. Currently, he is working on a comparative study of several urban communities as they struggle for renewal (School of Public and Environmental Affairs, Room 243, Indiana University, Bloomington, IN 47405. Tel: 812-855-0635, Fax: 812-855-7802, E-mail:dreingol@indiana.edu).

Clifford Singer: A professor of Nuclear Engineering at the University of Illinois at Urbana-Champaign, Clifford Singer served as an Urbana city alderman and representative to intergovernmental negotiations on waste disposal. He is a member of the executive committee of the University of Illinois Program in Arms Control, Disarmament, and International Security, has plutonium production and reprocessing in South Asia and Russia and on prospects for negotiations on greenhouse gas emissions between China and India. He has taught interdisciplinary courses in nuclear engineering and international security and is currently co-supervising research on global energy economics (Program in Arms Control, Disarmament, and International Security, University of Illinois at Urbana-Champaign, 505 Armory Drive, Suite 359, Champaign, IL 61820).

Susan Steinwell: An attorney at the law firm of Fredrikson and Byron, P.A. in Minneapolis, Minnesota, Susan Steinwell did her undergraduate work at Grinnell College and holds a master's from the University of Wisconsin-Madison. She received her J.D. in law from the University of Minnesota. She practices in the areas of real estate and environmental law and specializes in the area of Brownfields redevelopment. Steinwell represents clients in all types of real estate transactions, including acquisitions, leasing, and financing and assists clients with environmental issues including Superfund liability, wetlands regulations, environmental review, preservation, and permitting issues.

Jeff Zachman: Jeff Zachman is the Wellhead Protection Coordinator for the Minnesota Department of Agriculture. He received his master's in soil physics and a doctorate in soil biochemistry and microbiology from the University of Minnesota. He formerly worked for Braun Intertec Corporation, addressing the needs of private- and public-sector clients facing active or abandoned industrial and commercial site redevelopment. He also consults in the area of regulatory process, environmental investigation, and remediation methods and project financing. Previously, Zachman worked with the Minnesota Pollution Control Agency as a supervisor of Superfund-financed and responsible party site cleanups and as a project manager in the nationally recognized and award-winning Voluntary Investigation and Cleanup Program.

AUTHOR INDEX

267

SUBJECT INDEX

Addison, Illinois, 10, 37, 223–228,
238–241
Adoption. *See* Tax increment
financing, adoption decision
Alabama State Legislature, 38, 54
Allocation
area, 79–80
of tax increment revenues. *See* Tax
increment revenue, allocation
Arizona State Legislature, 41, 54
Arkansas State Legislature, 50, 54
Assessed value. *See* Property value(s),
assessed
Auction bid. *See* Competitive bid

Base assessed value. *See* Property
value(s)
Base year, 20–22, 59, 71, 79–80
Bell Lumber and Pole Company, 248
Benefits of tax increment financing.
See Tax increment financing,
perceived benefits
Blight(ed), 1, 3, 6, 18, 20, 32, 36–39,
49, 52, 56, 58–61, 64, 67–68,
72–73, 84, 88, 93, 105, 113–115,
120, 123–125, 129–132, 134, 141,
157, 159, 162, 168, 176, 185–186,
192, 194, 217, 223, 226, 229,
234, 238, 240, 246, 257–258
Bonds, 3, 8, 16–19, 27, 44, 48, 50,
52, 59, 61–62, 71–78, 83–85,
86, 93, 104, 114, 143, 167,
190, 193
See also Debt
general obligation (GO), 6, 16, 71,
75–78, 81, 93,
113,117,121,143, 188, 193
revenue, 6, 37, 63, 75, 113

tax allocation, 119, 121, 123, 134
tax increment, 61, 71–72, 83–84,
86
Brighton Corporate Park III, 248, 250
Brownfields, 10, 243, 244, 246,
252–255, 257
But for test, 39, 60, 159, 169, 176,
188, 234, 238, 246, 249, 259

California
fiscal stress, 9, 113–125
housing, 127–128
redevelopment agency, 51, 58–59,
82, 121–129, 130–132
tax increment financing in, 1, 17,
31, 37–39, 41, 44, 50, 51, 53,
58, 68, 72–78, 80–82, 84, 92,
97, 113–133, 159, 257
California State Legislature, 39, 44,
51, 54, 58, 69, 115, 120, 128,
129, 134, 135
Cash flow, 49, 203, 207, 258
Certificate of Completion of Response
Actions, 245
Chicago, Illinois
city of, 230–231, 234, 237–239
tax increment financing in, 9–10,
37, 105–106, 223–224,
228–240, 246
*City of Hartford v. Dean T. Kirley
and John C. Spielman (No 91-
1390-OA)*, 78, 86
Colorado, tax increment financing in,
59
Colorado State Legislature, 59, 69
Community Redevelopment Act, 114,
115
Community Redevelopment Law, 115

271